Romans 1-8

DENNY PETRILLO
JOE WELLS
GARRETT BERNETHY
BILLY CLABAUGH

An In-Depth Exegetical Study *with* **Practical Application** | The *Excel Still More* Workshop

KAIO PUBLICATIONS, INC.

Excel Still More: Romans 1-8
Copyright © 2025 by Kaio Publications
http://www.kaiopublications.org

All rights reserved. No part of this publication may be reproduced, stored in a retrieval system, or transmitted in any form by any means, electronic, mechanical, photocopy, recording, or otherwise, without the prior permission of the author, except as provided for by USA copyright law.

First printing 2025
Printed in the United States of America

Scripture quotations taken from the New American Standard Bible® (NASB),
Copyright © 1960, 1962, 1963, 1968, 1971, 1972, 1973,
1975, 1977, 1995 by The Lockman Foundation
Used by permission. www.Lockman.org.

The Holy Bible, English Standard Version® (ESV®)
Copyright © 2001 by Crossway,
a publishing ministry of Good News Publishers.
All rights reserved.
ESV Text Edition: 2016

ISBN: 978-1-952955-55-6

Grammar edited by Tonja McRady
Graphic Designer: Kristin Arbuckle

Contents

Preface v
Letter From the Directors vii
Introduction iv

Section One: *Learning*
Learning Romans 1 1
Learning Romans 2 19
Learning Romans 3 27
Learning Romans 4 33
Learning Romans 5 39
Learning Romans 6 45
Learning Romans 7 51
Learning Romans 8 57

Section Two: *Applying*
Applying: Lesson 1: *Acknowledgment the Power of the Gospel* 69
Applying: Lesson 2: *Recognize Your Need for God* 79
Applying: Lesson 3: *Accepting Justification by Faith* 89
Applying: Lesson 4: *Nestle into Peace and Hope* 97
Applying: Lesson 5: *Step into Your New Life* 107
Applying: Lesson 6: *Focus on Christ for Deliverance* 115
Applying: Lesson 7: *Walk Consistent with Your Freedom in Christ* 123
Applying: Lesson 8: *More Than Conquerors Through Jesus Christ* 131

Section Three: *Building*
Building: Romans 1: *The Acknowledgment of God: A Path to Diving Understanding* 141
Building: Romans 2: *The Truth of Who You Should Be* 159
Building: Romans 3: *What We All Have in Common* 177
Building: Romans 4: *Where Does Righteousness Come From?* 183
Building: Romans 5: *Your Potential Choices* 189
Building: Romans 6: *Sin, Death, Life!* 205
Building: Romans 7: *The Struggle Is Real!* 227
Building: Romans 8: *No Condemnation!* 241

Section Four: *Biblical Text*
Romans 1-8 247

About the Authors 262

Preface

Thank you for your interest in the Excel Still More Bible Workshop! Our hope is that this book will be of great use to you and your study as well as a great blessing to your ministry. The E.S.M. Bible Workshop is designed to take us into a deeper study of God's Word. The method is simple: Learn, Apply, and Build. We believe that in using this pattern of study, we can grow stronger in the Lord by digging deep, applying it to our lives, and building a stronger faith by using tools that we find in the text.

In years past we have attended workshops such as the Workshop in the Word held in Durango, Colorado. The workshop was designed to teach the New Testament books in an exegetical fashion by digging deep into the text to get a better grasp of knowledge from that text. After several years, the workshop ended, and we yearned for that type of workshop again.

Ideas were exchanged, conversations were had, and the workshop started to form. A name for the workshop that continued to stand out was from the words of Paul in 1 Thessalonians 4:1,10: "Excel Still More." It was then that the workshop was born, and we knew this was something we had to do.

Our goal is to simply provide a great workshop and study tool to help us in our everyday study of the Bible. A deep study of the context reveals many things about the writer and his writing. We want to help in providing tools to grasp the context of each text, make application to our lives, and find faith builders that will help us grow stronger in the Lord and in our everyday walk.

As we began to collaborate, we knew exactly whom we wanted to partner with for this wonderful project: Denny Petrillo and Joe Wells. Through their many years of study, teaching, and hands-on work for the Kingdom, they bring much knowledge and ability to the table that make them amply capable to delve into the text with us.

We are very excited about this endeavor because we believe that it is something that will help us on our path to Heaven! Our efforts are completely geared toward providing material that will help us grow as disciples of Jesus and continue to transform our lives. We also know that as our lives are transformed by God and His Word, we will be better prepared to live and share that Word so He can change and transform those around us.

So, throughout your time in this study, grow! Grow in the Lord and excel still more in your knowledge, application, and faith because your soul depends on it, your family depends on it, and the Church depends on it. Grow because the world needs you to excel in finding those who are lost and guiding them to Jesus. Grow because your family needs you to excel in teaching them about Jesus and showing them how to live, walk, and be like Jesus—moving mountains to direct the hearts and minds of the lost to our risen Savior!

Each year we will strive to put out a wonderful, Bible-filled workshop that lays a strong foundation for growth in the knowledge of God's Word. We hope and pray this book will wind up on the shelves of people all over the world and help us all continue to learn His Word, apply it, and build a stronger faith!

Excel Still More!

Letter From the Directors

Dear friends,

Thank you so much for your interest in the Excel Still More Bible Workshop! We truly want this work to be something that lifts you up in your study, faith, and relationship with the Lord.

Our hope in this great study is simple: to help you learn the text, apply the text, and build a strong faith. Our faith and spirituality are our foundation in Christ that will drive us to reach our goal of Heaven, and through this work we intend to do all we can to help you achieve this goal. As Christians we want to grow in the grace and knowledge of our Lord Jesus Christ, and we pray this book and workshop will be tools to help us all do that.

Our intent for this work is to provide an easy-to-use book with reliable resources, so you can gain profitable knowledge from the text. We are so thankful for all of the authors of this book. Their efforts and work in the Lord's Kingdom have blessed so many, and we are thankful for their contributions to the work of the Excel Still More Bible Workshop!

Our prayers are with you as you embark on this study of Romans 1-8. Grow as you learn, apply, and build to become a spiritual champion, fighting the good fight of faith for the Lord as a servant warrior to the King. Excel Still More, friends, and the Lord will bless you more abundantly than you ever thought possible!

Excel Still More Bible Workshop Directors

Introduction

The *Excel Still More* Bible Workshop is directed toward a deep study of a particular book or topic of the Bible. Our platform is a simple three-step pattern.

1. **Learn the text.**
2. **Apply the text.**
3. **Build off of the text.**

With these three objectives in mind, which we call the "L.A.B. Technique," we will be studying the book of Romans 1-8 in an exegetical, applicable, and buildable fashion. It is our goal to always be honest with the text in every way, by looking not only at what the writer had to say but also why he said it, who it was said to, and what it meant to them. By studying the text with an open and honest heart, we can be very open minded in the way that we study the text.

Paul wrote, *"Be diligent to present yourself approved to God as a workman who does not need to be ashamed, accurately handling the word of truth"* (2 Tim. 2:15).

We surely want to be accurate in our understanding of what the Holy Spirit has divinely given to us, so we can accurately handle that wonderful truth in our daily lives. This great truth that has come from God is what guides us as ministers, preachers, elders, deacons, fathers, husbands, mothers, wives, teachers, and followers of Jesus. To have salvation we must know the truth, to grow in our faith we must have the truth, and to lead the Church and our families, we must live the truth.

Jesus said, *"If you continue in My word, then you are truly disciples of Mine; and you will know the truth, and the truth will make you free"* (Jn. 8:31-32).

The truth is what we are interested in, it is what we are searching for, and it is what we want to live our lives by. The truth of God given through the Holy Spirit and written by the pen of man is the revelation of God's grace to mankind, revealing His plan of salvation given through His Son. God has revealed His Word and His way to us, blessing our lives beyond all measure by telling us of His creation, His power, His plan, His love, His truth, and His grace. Without the revelation of God given to all of humanity, we would not have any knowledge of God or His Son. How blessed we are that we have a God who loves us so much that not only did He send His Son, but He also gave us His Word to tell us about Him.

God has given us His Word. It tells us just how important the truth is, but it also emphasizes how vital it is that we grow in that truth. This is precisely where this workshop comes into play. We know the truth is important, and we know just how important it is for that truth to transform our lives in every way. However, it is up to us to put forth the effort to grow in His truth. It is an effort that should not be taken lightly. It is our hope that this workshop is yet another tool to add to your arsenal to fight against all that Satan throws at you as you build a stronger faith through the wonderful study!

Paul wrote, "*Finally then, brethren, we request and exhort you in the Lord Jesus, that as you received from us instruction as to how you ought to walk and please God (just as you actually do walk), that you excel still more*" (1Thess. 4:1).

To *"excel still more"* is to achieve that which is set in front of you. In our case Heaven has been set in front of us, and it is up to us to walk in a manner worthy of Heaven. When I excel, I grow; when I excel still more, I grow and grow and grow! What does this mean? It means that I never stop growing! I never stop growing in the truth of God's Word!

John wrote, "*But whoever keeps His word, in him the love of God has truly been perfected. By this we know that we are in Him: the one who says he abides in Him ought himself to walk in the same manner as He walked*" (1 Jn. 2:5-6).

I am to walk in truth as Jesus walked in truth, and the only way to begin to do that is to know the truth. Jesus Himself said that the truth would be that which would sanctify us (John 17:17). It is by that wonderful truth that we have become the sanctified (Acts 26:18; Heb. 10:10). Those who are sanctified are those who have been set apart, and those who are set apart are those who have been "*rescued from the domain of darkness and transferred to the Kingdom of His beloved Son*" (Col. 1:13).

We who are the set apart are to be set apart in every aspect of our lives—set apart in how we love, how we act, how we study, how we live, how we lead, how we follow, and by our knowledge of God's wonderful Word. For this task of growing in our knowledge of His truth, we at the *Excel Still More* Bible Workshop have developed a method of study that we hope will be of great value to you as you study the Word of God. This method is very simple and is the pattern of this book.

Each chapter will be separated into three sections.

Section #1: Learn—This section will cover the exegesis of the chapter. It is designed to go through the text in a verse-by-verse fashion, identifying key words, phrases, and verses. Every word in each verse is important because it gives you the meaning of what is being said. It is a well-known fact that the context of a verse is everything. Looking at the context allows us to define words of importance. This requires examining the original language in which the Scriptures were written. Those languages consist of Hebrew, Aramaic, and Kione Greek. Denny Petrillo will be leading us in the exegesis of Romans 1-8.

Section #2: Apply—This section will take all that we have learned in the exegesis and make application to our everyday lives. While the exegesis of the passage is of the upmost importance, the application is crucial as well. A person may know the Bible from front to back and have every word memorized, but if he isn't able to apply what he has learned, he has fallen short of what really matters. To apply the text is to grow from the text. It means that I realize the right way to live, love,

Learning Romans 1

and submit myself—now I want to do it. Paul wrote in Roman 12:2, "And do not be conformed to this world, but be transformed by the renewing of your mind, so that you may prove what the will of God is, that which is good and acceptable and perfect." The transformation of the heart is due to the realization that I must change. The Word is what tells me that I need to change and how I need to change. Therefore, the application portion is vitally important to the learning of each passage. Joe Wells will be directing our thoughts on exactly how we can apply each passage to our lives.

Section #3: Build—This section offers a practical approach to applying the lessons we've learned, guiding us to live out our faith more effectively. It builds on the foundation laid in the **Learning** and **Applying** sections, encouraging us not just to understand the principles, but to actively integrate them into our daily lives.

The format of each session is structured to be engaging and interactive, ensuring we reflect on the chapter's teachings. It begins with an introduction to set the context, then focuses on the chapter's key themes. The "Knowing the Keys" section identifies significant lessons and principles, giving us a framework for understanding the passage. Then, we delve into a detailed study of the chapter, exploring the text and its meaning in depth.

> Excel for the Lord, excel in His Word, excel in His ways, and excel in His work.

An activity is included to reinforce what we've learned. This hands-on portion actively engages us with the material, challenging us to think critically about applying these truths in real-life situations. The accompanying worksheet further supports this process, helping to structure our thoughts and encourage meaningful reflection.

Whether attending a workshop, participating in a class study, or working through the material independently, have your Bible and marking tools on hand. This session will push you to think profoundly and stretch spiritually as you apply the chapter's teachings. The ultimate goal is to grow in your faith, strengthen your relationship with God, and step into active discipleship. Garrett and Billy will lead us in these sessions.

Learning the text, applying the text, and building from the text (L.A.B) is vital to our daily walk. Incorporating these three methods of learning can and will give you the strength to handle all situations in life. It will better prepare you as a preacher, elder, or deacon in the Church. It will better prepare you as a father or mother, husband, or wife, as you strive to take your family to Heaven. It will provide you with the right tools to parent your children in the discipline and instruction of the Lord. Why? Because you will have the Word of the Lord in your "mind," you will live the Word in your "actions," you will be faithful to the Word in your "direction." Mind, action, and direction all pointed one way—toward the Lord.

The challenge of this book is simple: *Excel Still More* in all that you do. Excel for the Lord, excel in His Word, excel in His ways, and excel in His work. When you excel, so does your marriage, your family, your children, and the Church. By excelling still more in the Lord, you will bring about change that causes transformation to a world that usually does nothing but conform. So be the one who excels in all you do and be the effective change to a world that needs you!

Learning Romans 1

DENNY PETRILLO

INTRODUCTORY NOTES

I. High Praise for This Book

    A.   One does not need to search too deeply to find multiple authors who lavish praise on this book. To many it is not just the greatest epistle of Paul, it is the greatest book in the NT.

    B.   Martin Luther was impacted more by this epistle than any other. In his preface to the letter, he wrote: "This epistle is really the chief part of the New Testament and is truly the purest Gospel. It is worthy not only that every Christian should know it word for word, by heart, but also that he should occupy himself with it every day, as the daily bread of the soul" (Luther 1972:365). John Calvin said, "If we have gained a true understanding of this Epistle, we have an open door to all the most profound treasures of Scripture" (1960:5; cf. Schreiner, xxii).

    C.   William Tyndale noted: "No man verily can read it too oft or study it too well; for the more it is studied the easier it is, the more it is chewed the pleasanter it is, and the more groundly it is searched the preciouser things are found in it, so great treasure of spiritual things lieth hid therein" (From the prologue to Romans in Tyndale's English New Testament (1534 edition).

    D.   It has been said. "When you get Romans, Romans has got you."

II. Authorship and Authenticity of Romans

    A.   With so many epistles of Paul that have been doubted and questioned, it is refreshing that Romans has enjoyed virtually universal acceptance.

    B.   Thomas Schreiner said succinctly: "No serious scholar today doubts that Paul wrote Romans" (2).

          1. 1:1 refers to himself.

2. 11:13; 15:15-20 references himself as Paul.
3. Style and vocabulary are definitely Paul's.
C. Major discussion is regarding Tertius, who says in 16:22: "I Tertius, who write this letter, greet you in the Lord." There are three theories on this verse:
 1. *He (Tertius) is the true author of the epistle.* This is quickly rejected by the previous references pointing to Pauline authorship.
 2. *He was given general ideas from Paul and then formulated them into this epistle.* This kind of liberty was rarely given to an amanuensis.
 3. *Paul dictated the words and Tertius wrote it down word for word.* This is the most likely meaning and fits better with the concept of inspiration (cf. 2 Tim. 3:16).

III. Place of Writing and Date
A. The best evidence is that Paul wrote this epistle near the end of his third missionary journey and was preparing to return to Jerusalem (Acts 20:3-6). The best date, then, would be around 57 A.D.
B. Luke records that Paul spent three months in Greece before the journey to Jerusalem, almost certainly in the city of Corinth (cf. 2 Cor. 13:1, 10).
C. There are good indicators that also support Corinth as the location where the epistle was written:
 1. Paul commends to them a woman named Phoebe, who is from Cenchrea, a seaport adjacent to Corinth (16:1-2).
 2. Gaius, who apparently is hosting the apostle in his home, was baptized by Paul in Corinth (1 Cor. 1:14).
 3. Many think that Erastus is the same man who was the city treasurer in Corinth (see notes on 16:23).
D. "It was during the winter 57–58, or early in the spring of the year 58, according to almost all calculations, that St. Paul wrote his Epistle to the Romans, and that we thus obtain the first trust-worthy information about the Roman Church. Even if there be some slight error in the calculations, it is in any case impossible that this date can be far wrong, and the Epistle must certainly have been written during the early years of Nero's reign" (Sanday and Headlam xiii).

IV. Who Started the Church in Rome?
A. Theory #1: Established by Peter who served as an elder there for 25 years (Catholic view).
 1. The tradition that the church in Rome was founded by Peter (or Peter and Paul together) cannot be right. It is in this very letter that Paul enunciates the principle that he will "not build on another person's foundation" (15:20). This makes it impossible to think that he would have written this letter, or planned the kind of visit he describes in 1:8-15, to a church that was founded by Peter. Nor is it likely that Peter could have been at Rome early enough to have founded the church there (Moo 4).
B. Theory #2: Established by converts from the Day of Pentecost.
 1. Acts 2 does record people from Rome who were there (v. 10). These converts would

have then carried the Gospel message with them back home.
2. This view also is strengthened by the fact that Paul did not begin the church there, and it is impossible that Peter had established it.
3. "Some have suggested that Christianity was carried to Rome by Jewish visitors present in Jerusalem at Pentecost (Acts 2:10, 14). The assumption is that many of them were converted and were among the three thousand who were baptized that day (Acts 2:41). It is generally acknowledged that the Jews in Rome had a close connection with those in Jerusalem" (Mounce 23).
C. Theory #3: Established by converts of Paul.
1. This explains Paul's great love for them and his friendship with so many of them.
2. It also explains why Paul so strongly desires to come and see them.
3. Hiebert 170
D. The second theory has the greatest following, although the third theory has merit as well. The first theory has few proponents and is even being abandoned by some Catholic scholars.

V. Purpose of Writing

A. Exegetes know the value of searching for the four *P*s to identify the purpose of a book. Fortunately, in this book we have three of the four: Prevalence (key words), Prayers (1:9-12) and Petition verbs (12:1; 15:30; 16:17). We also have what could be considered a "thesis statement" in 1:16-17. Such statements can be equated to Purpose statements. If this is true, then this book has all of the four *P*s.

B. *Prayers* are always important because they reveal what is on the heart of the writer. In Romans, Paul is praying first that he makes it to Rome. It is clear from several sections (cf. 3:1ff; 6:1) that Paul's doctrines are being twisted and misrepresented. Paul hopes to come and personally set the record straight. Second, Paul is praying that the church be "established" (1:11; 16:25). He intends for this letter to be a grounding in the key doctrines of Christianity (chapters 1–11).

C. *Petition Verbs.* This epistle has three of these important verbs. These petition verbs are where a Greek writer intends to add special emphasis to a point being made (like a modern writer might use bold print or italics). Note the three times Paul uses petition verbs:
1. 12:1—The importance of this verse has been universally recognized as an important transition in the epistle. After finishing up 11 chapters of doctrine, Paul now moves to application. The petition verb draws special attention to that change of direction.
2. 15:30—Paul pleads with them to "strive together with me." While there is a personal appeal to pray for Paul's deliverance, the theme of a united action is a predominant concept in the book (cf. 14:7-8, 19; 15:1-13).
3. 16:17—Paul's enemies had done considerable damage to the cause of Christ and had adversely impacted the church at Rome. These self-serving false teachers needed to be identified and disfellowshipped. The importance of this petition verb is clear here. Paul could not emphasize more clearly the importance of dealing with these deceivers.

D. *Purpose Statement.* These kinds of statements frequently have the writer say something like "this is why I am writing this" (cf. John 20:30, 31; 1 Tim. 3:15). Romans has no such language. However, the way Paul sets up his words in 1:16-17 shows that these verses compose one of the core concepts of the book, if not *the* core concept. Paul says so clearly and powerfully that the Gospel is God's plan for mankind—for all of mankind. In the Gospel is found how one can become righteous.

E. *Prevalence* is a logical indicator of a book's purpose because the inspired writer continues to focus on a group of words. Such is certainly the case with Romans. Consider the list of key words below. Obviously with a book the size of Romans there are going to be several prevalent words. These words need to be identified and marked so that we are continually reminded of their importance.

Key Words

- God (θεός) —153x
- Law (νόμος) —86x
- Right/Righteousness/Justification (δίκη) —76x
- Faith (πίστις) – 66x
- Christ/Jesus (Χριστός) —67x
  - (Ἰησοῦς) —37x   104x total (add "Lord" = 152 references to Christ)
- Sin (ἁμαρτία) —60x
- Death (θάνατος) —50x
- Lord (κύριος) —48x
- Grace/Rejoice (χαίρω) —44x
- Life (ζωή) —41x
- Judge/Judgment (κρίνω) —37x
- Spirit/Spiritual (πνεῦμα) —37x
- Work (ἔργον) —36x
- Scripture/Writing (γράφω) —33x
- Gentiles/Nations (ἔθνος) —29x
- Knowledge (γινώσκω) —28x
  - (οἶδα) —16x
- Flesh (σάρξ) —28x
- Do/Make (ποιέω) —27x
- Glory/Glorify (δόξα) —25x
- Love (ἀγάπη) —24x
- Holy (ἅγιος) —24x
- Good (ἀγαθός) —22x
- Power/Be able (δύναμαι) —22x
- Think/Understand (φρονέω) —20x

F. Now that we have identified the four areas where Paul was emphatic, what overall themes/lessons can be learned? Consider the following themes (key words will be noted in bold):

VI. Themes

First, all are saved the same way—by **faith** in **Christ** (1:16-17). The Jews sought salvation through the **law**, but the law cannot save (3:27-28). It is the Gospel that reveals God's one plan. The Gospel is God's **power** to save and show how men can be **righteous/justified** (1:16).

Second, all men have **sinned** and fallen short of the **glory** of **God** (3:23). The problem with sin has plagued all who have lived except **Jesus** Himself (3:25). Sin brings **death.** God has provided the solution to our sin problem: **faith** in **Christ**.

Third, all need to understand the purpose of **law**. The Jews sought salvation through the Mosaic Law and maintained a belief that they could earn their salvation through law-keeping. However, if one pursues salvation through law-keeping, they are forfeiting their access to **grace** (6:14; 11:6). **Life** is found only in **Jesus**.

Fourth, the church needs to be established in the **knowledge** of **Scripture** (1:11; 16:25). That knowledge will protect her from false teachers (16:17) and show her the way to be freed from **sin** and become **righteous** (6:16-17).

VII. Rome and the Makeup of the Church

A. The city of Rome had a large population of Jews. Some have estimated that by the first century B.C. there were approximately 50,000 Jews in Rome. Life for the Jews in Rome was generally good, as they were a recognized religious group and allowed to worship according to their own laws. Christians initially were thought to be a subgroup of Judaism. However, once the Jews were able to convince the Roman authorities that such was not the case, Christianity became illegal and faced great persecution. In 49 A.D. Claudius "expelled from Rome Jews who were making constant disturbances at the instigation of Chrestus" (*Life of Claudius* 25:2). "This was the edict that caused Aquila and Priscilla to leave Rome and go to Corinth (Acts 18:2). Although Chrestus could have been the name of some Jewish agitator, it is more likely a corruption of the Greek Christos ("Christ")" (Mounce 24).

B. The church was made up of both Jews and Gentiles.
   1. Gentiles—"I am speaking to you who are Gentiles" (11:13)
   2. Jews—"If you bear the name Jew" (2:17)
   3. The long list of names in chapter 16 include a combination of Jewish and Greek names.
   4. This explains Paul's appeals for unity and acceptance (15:7) because the Gospel is God's plan for all of them (1:16-17).

VIII. Outlines

A. Mounce (57-58)

I. Introduction (1:1–17)
   A. Salutation (1:1–7)
   B. Paul's Desire to Visit Rome (1:8-15)
   C. Theme: Righteousness from God (1:16-17)

II. The Unrighteousness of All Humankind (1:18–3:20)
   A. The Gentiles (1:18-32)
   B. The Jews (2:1–3:8)
      i. God's Righteous Judgment (2:1-16)
      ii. Authentic Jewishness Is Inward (2:17-29)
      iii. The Faithfulness of God (3:1-7)
   C. All People (3:9-20)

III. The Righteousness Only God Can Provide (3:21–5:21)
   A. Received through Faith in Christ (3:21-31)
   B. Abraham, the Great Example of Faith (4:1-25)
   C. The Results of Faith (5:1-21)
      i. Peace and Hope (5:1-8)
      ii. Reconciliation (5:9-11)
      iii. The Gift of Righteousness (5:12-21)

IV. The Righteousness in Which We Are to Grow (6:1–8:39)
   A. No Longer Slaves to Sin (6:1-23)
      i. Dead to Sin, Alive in Christ (6:1-14)
      ii. Slaves to Righteousness (6:15-23)
   A. No Longer Condemned by Law (7:1-25)
   B. Living in the Spirit (8:1-39)

V. God's Righteousness Vindicated (9–11)
   A. The Justice of Rejection (9:1-29)
   B. The Cause of Israel's Rejection (9:30–10:21)
   C. Some Alleviating Factors (11:1-36)
      i. The Rejection Is Not Total (11:1-10)
      ii. The Rejection Is Not Final (11:11-24)
      iii. The Salvation of All Israel (11:25-36)

VI. How Righteousness Manifests Itself (12:1–15:13)
   A. Among Believers (12:1-21)

B. In the Word (13:1-14)
C. Among the Weak and the Strong (14:1–15:13)
VII. Conclusion (15:14–16:27)
   A. Paul and His Plans (15:14-33)
      i. Paul's Ministry to the Gentiles (15:14-22)
      ii. Paul's Plan to Visit Rome (15:23-33)
   B. Some Final Items (16:1-27)
      i. Commendation for Phoebe (16:1-2)
      ii. Greeting (16:3-16)
      iii. Warnings against False Teachers (16:17-20)
      iv. Greetings from Paul's Companions (16:21-23)
      v. Doxology (16:25-27)

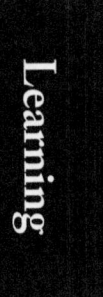

B. Bruce (73-75)

I. Prologue (1:1-15)
1. Salutation (1:1-7)
2. Introduction (1:8-15)

II. The Gospel According to Paul (1:16–11:36)

1. The theme of the Gospel: the righteousness of God revealed (1:16-17)
2. Sin and retribution: the universal need diagnosed (1:18–3:20)
   A. The pagan world (1:18-32)
   B. The moralist (2:1-16)
   C. The Jew (2:17–3:8)
      i. Privilege brings responsibility (2:17-29)
      ii. Objections answered (3:1-8)
      iii. All mankind found guilty (3:9-20)
3. The way of righteousness: the universal need met (3:21–5:21)
   A. God's provision (3:21-31)
   B. Two Old Testament precedents (4:1-8)
   C. The faith of Abraham (4:9-25)
   D. The blessings which accompany justification: peace, joy, hope, love (5:1-11)
   E. The old and the new solidarity (5:12-21)
4. The way of holiness (6:1–8:39)
   A. Freedom from sin (6:1-23)
         i. A supposed objection (6:1-2)
         i. The meaning of baptism (6:3-14)
         ii. The slave-market analogy (6:15-23)
a. Freedom from law (7:1-25)
         i. The marriage analogy (7:1-6)

        ii. The dawn of conscience (7:7-13)
        iii. The conflict within (7:14-25)
   b. Freedom from death (8:1-39)
        i. Life in the Spirit (8:1-17)
        ii. The glory to come (8:18-30)
        iii. The triumph of faith (8:31-39)
5. Human unbelief and divine grace (9:1–11:36)
   A. The problem of Israel's unbelief (9:1-5)
   B. God's sovereign choice (9:6-29)
   C. Human responsibility (9:30–10:21)
      i. The stumbling-stone (9:30-33)
      ii. The two ways of righteousness (10:1–3)
      iii. The world-wide proclamation (10:14-21)
   D. God's purpose for Israel (11:1-29)
      i. Israel's alienation not final (11:1-12)
      ii. Admonition to Gentile Christians (11:13-24)
      iii. The restoration of Israel (11:25-29)
   E. God's purpose for the world (11:30-36)

III. The Christian Way of Life (12:1–15:13)

1. The living sacrifice (12:1-2)
2. The common life of Christians (12:3-8)
3. The law of Christ (12:9-21)
4. The Christian and the state (13:1-7)
5. Love and duty (13:8-10)
6. Christian life in days of crisis (13:11-14)
7. Christian liberty and Christian charity (14:1–15:6)
   A. Christian liberty (14:1-12)
   B. Christian charity (14:13-23)
   C. The example of Christ (15:1-6)
8. Christ and the Gentiles (15:7-13)

IV. Epilogue (15:14–16:27)

   A. Personal narrative (15:14-33)
   B. Commendation of Phoebe (16:1-2)
   C. Greetings to various friends (16:3-16)
   D. Final exhortation (16:17-20)
   E. Greetings from Paul's companions (16:21-23[24])
   F. Doxology (16:25-27)

Learning Romans 1

C. My Outline

I. Introduction and Thesis Statement—1:1-17
II. Doctrinal Section—1:18–11:36
    A. All are under sin (1:18–3:31)
        1. Gentiles are under sin (1:18-32)
        2. Jews are under sin (2:1-29)
        3. Summary: Jews and Greeks are all under sin (3:1-23)
        4. The solution offered: redemption found by faith in Christ (3:24-31)
    B. Proof of solution #1: Abraham (4:1-25)
    C. Proof of solution #2: Our previous condition vs. now (5:1-11)
    D. Proof of solution #3: Comparing Adam with Christ (5:12-21)
    E. Proof of solution #4: The church's death to sin (6:1-23)
    F. Objection addressed: Law and Sin (7:1-13)
    G. The dilemma of the wretched man (7:14-25)
    H. Motives to holiness (8:1-39)
    I. The current condition of Israel and the Gentiles (9:1–11:36)
III. Practical Section—12:1–16:27
    A. The appeal to respond to God's mercy (12:1-17)
    B. Getting along with the world (12:18–13:14)
    C. Getting along with the church (14:1–16:20)
    D. Closing exhortations (16:21-27)

EXEGETICAL NOTES

Chapter Overview: Paul begins this great book by establishing that the Gospel was a part of God's eternal plan. This point is going to lay the foundation for the entire book, because the Gospel offers salvation only in Christ, and only through faith in Christ. This fundamental truth will bring Paul to what many consider to be the principal verse for all of Romans—verse 16. God has no other plan to save man. He has invested His power in the Gospel, and only in the Gospel. All men who believe can find salvation in the Gospel.

    This point established, Paul then begins his thesis that all men are guilty of sin. He will first deal with the Gentiles (vv. 18-32).

1:1—Paul does not need to defend his call to be an apostle in this book. His reference to himself is merely to point out that his life is devoted to the **gospel of God**. For this Gospel he was **set apart** (cf. Gal. 1:15; Jer. 1:5). If God did not place great importance on the Gospel, then why would He set men like Paul apart to preach it? The word **Gospel** (εὐαγγέλιον) occurs 10 times in Romans. It is well documented that the word means "good news." Certainly this good news is that there is salvation for all—apart from the impossible task of justification by law keeping. It is important to note that Paul calls it the **gospel of God**. Critics will claim that Paul's message was a lie and that he taught "let us do evil that good may come" (3:8). Later in chapter one Paul will call it the "gospel of His Son" (v. 9). Paul had so adopted this message of good news that it became a part of his character and personality. That is why he would say it is "my gospel" (2:16).

The word **servant** is a theologically significant term in this book. In chapter 6 Paul will establish that all men are servants of God or Satan, righteousness or sin (6:16-23). Paul made his choice to be a **bond-servant of Christ Jesus**. He was not forced to such servitude but accepts the position willingly. Paul will note that "Christ has become a servant to the circumcision…and for the Gentiles" (15:8-9). He will later commend Phoebe as a "servant of the church" (16:1).

1:2—The Gospel is not an afterthought of God (despite claims to the contrary by premillennialists). The OT prophets predicted **beforehand** the events of Christ, from His seed line (**David**) to the **resurrection**. Paul would tell Titus that his message provides "the hope of eternal life, which God, who cannot lie, promised long ages ago" (Tit. 1:2). It is natural that these prophets would have had an insatiable curiosity about this amazing message. Peter says they "made careful search and inquiry, seeking to know what person or time the Spirit of Christ within them was indicating as He predicted the sufferings of Christ and the glories to follow" (1 Pet. 1:10-11). The phrase **holy Scriptures** (γραφαῖς ἁγίαις) is significant because it is making a claim that makes these writings far superior to any human composition. They are **holy** because they originate from the holy God (1 Pet. 1:15-16) and are therefore without a single error or mistake. What makes this phrase even more remarkable is the word **Scriptures**. This word (γραφή) is an exclusive word that only applies to sacred writings (2 Tim. 3:16). Combined, we have a message that originated from the holy God and made its way to being written down. This is why we should have the utmost confidence in the words of the Bible. They are the words from God Himself (cf. 2 Pet. 1:19-21).

> The Old Testament continually points beyond itself to a time of fulfillment, the age to come. God made his promise "through his prophets" in the Old Testament. He entrusted his message to men chosen to speak for him. Beyond that, he allowed his message to be written down. What the prophets wrote became "Holy Scriptures." Here we have a brief summary of the method God chose in order to communicate with his people. Scripture originated with God. He used prophets to communicate his will, and they accomplished that purpose by writing down what God was pleased to reveal. The result was Scripture that is holy (Mounce 60)

1:3—The Old Testament prophecies had one focused subject: Jesus. They were **concerning His Son**. Paul would say in another letter "Therefore the Law has become our tutor to lead us to Christ, that we may be justified by faith" (Gal. 3:24). It is disappointing when modern religious groups continue to take OT prophecies and apply them to modern events. The OT was not designed for such. Rather, as these verses affirm, it was designed to prepare God's people for the coming of His Son and the saving message He would bring. Stating that Jesus was **born of the seed of David** is a significant Messianic phrase. Based on OT prophesies, the Messiah would be from the David line. "That Jesus was of the Davidic family is attested by both Matthew and Luke. It is theologically important because of the prophetic emphasis on a Davidic Messiah (Ps. 2:6-7; Isa. 9:6-7; 11:1-5; Ezek. 34:23-24). Thanks be to God that he was not only David's son but David's Lord (Matt.

Learning Romans 1

22:45)" (Owen 3). The phrase **according to the flesh** points to the human nature of Jesus. He is God, but the marvel of the Gospel is that He "became flesh" (John 1:14).

1:4—The human nature of Jesus was seen in the phrase "according to the flesh." Paul now moves to His divine nature. A **powerful** statement was made when Jesus was raised from the dead: It established that He was the **Son of God**. How did the resurrection prove this? *First,* because it was prophesied of the Messiah (Isa. 53:10). *Second,* Jesus had frequently predicted that He would rise on the third day (Matt. 16:21; 17:23; 20:19; cf. 26:32). *Third,* logic demands that Satan would have done everything within his power to keep Jesus from being raised. Yet he was "bound" (cf. Matt. 12:29) and unable to prevent this significant event. The resurrection is also a theologically significant concept in Romans. Paul will devote much of chapter 6 connecting the resurrection of Christ with the Christian's baptism. Peter will do the same in 1 Peter 3:21-22. This resurrection was **according to the Spirit of holiness**. This expression has two basic interpretations. First, "'Spirit of holiness' is a unique expression generally regarded as a Semitism conveying the same concept as 'Holy Spirit'" (Harrison 15). This would then be declaring that the Holy Spirit was the power behind the resurrection (cf. Acts 10:38). A second view is that Paul is referring to Jesus' own nature as one of holiness. According to this view, His perfection is why He could not remain in the grave. The more logical view is that Paul has in mind the Holy Spirit. "It would almost certainly be understood by Paul and the first Christians as denoting the Holy Spirit, the Spirit which is characterized by holiness, partaker of God's holiness" (Dunn 15).

1:5—Paul considers his **apostleship** a **grace** (gift) that Christ has given him and his fellow apostles (**we** received). Their mission was clear it was to bring about the **obedience of faith**, a theme that he also concludes the epistle with (16:26). It is vital that this phrase be understood here, because **faith** is one of the predominant ideas in this book yet is frequently misapplied. The merging together of the word **faith** and the word **obedience** shows that genuine faith is not just a mental conviction or belief. Faith, when it is a Biblical faith, is coupled with **obedience**.

> The obedience of faith expresses the purpose of God in giving Paul his gift of apostleship. The carrying out of his ministry would result in an obedience of faith among the nations or Gentiles, *ethnesin*, for the sake of Jesus's exalted name. Paul intentionally speaks of the obedience of faith because he does not want to leave the impression that his message is about justification by works. When Paul uses the word *works* in Romans, he is talking about the mentality of earning one's salvation or doing things to merit one's salvation. He clearly denies this as a possibility (Rom. 4:4-5). But submitting to Jesus and living in His grace does require obedience. It is an obedience that trusts in the redemptive work of Christ, not in one's ability to merit salvation. The phrase *obedience of faith* is used in the conclusion of the epistle as well (Rom. 16:25-26). The nations are the Gentiles to which Paul was made a special minister (Acts 9:15; Rom. 11:13; Eph. 3:2) (Owen, Teacher's, 4).

1:6—The word **called** (κλητός) is sometimes applied to the Calvinistic doctrine of "unconditional election." That is, God calls those whom He has already predetermined for salvation. Such is a concept foreign to the Gospel of Christ and the doctrine of the New Testament. There is no question that God calls. The question is how He does it. Paul answers this question in 2 Thessalonians 2:14 when he says that God "called you through our gospel." When one responds to that Gospel call in obedience, He then is referred to as the chosen, elect, and the called.

1:7—Paul considers it an honor to address the people of God; people who are *first* **beloved of God**, and *second* are **called as saints**. That first designation shows that even though God loves all of humanity (John 3:16), there is a special love reserved for His people. To them he provides His promises of eternal life (4:13, 16, 20-21; 15:8; 1 Pet. 1:4), His spiritual blessings (8:31-39; Eph. 1:3), and the indwelling of the Holy Spirit (5:5; 8:9; Acts 2:38; 5:32).

Called as saints. "The word "saints" (from the stem "holy") is not a description of the moral character of the Christians but refers to the fact that they belong to God (see NEB "his dedicated people"). In the same way that the Israelites in the Old Testament were God's people, so those who belong to Jesus Christ are also God's people" (Newman and Nida 13). Bruce also makes a good comment here: "Because they are the well-loved people of God, they are called to be holy as he is holy (Lev. 19:2, etc.; 1 Pet. 1:15-16). He has summoned them to be set apart for himself; they are saints by divine vocation" (80).

THE GOSPEL OF GOD (Romans 1:1-7)

Intro: By following Paul's use of prepositions, we can follow the path of the Gospel to man:

Part One: God promised to send man "good news"
Part Two: *Through* His prophets
Part Three: *In* the Holy Scriptures
Part Four: *Concerning* His Son (3 points about Son)
Part Five: *Through* Apostles (3 points about apostles)
Part Six: *To* you
        a) Called of Jesus Christ
        b) Called as saints

Learning Romans 1

SET APART: PREACHING IN THE 21 CENTURY (Romans 1:1)

Intro: As a Gospel preacher Paul was "set apart for the gospel of God." Any preacher worth his salt sees himself as a man of God set apart for a special task (based on Lanier 3).

1) **We are set apart to obey the Gospel.**
   A.   We cannot expect others to obey what we will not.
   B.   Preacher set the standard of the dedicated life.

2) **We are set apart to preach the Gospel.**
   A.   The Gospel must be preached. We are the "earthen vessels" through which God delivers His saving message to the world.
   B.   There are many lost who have never heard this eternal plan of God

3) **We are set apart for the confirming of the Gospel.**
   A.   We live in unsettled times. People desperately need the truth of God!
   B.   The Gospel needs to be confirmed again and again. This way believers will not be deceived by "every wind of doctrine."

WHY PREACHERS PREACH (Romans 1:11-13)

1. To help establish and strengthen the church

2. To encourage the church

3. To be encouraged by the church

4. To obtain fruit from the church

1:8-10—When you are as zealous for the Gospel as Paul was, you are excited and encouraged to see and hear of others who are just as zealous. The **faith** (personal conviction) of the Roman Christians was real, and **the whole world** knew it.

1:11-13—The church at Rome apparently did not have the apostle Peter dwelling there, because they were without **spiritual gifts**. Paul desired to go there to **impart** (through the laying on of hands [Acts 8:18; 2 Tim. 1:6]) this gift. The purpose of these manifestations of the spirit was to **establish** the church (στηρίζω). This word clearly indicates the divine purpose for such gifts in the early church. She was dependent upon such gifts to assure doctrinal accuracy, enhance growth, and congregational stability. The gifts Paul has in mind here are not those of 12:3-8, for it is clear the church already possessed those gifts.

1:14-15—Paul's divine call put him under **obligation** to **preach the gospel**, a task that he was **eager** to do, especially to those in **Rome**. It is significant to note that it was the Gospel he wanted to preach to those who were *already* Christians. This shows that the NT knows no distinction between the Gospel (for the lost) and the doctrine (for the church). This heretical teaching was initially invented to eliminate doctrinal teachings such as marriage, divorce, and remarriage for those outside of Christ.

1:16-17—Considered the thematic foundation for the letter, these two verses present God's one and only offer for salvation: faith in the Gospel of Christ. It is here noted as the **power** of God for **salvation**. Certainly no one would limit God's power, but yet *He* has determined to dispense that saving power only through this medium. It is up to man to conform to the divine plan. Why? Because only in the Gospel is the **righteousness** of God **revealed**. This righteousness (δικαιοσύνη) is arguably the most important word in this epistle. It represents God's way to declare man as justified, holy, and treated as sinless. This comes *only* by **faith**.

1:18-19—In verse 17 Paul noted that the "righteousness of God" has been "revealed." He now turns to something else that has been **revealed**—the **wrath of God**. The anger of God is here specifically devoted to those who have ignored undeniable evidences that God exists. Those evidences are provided from God's creation. The reason these men **suppress the truth** is because they have determined that they wanted to pursue **unrighteousness**.

PAUL, THE READY MAN

1. Ready to preach the Gospel (Rom. 1:15)

2. Ready to suffer for the Gospel (cf. Acts 21:13)

3. Ready to spend and be spent (2 Cor. 12:15)

4. Ready to be imprisoned (2 Tim. 2:9, 10)

5. Ready to die (2 Tim. 4:6, 18) (Lanier 3).

Learning Romans 1

THE TRUE PREACHER (Romans 1:14-16)

Intro: Paul describes himself as a preacher with three beautiful "I am" statements. These statements form a foundation for the modern preacher. He…

1. **Is under obligation.**
   A. To people of all nationalities
   B. To people of every intellectual level social class or gender
   C. Foremost, to God (who demands that we preach the truth!)
2. **Is eager to preach the Gospel.**
   A. Is always excited about the saving message
   B. Demonstrates a love and enthusiasm for his message
   C. Notice *what* is preached. Not man's opinions, but God's Word (2 Tim. 4:2).
3. **Is not ashamed.**
   A. This world is full of compromising preachers (cf. 2 Tim. 4:3-4).
   B. Boldness in preaching is essential (cf. Eph. 6:20).
   C. Not ashamed of the person, power, or purpose of the Gospel

1:20-21—The exegete will note the many verbs that describe what the creation is capable of doing in regard to man's knowledge of God: **known, evident, understood, clearly seen, knew**. This creation teaches the observant much about the nature and character of God, specifically His **invisible attributes**. Those who ignore the clear evidences are described as **futile** (ματαιόω—that which is worthless or stupid), **foolish** (ἀσύνετος—without understanding, senseless; cf. 1:31), **fools** (μωραίνω—we get *moron* from this word. It is an aorist passive, demonstrating that, through their ignorant rejection of the creation-evidence, they were made fools).

Man's logical response should have been: (a) to **know God**, even though no other information, e.g. human or written, was provided; (b) to **honor Him as God**. The word *honor* (δοξάζω) means to praise and glorify; (c) to **thank** God. The thinking person recognizes the multitude of blessings found in such a wonderful and beautiful world. He responds with gratitude.

1:22-23—Evolutionists and idolaters **profess to be wise** but are clearly **fools** (cf. Ps. 14:1). Through human reasoning they determine that such a universe could transpire by chance (talk about faith!) and **exchange** the glorious and perfect God for that which is vastly inferior—**images** of various creatures. God is described as **incorruptible**. This word (ἄφθαρτος—"pertains to imperviousness to corruption and death, imperishable, incorruptible, immortal"—BDAG 155) means that God, unlike that which is created, is incapable of growing old or dying. Clearly what is eternal is superior to that which can't survive. Only a fool would choose the temporary for the eternal. They made a choice to "exchange" the glorious God for a stick.

WHO IS GOD MAD AT? (Romans 1:18)

Intro: There are certain kinds of men who provoke God's wrath. Yes, it is true that God gets angry! Paul identifies such men:

1. **Ungodly men**
   - A. These are men who consciously determine to ignore the divine pattern.
   - B. They practice all that is foreign to the holy nature of God.
   - C. They want to live exactly opposite of what is described in 1 Timothy 1:5.
2. **Unrighteous men**
   - A. These are men who determine to practice evil instead of good.
   - B. The use of this word (ἀδικία) stands in contrast with the righteousness (δικαιοσύνη) that was revealed by God (v. 17).
3. **Truth-suppressing men**
   - A. The word *suppress* (κατέχω) means to hinder or hold back. "To prevent the doing of something or cause to be ineffective, prevent, hinder, restrain" (BDAG 532).
   - B. These men are making a determined effort to "bury the truth."

GOD'S INVISIBLE ATTRIBUTES (Romans 1:20)

Intro: The creation is a powerful witness to God. Paul says that one, without another witness, is able to identify two attributes of God simply by looking at the marvelous creation.

1. **Eternal Power**
   - A. One cannot help but be in awe of the power it would take to bring this universe into existence.
   - B. This power had to be a permanent possession of God, for the world needs to be sustained.
2. **Divine Nature**
   - A. Through the creation one can determine God's goodness, love, compassion, etc.
   - B. God didn't have to create it this beautiful! He could have put us on a planet like Mars.
   - C. Every tree, river, mountain, sunset is a testimony to God's nature.

Learning Romans 1

1:24-25—Paul begins this section with the word **therefore**. In view of the foolish choices made by those who exchanged God for creatures, **therefore** God **gave them over**—or gave up on them. This idea is repeated three times (vv. 24, 26, 28). A heart so hardened, so evil, that it would reject clear, undeniable evidence is a heart beyond recovery. God continually tries to win men to Him (1 Tim. 2:4; 2 Pet. 3:9). Sadly, there comes a point when men are beyond the point of return (2 Thess. 2:10-12). Once God gives up on them, they are no longer restrained, and thus plunge into unthinkable evils. Foremost in this category is **lust**, **impurity**, and the dishonoring of their **bodies**. It is clear that Paul has in mind both idolatry and homosexuality.

1:26-27—God's release of these is **for this reason**: idolatry. This release signaled the onset of **degrading passions** where men exchange that which is **natural** (sexual relations between a man and a woman) with that which is **unnatural** (lesbianism and homosexuality). These are **indecent acts** that will certainly bring the **due penalty** (ἀντιμισθία—the logical response of punishment. (BDAG defines this word as "requital based upon what one deserves, recompense, exchange," 90). The statement that they will receive this punishment **in their own persons** seems to indicate temporal (VD, Aids, etc.) as well as eternal consequences. See the special study on Homosexuality: A Biblical Study from Romans 1:26-27.

1:28-31—This judgment is of their own doing, for Paul notes that they did not **see fit** to recognize God and His authority. This choice led them to a type of anti-knowledge, where they purposely determine to know as little about God as possible. They do not want to discuss Him, choosing rather to have a **depraved mind** (a mind that fails to pass the test of being logical and sensible). A depraved mind will freely engage in a variety of evils, many of which are here listed by Paul (21 attributes are listed—ending with a powerful group of five alpha-negative verbs).

1:32—In Greek a quotation is frequently preceded by ὅτι—"that." This is the case here. These men fail to respect the **ordinance of God**, which is "**those who practice such things are worthy of death**." God has spoken! He identified sinful practices and announced the consequence (**death**) to those who **practice** (πράσσω) these things. The hideousness of these activities is seen in two declarative statements of Paul. *First*, the fact that they practice these sins (**do the same**), but *second*, they **give hearty approval to those who practice them**. We say, "misery loves company." Well, so do those who engage in sinful activities. These evil men encourage others to join them in their rebellion to the soul-saving laws of God.

Homosexuality: A BIBLICAL STUDY (Romans 1:26-27)

Intro: In our world today, there is much discussion about the practice of homosexuality. There are even some who profess to be Bible-believers who argue that the practice of homosexuality is acceptable to God and not condemned anywhere in Scriptures. Such is clearly not the case. Here Paul uses four words that describe how God views the sins of homosexuality and lesbianism.

1. **Homosexuality is a "degrading passion"** (v. 26).
    - A. Greek: ἀτιμία—dishonorable, disgraceful, shameful
    - B. Vile (KJV, NKJV), Shameful (NIV)
    - C. *Atimia* is generally translated in the NT by dishonor, e.g. of a man's long hair (1 Cor. 11:14; RSV "is degrading"), of the dead body (1 Cor. 15:43), of the apostles "in honor and dishonor" (2 Cor. 6:8). RSV renders *atimia* by "ignoble" in 2 Tim. 2:20 which speaks of various kinds of vessels.

2. **Homosexuality is "unnatural"** (v. 26).
    - A. Greek: τὴν παρὰ φύσιν
    - B. Certain things are a part of God's natural world—the way He created and intended them to be. If Paul is not saying that unnatural things are unacceptable things to God, what is he saying? Why even call homosexuality unnatural if there is nothing wrong with doing that which is unnatural?
    - C. Nature shows how a man and a woman's body is compatible.
    - D. Nature shows this is the only way to procreate.

3. **Homosexuality is an "indecent act"** (v. 27).
    - A. Greek: ἀσχημοσύνη—shameless, unseemly, shameful
    - B. "Behavior that elicits disgrace, shameless deed" (Bauer 147)
    - C. This word never means anything acceptable to God, but represents that which is rejected by God (cf. Rev. 16:15).

4. **Homosexuality is an "error"** (v. 27)
    - A. Greek: πλάνη—perversion (NIV), delusion, deceit
    - B. This word represents a deviating or leaving the divine pattern, "wandering from the path of truth, error, delusion, deceit, deception" (Bauer 822).
    - C. Matthew 27:64; Ephesians 4:14; 1 Thessalonians 2:3; 2 Thessalonians 2:11; James 5:20.

Learning Romans 2

DENNY PETRILLO

EXEGETICAL NOTES

Chapter Overview: In chapter 1 Paul established the sinfulness of the Gentiles. In this chapter he turns to his own people—the Jews. They were very judgmental of the Gentiles, condemning them for their sinful excess, yet Paul notes that the Jews "practice the same things." His goal of this chapter is twofold: (a) to show that the Jews are under condemnation because of sin, and (b) to show that the true Jew is one who is circumcised in the heart by the Spirit.

2:1—One can almost see the Jews nodding in enthusiastic agreement of Paul's scathing condemnation of the Gentiles in 1:18-32. Now, Paul makes an unanticipated turn—now pointing the finger clearly in the direction toward "you" (the Jews, v. 17). As the Gentiles were **without excuse** (1:20), so equally are the Jews. If the sins the Gentiles committed are worthy of **condemnation**, then logically the Jews, who **practice the same things,** are guilty; for they have **judged themselves**.

2:2—The honest Jew knows that the **judgment of God** is against such sins (no matter who commits them—Gentile *or* Jew). As a matter of fact, this judgment **rightly falls** upon those who **practice such things**. The phrase *rightly falls* is literally ἐστιν κατὰ ἀλήθειαν—a phrase meaning "according to truth." The Jews had created a view that God gave special indulgence to them. The "truth" of God's word, however, provided no basis for such a race distinction.

2:3—Paul challenges the self-pious Jew with a penetrating question, one that certainly requires a no answer. They will *not* **escape the judgment of God**, because they **practice** (πράσσω) the same things the Gentiles practiced. It is clear Paul is emphatically pointing out that they **practice** these sins, using this word in every verse thus far.

2:4—Paul appeals to logic. Have they **supposed** (καταφρονέω—dismiss, shove aside) that God will not hold them accountable? God has shown incredible attributes (Paul names three: See Sermon Seed "How God Leads Men to Repentance") to bring about the **repentance** of the Jew. They deserved God's wrath (cf. 1:18).

HOW GOD LEADS MAN TO REPENTANCE (Romans 2:4)

Intro: The Jew, practicing the same sins as the Gentiles practiced, were deserving of God's wrath. Yet God gave them three indescribable gifts—all for one primary goal: repentance. Paul precedes these three gifts, noting that God has an abundant supply ("riches") of all three.

1. **The kindness of God leads men to repentance.**
   A. Χρηστότης—kind, loving, good, merciful
   B. God has shown kindness instead of wrath, love instead of anger.
   C. This word is also found in Romans 11:22.

2. **The forbearance of God leads men to repentance.**
   A. Ἀνοχή—restraint, lenience, tolerance
   B. God could have easily destroyed the sinners, but He demonstrated a loving restraint, in hopes that this restraint would bring about the desired response.
   C. This word is also found in Romans 3:25.

3. **The patience of God leads men to repentance.**
   A. μακροθυμία—endurance, slow to act, fortitude, patience
   B. This word includes the element of time. God demonstrated forbearance by not *immediately* punishing the Jews. But He did more—He allowed their wickedness to continue over time, exhibiting a slow to wrath quality.
   C. This word is also found in Romans 9:22 (cf. 1 Tim. 1:16; 1 Pet. 3:20; 2 Pet. 3:15; see also Ex. 34:6).

Conclusion: The Gospel preacher would do well to exercise these same qualities when dealing with the lost. They deserve our kindness, forbearance, and patience.

2:5-6—Did the gifts of God mentioned in verse 4 bring the Jews to repentance? No, because they were characterized as having **stubbornness** and an **unrepentant heart**. These words reflect an arrogance and insensitivity to God's Word. It is as if the Jews were confident they knew *better* than what the OT Law clearly indicated (v. 6 quotes Ps. 62:12). But there is a **day** of God coming, which will reveal God's **righteous judgment**. This conforms that it would have been unjust for God to save the Jews despite their wickedness. God's righteousness *demanded* that they receive **wrath**.

2:7—Some have argued that these verses contradict the faith theme of Romans and therefore should be viewed as the mantra of the work-salvation mentality. However, such is not the case. These verses prove to illustrate the truth of Psalm 62:12 that God will render to every man according to his deeds. In Romans it is *not* correct to say that faith requires that one do *nothing*. Instead, faith moves forward in obedience, trusting God's grace for salvation. Paul is still operating on the principle of 1:5 – "the obedience of faith." These who are here seeking God's reward are not doing the good deeds because they believe they earn or merit God's glory. One must read this into the text—but it is not there. Rather, Paul is basing this discussion on the statement in verse 6: "God will render to every man according to his deeds." If one trusts in God and practices the "obedience of faith," are they not doing what God requires? And, if they are doing what God requires, should they not anticipate His **glory and honor and immortality** and **eternal life**?

At the very least, it is safe to say that he is not contradicting what he says later about the impossibility of having salvation by means of the works of the law (3:20). Far from teaching a system of salvation by works, the statement of v. 7, rightly understood, teaches the opposite. "The reward of eternal life...is promised to those who do not regard their good works as an end in themselves but see them as marks not of human achievement but of hope in God. Their trust is not in their good works, but in God, the only source of glory, honour, and incorruption" (Harrison 29).

The word **glory** (δόξα) means "honor as enhancement or recognition of status or performance, fame, recognition, renown, honor, prestige" (Bauer 257). The word carries the idea of "brightness" or "splendor." "When applied to men or earthly powers with the meaning of splendour, radiance, glory, *doxa* reflects OT usage: e.g. "all the kingdoms of the world and the glory of them" (Matt. 4:8 par. Luke 4:6; Matt. 6:29; 1 Pet. 1:24)" (Aalen 46).

The word **honor** (τιμή) means "manifestation of esteem, honor, reverence" (Bauer 1005). It appears that *glory* involves verbal recognition (like a lifting up or praise), and *honor* is an actual rendering of a gift or reward. When widows are "honored," they receive financial help (1 Tim. 5:3).

The word **immortality** (ἀφθαρσία) means "the state of not being subject to decay/ dissolution/ interruption, incorruptibility, immortality" (Bauer 155). In this life God has given us bodies that are designed to grow old and tired (cf. 2 Cor. 5:1-4). The word is somewhat rare in the NT, found also in 1 Corinthians 15:42, 50, 53, 54; 2 Timothy 1:10.

In rendering "immortality" it may be necessary to employ an entire clause, for example, "that people will not die." However, in 2 Timothy 1:10 "life and immortality" may be best understood as a phrase in which "immortality" is a qualification of "life," and therefore one may translate "revealing immortal life through the Gospel" or "revealing by means of the good news the life that does not end" (Louw and Nida 267).

The phrase **eternal life** (ζωὴν αἰώνιον). The word **eternal** (αἰώνιος) "pertains to a period of unending duration, without end" (Bauer 33). The word **life** (ζωή) is "life in the blessed period of final consummation" (Bauer 430). When both words are used together, they capture not just an eternal existence. Rather, the phrase includes the *quality* of that eternal state. It will be the best of being alive.

2:8—Paul uses three phrases to describe those who are outside of God's favor. *First*, he says they are **selfishly ambitious**. This is one word in the Greek (ἐριθεία) and means a self-seeking pursuit that is absent of consideration of others and especially without consideration of the divine will.

Even at an early stage, different people gave the word different senses in the absence of any control of the meaning by derivation. For many it probably had no more than the general sense of baseness, self-interest, ambition, contention etc. But in Rom. 2:8 contention or strife is rather too specialised, and we do best to see a reference to the despicable nature of those who do not strive after glory, honour and immortality by perseverance in good works (v. 7), but who think only of immediate gain (Büchsel 661).

Second, Paul says they **do not obey the truth**. This indicates that they know the truth (cf. 1:32) but they have made a conscience decision to reject it. They have charted out a different course for their lives, and it does not include following God's laws.

Third, Paul says they **obey unrighteousness**. In chapter 6 Paul will argue that all men are slaves. Some choose to be slaves of sin, and others determine to be "slaves of righteousness" (6:18). These Christians in Rome, by their "obeying from the heart that form of teaching" (6:17) had made the transition to obeying sin (Satan) to obeying righteousness (God). That language has a clear link to what Paul is saying here. These evil self-seekers are submitting themselves to the unrighteous deeds of men. They care more for earthly pleasures and material wealth. They are not going to practice what is right but are going to submit to what is wrong.

Paul now begins the list of four nouns that describe the fate of those who practice evil.

The word **wrath** (ὀργή) means "strong indignation directed at wrongdoing, with focus on retribution, wrath" (Bauer 720). Paul had earlier used this word when he declared that the "wrath of God is revealed from heaven against all ungodliness and unrighteousness of men" (1:18).

The second word used is **indignation** (θυμός). This word means "a state of intense displeasure, anger, wrath, rage, indignation" (Bauer 461). This word captures God's utter disgust with those who reject His holiness and defiantly embrace wickedness. This overt dismissal of God and His love warrants His disgust.

2:9—The third word Paul uses to describe the fate of those who do evil is **tribulation**. This word (θλῖψις) means "trouble that inflicts distress, oppression, affliction, tribulation" (Bauer 457). It is an adversity that God will bring into their lives that includes both mental and physical punishment. Jesus is describing the impact of this when He describes Hell as a place of "outer darkness" and "in that place there shall be weeping and gnashing of teeth" (Matt. 8:12; cf. 13:42, 50; 22:13; 24:51; 25:30; Luke 13:28).

Paul's fourth word is **distress**. This word (στενοχωρία) means "a set of stressful circumstances, distress, difficulty, anguish, trouble" (Bauer 943). This word is frequently used to describe events that destroy enjoyment and the quality of life (8:35; 2 Cor. 6:4; 12:10). In Hell these God-rejectors will be enduring the anguish of knowing they will never again enjoy the good things of life; nor will they benefit from the presence of God (cf. 2 Thess. 1:7-10).

These four punishments will be for **every soul of man who does evil**. God's judgment will be fair, since He is the perfect Judge (James 4:11). If a man decides to do **evil**, He will be the recipient of these four punishments of God. It does not matter if the offender is a **Jew** or a **Greek**. The **Jew** foolishly thought that they would escape God's judgment since they were Jews and descendants of Abraham (2:2-3).

2:10—Deeds of obedience are indicators of genuine faith (1:5; 6:17; 16:26). Paul lists four blessing sought by those who **obey the truth**, in contrast with four consequences for those who **obey**

Learning Romans 2

unrighteousness. It is interesting to note that these eight words have similar meanings to each other but still possess some important differences (See Study: Life Choices: A Study of Romans 2:6-10). Paul repeats two of the earlier blessings (**glory and honor**) and then adds one more—**peace** (v. 10). Paul is making it clear that each individual determines what kind of reception he will receive from God. It doesn't matter if he is **Jew** or **Greek** (repeated twice). God's judgment will be based on every man who **does evil** or **does good**.

LIFE CHOICES (Romans 2:6-10)

Intro: Paul will state that all men are slaves to that which they "obey" (Romans 6:16). This section serves as an intro to that discussion. Look carefully at the chart below. It draws together eight principle nouns. These eight nouns can be divided into two important categories: those who "obey the truth" versus those who "obey unrighteousness" (v. 8). Those who obey the truth do so because they "seek" for four amazing divine promises (glory, honor, immortality, and eternal life). On the other side are those who obey unrighteousness. By making the choice to live this way there are four terrifying promises from God (wrath, indignation, tribulation, distress).

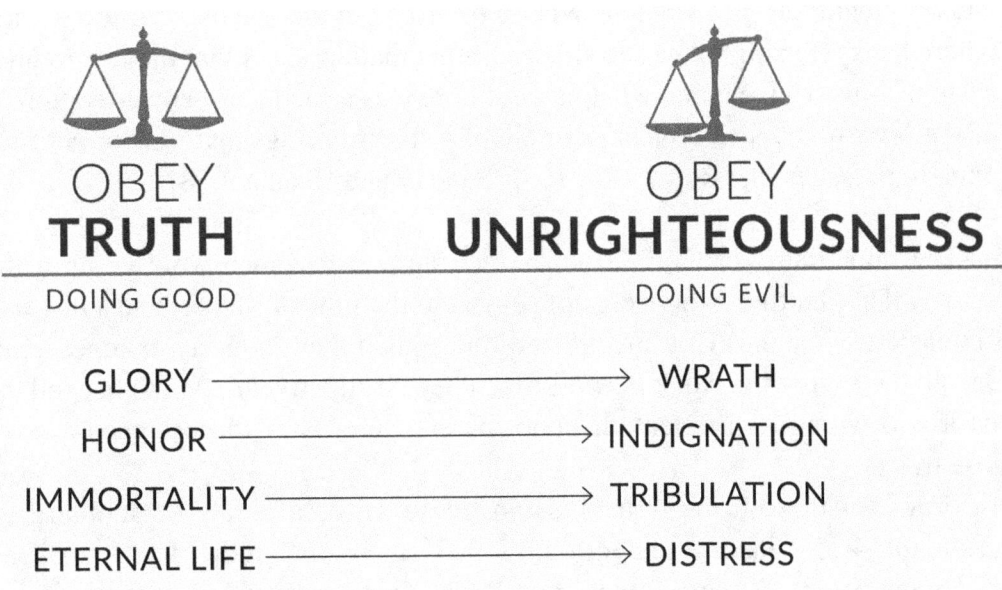

What distinguishes these two categories? In addition to the fact that one obeys the truth and the other does not is that the first group perseveres in "doing good" (v. 7) whereas those who obey unrighteousness "do evil" (v. 9). It is also interesting to note how these words line up. The arrows connecting the words (for example, glory with wrath) portray the *exact opposite* reactions from God.

2:11—God's impartiality demands that judgment be based upon a man's response to His will. The litmus test for God's wrath is sin, and it does not matter if one has **sinned** under the Mosaic Law or without it. Ultimately God will judge men based upon their response to law (Mosaic for the Jews, the "moral law" for the Gentile). It is important that one understand the context of this statement. God has **no partiality** when it comes to *judgment* (Acts 10:34; Eph. 6:9; Col. 3:25). It is not true that He is impartial in his dealings with man during this life (cf. Matt. 13:12; 25:15).

2:12—Part of the challenge of this section is how Paul is using the word **law**. Many translations insert a definite article, and capitalize the *L* in *law*, making the discussion include only the Mosaic Law. Such is the case with the NAS which reads **"for all who have sinned without the Law will also perish without the Law."** However, the Greek does not include the definite article. This is because Paul's point is that whatever law one is under will be the basis of that person's judgment (**will be judged by law**).

2:13—The Jews were those who frequently were **hearers of [the] law**. Daily activities and synagogue worship involved long readings from the Torah. Yet they did not apply what they heard to their daily lives. They were, in fact, law breakers (v. 23). Paul says the **doers of law will be justified**. In context, God will fairly judge both Jews and Gentiles. His judgment will be based upon how men have responded to, and obeyed, His law.

> St. Paul regards the pre-Messianic period as essentially a period of Law, both for Jew and for Gentile. Hence when he wishes to bring out this, he uses νόμος without art, even where he is referring to the Jews; because his main point is that they were under "a legal system"—who gave it and what name it bore was a secondary consideration. The Law of the Jews was only a typical example of a state of things that was universal. This will explain passages like Rom. 5:20, 10:4 (Sanday and Headlam 58).

2:14-15—The impartiality of God did not affect the fact that men were going to be judged by different laws. The Gentiles, who were not subject to the Law of Moses, had a **law to themselves**, a law of **conscience** which is God-instilled attitudes in all men (honesty, kindness, integrity, etc.). How then, did they **show the work of the Law**? They "instinctively" (v. 14) obeyed the Law. They knew that it was wrong to lie, steal, dishonor parents, etc. They did not need a law to tell them about those traits.

> In order for there to be transgression, there must be a law or standard to transgress (Romans 4:15). Paul repeatedly says that sin is not credited to man apart from law (Romans 5:13). The principle, says Paul, does not just apply to the Law of Moses, but to any other law as well. The same principle applies to the pagan world, the world with no formal knowledge of God, and his written Word. Those people have a natural, societal law that shapes their conscience. As a result, they have a sense of right and wrong that develops in their minds. It is this standard they have transgressed. The thoughts of the pagans accuse them of sin because they realize they have violated their own standard of good and evil (Owen, *Teacher's Commentary*, 24-5).

Learning Romans 2

2:16—Paul concludes this section by referring to his **gospel**, in which God will judge all men **through Christ Jesus**. Distinctions between Jew and Gentile are eliminated under the banner of the cross (Eph. 2:16; 2 Thess. 1:7-9). In chapter 7 Paul will demonstrate how the Mosaic Law has been removed. He will say that the Jew has "been released from the Law" (7:6). He will also remind the Gentiles that they are now accountable to the Gospel of Christ (11:22, 32; 15:7-13). This is why the Great Commission calls Christians to take the good news into all the world (Matt. 28:18-20). No person can find salvation without the Gospel of Jesus.

2:17-20—Paul now returns to the sinfulness of the Jews. He begins, however, by identifying five advantages they had, advantages which should have led to four responsibilities (see Sermon Seeds). Yet they had failed to live up to those responsibilities.

2:21-23—The Jews taught others but failed to **teach** themselves. They vigorously preached against **stealing, adultery, idolatry,** and **the breaking of the Law**. Paul said the Jews **rob temples**—a difficult phrase but probably meaning that they had no problem stealing from the pagan temples (thinking that such was acceptable, since God disapproved of these temples in the first place, cf. Acts 19:37).

2:24—The conduct of the Jews was a horrible reflection upon the character of the God whom they claimed to serve. As a result, the Gentiles **blasphemed** the **name of God**. Paul makes it clear that they did this **because of you**. Rather than be a shining example of how people of the true and living God behave, they mirrored (and in some cases exceeded) the wickedness of the world. This verse has powerful implications for God's people today. If we do not "come out and be separate," how can we be the salt of the earth and the light of the world? (2 Cor. 6:14-17; Matt. 5:13-14).

There were certainly some Jews (like Paul himself) that represented Judaism well. Therefore, it would be a mistake to take these words as a blanket indictment on all of Judaism. "It is not, then, that all Jews commit these sins, but that these sins are representative of the contradiction between claim and conduct that does pervade Judaism" (Moo 165).

2:25-27—The Jews believed that their **circumcision** was a ticket into Heaven. Paul notes that circumcision is of **value** only when one **practices law**. He continues this argument by maintaining something that would be an extreme insult to the Jew: that a Gentile, who **keeps the requirements of the Law** will be **regarded** (by God) as one who is of the **circumcision**, and the one who is disobedient (the Jew) will be regarded as one who is uncircumcised. Paul remains "on a roll" in offending his Jewish kinsmen. Whereas they thought they were qualified to judge the Gentiles (v. 1), he now says that these obedient Gentiles will **judge you**.

2:28-29—These verses are very important and contribute directly to Paul's primary argument. The "true Jew" has a "circumcised heart." The way a genuine child of God is now identified is not from some **outward** sign. The true child of God **is one inwardly**; that is, he or she lives faithfully to God's Word. Their **heart** is committed to God, and it is His **praise** (ἔπαινος) they seek, not that of men (cf. 2:7, 10).

ADVANTAGES & DISADVANTAGES A COMPARISON BETWEEN OT JEWS AND NT CHRISTIANS

Intro: The Jews were the chosen race of the Old Testament. Christians are the chosen race of the New Testament. By looking at Paul's description of the Jews, there is much to learn about what kind of people we should be today.

1. **Advantages for the Jews**
    A. Bore the name "Jew." This name becomes synonymous with the chosen people of God.
        i. Today: We wear the name "Christian." It is the only name one can wear and be a child of God (Acts 4:12).
    B. Rely upon Law. The Jews depended upon the Law to discern the will of God.
        i. Today: We look to God's new law (Heb. 8:10) to be approved of God (2 Tim. 2:15).
    C. Boast in God. The Jews made claim to a special relationship with God—one that was not shared with the world.
        i. Today: Christians only are God's people (1 Pet. 2:9-10).
    D. Know His will. The Jews prided themselves that they knew what the only true God wanted while the world remained in ignorance.
        i. Today: Christians must know His will in order to be a part of the new covenant (Heb. 8:11; 1 John 2:27; John 6:45).
    E. Approve the things that are essential. The law had taught the Jew what was important versus the unimportant.
        i. Today: Christians follow the doctrine of Christ (1 Tim. 6:3).

2. **Responsibilities of the Jews/Christians**
    A. A guide to the blind
    B. A light to those in darkness
    C. A corrector of the foolish
    D. A teacher of the immature

Learning
Romans 3

DENNY PETRILLO

EXEGETICAL NOTES

Chapter Overview: This chapter begins with Paul addressing a Jewish argument he has encountered as he has preached this message of salvation by faith for all men. The Jews responded by arguing that his message reduced the Jews to insignificance and encouraged sinful behavior (vv. 1-8). He follows this discussion with a series of Scriptures to establish the sinfulness of all men (vv. 9-18). This being the case, how might a man acquire justification? Paul argues conclusively (vv. 19-31) that the righteousness of God is "through faith in Jesus Christ" (v. 22).

3:1-2—In view of what Paul said in chapter 2, the Jew would object that Israel no longer has any **advantage**. Paul reminds them that they were **entrusted** with God's precious **oracles**. God had chosen Israel's prophets to reveal His message to mankind. They were given a head start on understanding and embracing God's plan. Yet, as he will say in verse 9, the Jews have no advantage in that they have also sinned against God (as did the Gentiles).

3:3-4—However, **some** Jews did not believe those oracles (regarding the Messiah). Did that mean they did not originate from God? Is God going to do away with those oracles if He did not achieve 100% acceptance? Such is foolishness, and the Jew knew it. God is going to be true to His Word even if **every man** rejects it. Man is in no position to **judge** God (quote from Ps. 51:4). Paul says that in every way God need to **be found true**. In chapters 9–11 Paul will spend considerable time discussing the current condition of the Jews. Galatians 3:19 shows that the Law was "added" to the promise "until the seed should come." So the Law was always designed to be temporary. What was greater was the promise, and that promise included the Gentiles (see 4:13).

3:5-6—Paul offers an argument cloaked in **human terms**—that is, it is human logic and does not necessarily agree with the truth of God. This argument is a fanciful one, suggesting that man's sin is not such a bad thing. Why? Because man's sin **demonstrates** the **righteousness of God**. Why, then, would God **inflict wrath** against those who made Him look good? To this argument Paul responds **may it never be!** If such were true, then God would never be able to **judge** (condemn) anyone (one might even assume that He would condemn those who tried to be righteous, because they took away some of the glamour of God's holiness!)

3:7-8—Paul preached zealously about God's grace and man's need for that grace (because of his many sins). This led some, who misunderstood the message, to suggest that Paul actually encouraged sinful behavior. They reasoned as follows: (a) grace comes because of sin; (b) more sin requires more grace; (c) grace is a good thing; (d) therefore we should sin more to bring in more grace.

This reasoning provokes two responses from Paul:
1) If this fanciful argument is true, then I should be praised by others because of my **lie** (his message of grace and salvation). After all, this false doctrine I'm preaching **abounded to His glory**. Therefore, rather than being **judged as a sinner,** he should be praised, because he's doing such a good job of making God look good! (v. 7)
2) Paul then follows with a question based upon the logic of verse 7. Why shouldn't Paul preach **let us do evil**, so that **good may come** (in two ways: it brings more grace, and it makes God look good). There were even some **slanderously** reporting that this is exactly what Paul was preaching!

Paul never taught that grace provided permission to sin. He will specifically address this point in chapter 6. In the meantime, he has a word for such critics: **Their condemnation is just**.

GOD & THE SINS OF MAN (Romans 3:1-8)

Intro: Some had conjured up a creative argument in order to justify their sin. They contended that God did not have a problem with sin because it contrasted His holiness with man's imperfections. In this text we can better understand what God wants from man.

1. God wants us to reflect His holiness, not contrast it.
2. God wants us to live sinlessly but provides grace when we do sin.
3. God's judgment will be based upon how man has dealt with sin.

3:9—By repeating the phrase **what then** (Τί οὖν) Paul is now returning to the question in verse 1. The Jews did have some advantages, but the bottom line is they are guilty of sin, as are the Gentiles. Therefore are **we** (Jews) **better than they** (Gentiles)? His answer (proven in chapters 1 and 2): **Not at all**. The fact is **both Jews and Greeks are all under sin**.

The phrase (Τί οὖν) is a frequent literary devise used by Paul, often in response to Jewish arguments (cf. 3:1, 9; 4:1; 6:1, 15; 7:7; 8:31).

3:10—The truth that all men are under sin is well documented in the Old Testament. Paul quotes portions of seven OT passages, all but one (Is. 59:7; v. 15) coming from the Psalms.

His first quote sets the stage for all of the quotes: **There is none righteous, not even one**. This powerful passage (from Ps. 14:1-3) offers that there are **none** righteous (whether Jew or Greek). This coincides with verse 23 ("all have sinned"). The Greek has a phrase translated into the English "none" (οὐκ ἔστιν). This exact phrase will occur six times in this section (vv. 10, 11 [2x], 12 [2x], 18), clearly

Learning Romans 3

proving the point that *no man* can claim to be **righteous**. Paul is not concerned whether one is less a sinner than another (for example, whether Jews are less sinners than are the Gentiles). All men have a sin problem, and all men are going to have to do something about that sin problem.

3:11-12—Man's ignorance of what God wants is at the root of the problem. They do not **understand** God, neither do they **seek for God** (because they are too interested in pursuing sin). As a result, they have become **useless** to God (who cannot use these sinful vessels to accomplish His will; cf. 2 Tim. 2:21).

3:13-18—Paul here begins to specify the variety of sins that men have committed (misusing their **throats, tongues, lips, mouth, and feet**), making them useless to God. See Sermon Seed: Rushing to Do Evil. All of these sins are committed because men have no **fear of God**.

RUSHING TO DO EVIL: BODIES GIVEN TO SERVE UNRIGHTEOUSNESS

Intro: Paul will later say that we need to give the "members of our body" to God as instruments of righteousness (6:12, 13). Here he notes how men use those members to serve unrighteousness.

1. **Throat**
   A. An open grave (Ps. 5:9; 140:3)
   B. We put the decaying body deep into the earth because we don't want to see the corruption. These men make no attempt to hide their evil way.
2. **Tongues**
   A. Keep deceiving (Ps. 5:9; 140:3)
   B. They undermine the fabric of society through deception.
3. **Lips**
   A. Like the poison of asps
   B. Men do not appreciate the danger until they are bit. Lying is like the poison of a venomous snake.
4. **Mouth**
   A. Full of cursing—they have no qualms about blaspheming God or profaning man.
   B. Full of bitterness—they do not like this life but are continually critical and unsettled.
5. **Feet**
   A. Swift to shed blood
   B. Men know no limits—even to the point of taking human life.
   C. Where their feet take them (people they encounter) brings (a) destruction and (b) misery.
   D. They have not walked in the "path of peace" which comes from knowing and doing the will of God.

Conclusion: How can men plunge to such depths of wickedness? The answer is clear: "There is no fear of God before their eyes" (cf. Eccl. 8:11; Prov. 1:7).

3:19-20—The **law** has spoken (see Sermon Seed: The Law). Paul just supplied quotations from seven separate Old Testament texts. Would any man dare maintain that he is without sin? Certainly those **under the Law** (the Jew) would have no response (**every mouth may be closed**) to what the law made clear—every man has a sin problem and every man is **accountable to God**. This being the case, where is man going to go to address this sin problem? Are they going to be able to appeal to their own righteousness through law-keeping (**works of law**)? The hard facts are that **no flesh will be justified in His sight** through this approach (because the Law demanded perfection). Both Jews and Gentiles realize that they have failed to meet God's standards.

3:21-22—In 1:16-17 Paul maintained that the **righteousness of God** was revealed in the Gospel. Therefore, it established that this righteousness came **apart from law**. The **Law and the Prophets** both **witnessed** that God would eventually provide a system of justification apart from the Law, and one that was based upon **faith** (Hab. 2:4; Jer. 31:31-34; Zech. 13:1; Is. 53; cf. Gal. 3:6-13; 1 Pet. 1:10-12). This righteousness comes **through faith in Jesus**, and it is offered for **all who believe** (bringing us back to 1:16-17).

3:23—It is clear that this system is in contrast to one where man trusts in his own goodness to save him. That approach won't work for one simple reason: **all have sinned** (cf. 2:12). Who is God going to give **glory** to? The self-righteous Jew? The Gentile who has violated God's moral law? Since all have sinned, there are none left to receive this glory. Yet Paul will eventually show that in Christ one can expect to receive this glory (2:10; 8:18). Paul uses a past tense verb (**all have sinned**) and a present tense (**fall short**) to show that the sin problem continues with all humanity.

3:24-26—Man's justification is a **gift** (δωρεάν), and that gift is **grace**. Yet that gift came only through the **redemption** (ἀπολύτρωσις) found only in Christ, who was made a **propitiation** (ἱλαστήριον)—a sacrifice that satisfied God's demand for justice. This sacrifice allowed God to be both **just** and the **justifier**—but only to believers.

3:27-28—Since all men have sinned, and since salvation is found only as a gift by faith in Christ, where is the place for **boasting**? There is no place for the self-righteous to stand up and proclaim his own goodness, because he has no such inherent goodness (cf. 2:17). Thus this boasting is **excluded**. What disqualified one from boasting: the law of **works** or a **law of faith**? It has to be the law of faith, because a law of works *encourages* boasting. A law of faith shows man's complete dependence on a force outside of himself for salvation. The expression **law of faith** is curious—combining terms that seem, on the surface to be contradictory. Paul is not here referring to the "laws" given by Christ and the apostles (which would mean, essentially, that we went from one law system to another). We are no more able to perfectly obey the law of Christ then the Jew was able to perfectly obey the Law of Moses. Instead, Paul is saying that God has laid down a new law which states that righteousness is given based upon man's trust in the blood of Jesus rather than anything he has done.

THE LAW (Romans 3:19-21)

Intro: God used Law to establish man's need for a Savior and his need for grace. We can learn a lot about the plan of God by studying what Paul says about the Law.

1. **It closes every mouth (v. 19).**
   A. It establishes the perfection of God verses the imperfection of man.
   B. No man can establish a legitimate argument that he does not need the Gospel.
   C. Neither can any man maintain his sinlessness (v. 23; 1 John 1:8-10).
2. **It makes all the world accountable to God (v. 19).**
   A. Both Jew and Gentile
   B. All men are lost, yet all men are going to have to stand before God for judgment (2 Cor. 5:10; Rev. 20:11-14).
3. **It provides knowledge of sin (v. 20).**
   A. The law has revealed the mind of God. It established what is right and what is wrong.
   B. Through the Law man knows what sin is, and he is constantly reminded that he stands in violation of that law.
   C. With the Jew, he would have God's written Law.
   D. With the Gentile, he would have God's moral law, that standard of right and wrong that he knew intuitively.
4. **It bore witness to a new system of justification (v. 21).**
   A. No one who studied the OT would maintain that God planned on keeping the Mosaic Law in place forever.
   B. From Abraham on, it was clear that God would justify one through faith (Gen. 15:6).
   C. All men will now be judged through the Gospel of Christ (2 Thess. 1:7-10; 1 Pet. 4:17).

This verse defines the "law of faith" of verse 27. It is a law that states that **man is justified by faith**. And, in case someone might respond, "Yes, faith coupled with meritorious works," Paul says—**apart from works of law**.

3:29-30—The Law of Moses was given specifically to the Jews (3:1-2; Deut. 5:1ff; Ex. 19:5-6). This being the case, then man could only be saved if (a) he was a Jew and (b) he kept the Law perfectly. But the Jews couldn't keep the law perfectly, and besides, they do not have sole possession of the Lord as their God (even though that is what they said). But God is also the **God of the Gentiles**, and since **God is one**, he will justify both the Jew (**circumcised**) and Gentile (**uncircumcised**). Some have tried to find a distinction in the terminology **by faith** (ἐκ πίστεως) verses **through faith** (διὰ τῆς πίστεως). However, Paul's point has been that each are justified *in the same way*. I believe Paul uses the different prepositions to underscore his primary thesis—anyway you approach it, one is still justified by faith!

3:31—The Jew would conclude that, according to Paul, the Law was useless (thus an insult to God and to Moses). Paul says that such an argument is far from the truth. The Law is not **nullified** but rather **established**. It was not meant to justify but to educate man, showing them their need for a Savior. In this way **we establish the Law**.

WHERE THEN IS BOASTING? (Romans 3:27)

1. **We cannot boast that God owes us salvation because, in and of ourselves, we are imperfect.**
    A. As free moral agents we must accept the consequences for our own actions.
    B. Cf. James 1:13-14.
2. **We cannot boast that God owes us salvation because we have a flawless record of obedience to His law.**
    A. There is none righteous (3:9); all have sinned (3:23).
    B. One sin brings man under the consequences of law—judgment and condemnation. From that point on he needs help, mercy, and forgiveness.
3. **We cannot boast that God owes us salvation because we have inherent goodness and righteousness.**
    A. Again, there is none righteous (3:9).
    B. God expects His people to be good, moral people. That doesn't mean that such goodness merits salvation.
    C. If *any* sin is involved, man needs a Savior.

Conclusion: "This does not depreciate the importance of obedience on the part of a Christian. It simply says that justification is an act of grace on the part of God to the believer, and that it can never be earned by commandment keeping" (Owen 25). . Thus, we have no grounds for boasting. . We can only humbly and gratefully accept God's gift, offered through the blood of His Son.

Learning
Romans 4

DENNY PETRILLO

EXEGETICAL NOTES

Chapter Overview: Paul knew that his point (justification by faith) would not convince any Jew unless he could establish that the father of the Jews, Abraham, was also justified by faith. Therefore, this chapter is devoted to showing that Abraham was justified by faith before circumcision and before there was a Law of Moses. The promise of justification by faith is a promise for Jew and Gentile alike, since Abraham is the "father of us all" (v. 16).

4:1—**What shall we say** (Τί οὖν) is the typical phrase when Paul is addressing a Jewish argument or introducing a new argument (3:1, 9; 6:1, 7; 8:31; 9:14; 30). Certainly, the Jew would have asked about Abraham and his salvation in light of Paul's teachings regarding the Old Testament. He notes that Abraham is our forefather **according to the flesh**, a phrase he also used to describe Jesus in 1:3. He is about to show that Abraham is the spiritual father of all who come to God by faith—a connection to Abraham that is far more important than the "in the flesh" connection.

4:2-3—The Jew might maintain that Abraham was justified by his works. Paul says that if he was **justified by works**, he has **something to boast about; but not before God**. This means either: (a) He would never boast to God, because God would know the truth; or (b) He wouldn't dare boast before God, because he knows God knows the truth—he didn't live perfectly. The Scriptures, however, answer the question on how Abraham was justified: **Abraham believed God**. This verse (Gen. 15:6) is quoted a remarkable three times in this chapter (vv. 3, 9, 22). It proves that Abraham's faith is why God made him righteous.

4:4-5—By **works** Paul means one who has determined to earn, or merit, his own salvation by law-keeping. If one managed to do this his **wage** (salvation) would not be considered a **favor** (χάρις—lit. grace. He wouldn't need grace) because he earned it; it was that which was owed him. The one who **does not work** refers to one who is trying to earn or merit his salvation through obedience.

WHAT DID ABRAHAM FIND (Romans 4:1-5)

Intro: Perhaps no OT figure would have a greater impact on Jewish thinking than that of Abraham. If Paul were to successfully argue his case about justification by faith, he would need to demonstrate this truth through the example of Abraham. Paul asks the question, "What did…Abraham our forefather…find?"

1. Did he find that one can be justified by works?
   A. If so, he has reason to boast.
   B. If so, he would not boast before God.
   C. If so, the OT account would be false.
   D. If so, then salvation would be owed and not a gift of grace.

2. Did he find that one can be justified by faith?
   A. The OT account affirms that "Abraham believed God"—so we know he approached God through faith rather than through the works mentioned in verse 2.
   B. The text says that it was **credited** (λογίζομαι)—a word that means "added to one's account." Before, Abraham was spiritually bankrupt. Now his account has a deposit: righteousness.

PAUL AND JAMES

Martin Luther called James "an epistle of straw" because he thought it contradicted the clear teaching of salvation by faith in Romans. Luther misunderstood what both were saying.

Paul: Work = refers to an attempt by man to earn or merit his salvation. He does not believe he needs God's gift of grace.

James: Work = that which is done to show or prove the existence of faith. It is not done to earn salvation.

4:6-8—Paul will return to Abraham shortly. However, he wants to quickly establish that the "salvation by faith" principle was not unique with Abraham, nor was it removed through the Law of Moses. He begins by saying **just as** (καθάπερ) **David**…. David is one who lived after the Law of Moses was put into place. Yet he spoke of the **blessing upon the man whom God reckons righteousness apart from works** (he found the same thing—"just as" Abraham found). The word **blessing** (μακαρισμός) refers to the man approved of God. The man who comes to God in faith, rather than attempt to reach him through perfect obedience, is approved. Paul quotes David's words in Psalm 32:1, 2. These verses establish that a man has failed to live perfectly (has committed **lawless deeds**) yet his sins have been **covered** and are not **taken into account**. The only way this can happen is if he came to God by faith.

Learning Romans 4

4:9-10—Faith has nothing to do with being a Jew or Gentile. Abraham, whose faith brought **righteousness,** was awarded that righteousness before he was **circumcised**. Therefore God's righteousness has nothing to do with circumcision. It was in Genesis 15 that Abraham was declared by God to be righteous. It was in Genesis 17 that God gave Abraham the covenant of circumcision. Therefore, since justification has nothing to do with circumcision, there is no reason to argue that Gentiles can't be justified.

4:11-12—God did it this way so that Abraham might show himself to be the **father of all who believe**, and that **righteousness might be reckoned to them** because of their faith. Paul calls circumcision a **seal of the righteousness of the faith he had while uncircumcised**. God used circumcision as an identifying mark to confirm or acknowledge that Abraham was declared righteous by faith. This is why one should not consider baptism the "Christian circumcision." Abraham was saved before circumcision. One cannot be saved before baptism (see Rom. 6).

FINDING SALVATION

Intro: Men long to be with God. Their attempt to reach Him will lead them on two distinct paths. Paul discusses these two methods of justification as well as provides two examples.

1. **Two Examples**
   A. Abraham
      1. Did not trust in his own goodness
      2. Believed God, and that belief was reckoned to him as righteousness
      3. Found that righteousness apart from circumcision
   B. David
      1. Was grateful that a "lawless man" could be forgiven
      2. Was grateful that the Lord would not "take into account" the sins of the man of faith

2. **Two Methods**
   A. Works
      1. An attempt to earn salvation the way one earns his paycheck
      2. When I get my check, I don't thank the treasurer for his kindness and the "gift" of this check. I worked hard, I earned it. There was no "favor" bestowed.
   B. Faith
      1. A recognition that one cannot live perfectly (work his way into heaven) and therefore is going to have to throw himself before the mercy of God.
      2. Is putting his trust/confidence in the blood of Christ
      3. Is a plan available to all—not just Jews.

Conclusion: All men are called to "follow in the steps of the faith" of Abraham. He still obeyed God, but that obedience was not what merited his salvation. We obey, but the blood saves.

4:13—Paul makes reference to the **promise** given to Abraham (or to his **descendants**) that he would be **heir of the world** was a promise that preceded the law by 600 years. Paul's argument is that this promise had to be based either on (a) **Law**—but that won't work because there was no law at that time or (b) **Righteousness of faith**—this has to be it because it is what is supported by the OT texts, and it is the only option left. This promise, that through Abraham all the nations of the earth would be blessed (Gen. 22:17f) is one that clearly must include the Gentiles.

4:14-15—If this promise applies only to the Jews (**those who are of the law**), then two critical parts of God's plan for man is made valueless: (a) **faith**, including the faith of Abraham, is **void** (κενόω)—worthless, useless. No Jew would want to say that, because it would go against what the OT clearly says (Gen. 15:6); (b) **promise**—that which offered blessings for Abraham's children is **nullified** (καταργέω)—empty, worthless. This promise said "all" the nations of the earth would be blessed.

The **law brings about wrath** by identifying sin and its consequences. But where there is no law, **neither is there violation**—because none can keep it perfectly. The Jews were well aware of the Law, and equally knew they were guilty of breaking that law—so what were they going to be able to do about it? How could they become justified?

4:16-17—**For this reason** refers to the fact that man cannot be justified by law-keeping and therefore must have another alternative. But justification can be obtained **by faith**. And the reason faith accomplishes justification is because it brings **grace**. This makes the **promise** guaranteed (**certain**) to **all** (Jew and Gentile alike). This confirms the statement of Genesis 17:5 and verifies that Abraham's faith was approved by God. His faith was one that believed in spite of evidences for unbelief (being **dead**—referring to Sarah's womb and to their being dead with old age).

4:18-19—Abraham had a lifetime of experiences, experiences that taught him that old men don't father children, old women don't bear children, and closed wombs don't open up. All of this was **hope against hope**, yet Abraham **believed.** He believed in God's promise to him and was convinced that somehow God would fulfill that promise. Astonishingly, Abraham did not become **weak in faith**, even as he thought about his own **body** and the **deadness of Sarah's womb**. How did he not become weak in faith in view of such negative evidences? This is why Abraham is such an important example to advance Paul's argument. We might ask "How can I be forgiven simply by believing in Christ's blood?" The evidence might suggest that we need to somehow earn God's forgiveness through works. Yet, we must simply believe what God said: He will justify the one who has faith in Jesus (3:26).

4:20-22—It was God's **promise** that kept Abraham going. He just thanked God for the promise and its eventual fulfillment. How God was going to do it wasn't Abraham's concern. He simply believed that He would do it, and knew He was all-powerful and thus had the ability to perform. It is on the basis of this kind of faith that Paul begins verse 22 with **therefore**. Since Abraham approached God with this kind of faith, God responded by reckoning **righteousness** to Abraham. This has Paul returning to the original point in verse 3—all of this happened because of Abraham's faith.

ABRAHAM: JUSTIFIED BY FAITH

Abraham: An Example of Justification by Faith

HOW? ⟶ BY FAITH
Romans 4:2-3

WHEN? ⟶ BEFORE CIRCUMCISION
Romans 4:10-12

WHY? ⟶ BECAUSE HE OBEYED
James 2:21-23

Abraham's Faith

WHAT PROMPTED IT? ⟶ The power of the promise of God (Gen. 12:1-3)

HOW DID IT WORK? ⟶ It encouraged him to do things beyond his dreams (Heb. 11:8-10)

WHAT DID IT DO? ⟶ It made him righteous by God (Gen. 15:6; Rom. 4:2f)

4:23-25—Paul now moves to his application. This wasn't written for **his sake**—because it was written well after he was dead. So why was it written? God wanted it to stand as a lasting example to future generations on how to please Him. God is now offering us a promise—one that in many ways seems as unbelievable as that given to Abraham. Yet if we can **believe in Him who raised Jesus,** righteousness **will be reckoned** to us. The fact that Jesus was **delivered up**, and then **raised**, was all for us. What else does God need to do to prove His desire to redeem us? God offers us the same assurance: **to whom** it will be **reckoned**.

RESPONDING TO GOD'S PROMISE
(A CASE STUDY IN THE FAITH OF ABRAHAM)

Intro: God did not reserve all His promises for Abraham. We've been given a few too. What God wants is simple. He wants us to respond to His promises the way Abraham responded.

1. Abraham did not waver in unbelief.
- A. He showed a consistency and a conviction in God's promises.
- B. This does not mean that he did/said some things that indicated he didn't fully understand *how* God was going to do it.

2. Abraham grew strong in faith.
- A. Whereas most people would weaken considerably when there are such overwhelming odds against them, Abraham kept his focus on one thing: God's promise.
- B. He used God's promise as a springboard to grow even stronger in his personal faith.

3. Abraham gave glory to God.
- A. There would be a great temptation to become disgruntled with the way God is handling this. Why does He have to make it so hard to believe?
- B. People of faith just accept God's marvelous promises and thank Him for those promises.

4. Abraham became fully assured.
- A. He believed that if God said it that settled it.
- B. He knew that, somehow, God was able to meet His promises.

THE STEPS OF ABRAHAM'S FAITH (LANIER)

1. Abraham had a faith that accepted God's Word at full face value without quibble.

2. Abraham had a faith that accepted God's way in preference to his own.

3. Abraham had a faith that obeyed God in spite of the cost.

Learning
Romans 5

DENNY PETRILLO

EXEGETICAL NOTES

Chapter Overview: This chapter is easily divided into two parts. In verses 1-11 Paul discusses the effect being justified by faith has on the Christian. In verses 12-21 Paul specifically addresses how man got into this sin problem and what God did about it. He makes a comparison between the work of Adam versus the work of Christ.

5:1-2—Paul begins with **therefore**, probably indicating that he wants to sum up the points made in the first four chapters (all men are sinners, but all men can find justification through faith in Christ). He now wants to specifically address those who are already Christians (**having been justified by faith**). Even though 3:23 is true, they are not waiting to be justified (or hoping to be justified)—they are now. This justification has impacted the Christian's life in four distinct ways (see Sermon Seeds). The emphasis on this section is clearly linked to Jesus. All this comes **through** Him.

5:3-4—Earlier Paul had said that boasting in self was excluded (3:27). But there are certain areas in which a Christian can boast, and **tribulations** are one of them. Paul offers three reasons why we can **exult** in our **tribulations**. (a) It brings **perseverance** (ὑπομονή), a word that means steadfast endurance. A suffering Christian can develop a quality that enables him to suffer through anything (2:7; 8:25); (b) It brings **proven character** (δοκιμή). This is a word that refers to a testing and a passing the test. One is approved only because he has demonstrated the kind of character that stays with God even in the face of tremendous tribulations; (c) It brings **hope**. A person who continually gives in and doesn't remain steadfast has no expectation of salvation. He has failed the divine test.

5:5—God is not going to let down those who have put their hope in Jesus (10:11). Proof of this is found in God's **love**, and God's love has been demonstrated when He gave us the **Holy Spirit**. God only gives the Holy Spirit to those who are holy/separated. The Holy Spirit is our guarantee that we will be saved (Eph. 1:14).

RESULTS OF JUSTIFICATION (Romans 5:1-4)

Intro: Christians need to be reminded why they became Christians. Far too many struggle with guilt, self-condemnation, and doubt. This is not God's plan for His children. In this awesome section, Paul details what has been brought into the life of the Christian as a result of his justification.

1. Peace
- A. This is not a promised peace with men, but with God.
- B. There is no more enmity because of sin.
- C. The word (εἰρήνη) means "to join that which was separated."
- D. This is the attitude that is to dominate our lives (Phil. 4:6-7).
- E. This is not a peace that the world can give (John 14:27).

2. Grace
- A. Faith in Christ created a relationship with Him. That relationship led Him to introduce us to "grace."
- B. One cannot receive or know grace except through Jesus.
- C. We "stand" in grace (ἵστημι—stand is in the perfect tense, indicating a state that was true in the past and continues into the present). This represents assurance and security.

3. Hope
- A. This word (ἐλπίς) depicts desire + expectation (not like English word *hope* which reflects a measure of doubt).
- B. We are saved by hope (8:24) and are looking for it (2:7, 10).
- C. As a result of baptism, we have a living hope (1 Pet. 1:3), and this hope is an anchor for our souls (Heb. 6:18-19).

4. Tribulation
- A. It goes with the territory of being a Christian (James 1:2ff).
- B. The Christian uses tribulation to improve and grow.

5:6—Paul established the fact that all men are guilty of sin in the first four chapters. Now he uses four words that detail our former condition (see Sermon Seeds). Paul uses a preposition that is a sermon all in itself. He says that Christ died **for** the ungodly. The word **for** is ὑπέρ and means "in the place of." Robertson notes: "We were under (ὑπέρ) the curse; Christ became a curse over (ὑπέρ) us and so between us and the overhanging curse which fell upon him instead of us. The use of ὑπέρ for substitution is common in the papyri and in ancient Greek as in the N.T." (John 11:50; 2 Cor. 5:14). See A.T. Robertson, *Word Pictures*, p. 294.

Learning Romans 5

WHAT YOU WERE. WHAT YOU ARE NOW.
A STUDY IN THE CHRISTIAN JOURNEY (Romans 5:6-11)

Intro: It has been said that one cannot appreciate where he is unless he appreciates where he has been. Paul seems to concur, reminding us of our former state and then contrasts that with our present state.

1. **What you were:**
   A. Helpless
      (1) Greek—ἀσθενής means weak, unable to save ourselves.
      (2) It is important that we recognize that there was never a chance that we could, somehow, pull ourselves out of this condemnation.
   B. Ungodly
      (1) Greek—ἀσεβής means one who represents all that is against the nature, purity, and holiness of God.
      (2) This is a direct insult to the character of God. It is one who says "I don't want to be like you. I want to be exactly the opposite."
   C. Sinners
      (1) Greek—ἁμαρτωλός means one who has failed to meet the divine standard and thus is disapproved.
      (2) Man was in violation of God's Law, failing to live up to the standard He has set.
   D. Enemies
      (1) Greek—ἐχθρός means an opponent, standing over against one in a trial, an adversary.
      (2) Friendship with world creates enmity—James 4:4.

2. **What you are now:**
   A. Loved (v. 8)
      (1) Paul has much to say about God's love (1:7; 5:5, 8; 8:35, 37, 39; 9:25; 11:28; 14:15; 15:30)
      (2) It is truly amazing that God could love the unlovable!
   B. Justified (v. 9)
      (1) One of the most important concepts in this book (see Introduction)
      (2) The idea is that God now treats us as if we had never sinned!
   C. Saved (vv. 9, 10)
      (1) Carries the idea of "deliverance"—deliverance from the terrors of Hell!
      (2) Another important concept in this epistle: 1:16; 5:9, 10; 8:24; 9:27; 10:1, 9, 10, 13; 11:11, 14, 26; 13:11
   D. Reconciled (vv. 10, 11)
      (1) The word means "reestablishment of an interrupted or broken relationship, reconciliation" (BDAG 521).
      (2) Because of what we were (four points above), we had severed our relationship with God (cf. Is. 59:1-2). Thankfully, Jesus repaired that severed relationship.

5:7—This verse has been interpreted in various ways but seems to indicate that men will rarely give up their lives for others. They won't die for a **righteous man** (since most people don't care for religious "fanatics") and a few might die for a **good man** (one who is benevolent). If people won't die for the best this world has to offer, then they certainly won't die for the contemptible, despicable people of the world. Yet God did just that.

5:8-9—God **demonstrated His love** by sending Jesus (same point as in John 3:16). God proved His love by this one sacrificial act. What magnifies the gift is that God sent Christ to die for **sinners**—the contemptible people mentioned above.

In an attempt to capture the magnitude of the gift, Paul says **much more then**. Not only have we been justified (returning to the thought of v. 1), but we shall be **saved from the wrath of God**. It is important to note not only what we shall receive, but also what we shall *avoid*.

5:10-11—Paul adds another **much more**. By following his reasoning, he lays the foundation of justification, adding much more—salvation from wrath, adding reconciliation, then adding **saved by His life**. Paul wants the Christian to capture the beauty and significance of God's act for us in Christ.

5:12-21—**Special note on this section:** It has long been maintained that Romans 5:12-21 is one of the most difficult sections in the entire NT. The old joke (perhaps no joke?) was that Peter had his scroll opened to Romans 5 when he said that some of what Paul said was "difficult to understand" (2 Pet. 3:16). The critical point of interpretation rests on how we should understand three words: *righteousness*, *death*, and *life*. There are two major interpretations:

1) **Death = physical death; Life = physical life**. This interpretation maintains that Adam brought physical death into the world and Jesus (through the cross) gave man the gift of physical life. It argues that Adam should have died on the day he ate, but he didn't die, having been given a gift of extended time. Equally, all men deserve to die the minute they commit their first sin. But they don't. Why? Because of the gift of Christ, a gift that allows them time to enjoy a physical life.

2) **Death = spiritual death; Life = spiritual life**. This interpretation maintains that Adam introduced spiritual death (separation from God) into the world and that all men followed suit *only when they sinned*. Since all men sin, they have unfortunately followed the bad example of Adam. Christ, however, has introduced spiritual life (reconciliation to God). Just like man does not have to sin, so also man does not have to accept the gift of Christ.

I agree with the second (spiritual death/life) position. My reasons will be given in the following discussion.

5:12—It is important to note that this section begins with **therefore**. This means that Paul is not moving to a new point (which, if physical death were the correct position, he would be doing). The fact that we were *spiritually dead* is apparent from the four descriptive terms given in verses 6-10. Adam is here presented as the protasis to Christ. **Through** him something entered into the world— **sin**; and **death through sin** was a logical consequence. But that death wasn't *because of*

RESULTS OF JUSTIFICATION (Romans 5:1-4)

1. Paul is making it clear that both death and life are conditional. The physical death position makes it mandatory.
2. People die at all stages of life. This makes the "gift of Christ" greater for some than for others, making Him a respecter of persons (which 2:11 says God has no partiality).
3. Why do babies die? Why did the "gift of Christ" (physical life) fail in these cases?
4. The interpreter has to re-interpret three key words: *death*, *life*, and *righteousness*. In Romans Paul is speaking of spiritual death and life (6:11, 23; cf. Eph. 2:1, 4-5). *Righteousness* in Romans refers to God's removal of man's sin—treating him as if he had never sinned. This position makes "the gift of righteousness" (v. 17) physical life. There is no place in Romans where righteousness is used in this way.
5. If Christians "reign in life" then they should never die (v. 17). But the fact that they still die shows that they do not "reign."
6. This view makes Jesus' gift only temporary, and less of a gift for some than for others.
7. Of what value is this information (if this position is true)?

Adam, but **because all sinned**. Upon this clause should rest the entire interpretation of this section. This has been a key concept in the previous chapters (cf. 3:23).

5:13-14—Even before the Law of Moses was given people were guilty of sin (breaking moral law, for example). God did not **impute** sin in areas where there was no law. People before the law could be like Abraham and live spiritually. However, **death reigned** even over those who did not imitate the sin of Adam.

5:15-16—The **free gift** is justification, and is **not like the transgression** because it originates from God. Paul notes that the **many died** by the **transgression of the one**. Adam introduced something into the world, and the rest followed suit. They didn't have to sin but they did (choosing to follow Adam). Equally, Christ is introducing something into the world which all men can take advantage of (it is their choice).

5:16—Again Paul notes that he is making a contrast. The gift is different from the condemnation. When Adam sinned, the **judgment** came, **resulting in condemnation**. On the other hand, the **free gift** came in spite of **many transgressions**, providing God's forgiveness and **justification**. Before Adam there was no sin. After Adam the world knew sin. They followed suit, and therefore it is maintained that the consequences of sin originated with Adam (but comes to all *because all sinned*—v. 12).

5:17—Thanks to Adam's poor example, **death reigned through the one**. Death in this context refers to separation from God. It is in this verse that it becomes clearer what Paul is talking about. The student should focus on the word **receive**. The physical death position offers no choice. Man is given the "gift" from Adam (whether he wants it or not) and man is given the "gift" of Christ (physical life) whether he wants it or not. However, Paul is talking about something that people can **receive**. One can decide to accept what Adam brought (by sinning), or one can accept what Christ brought (through faith). If he/she accepts Christ's gift, then the result will be to **reign in life** (spiritually live—forever).

5:18-19—As noted in verse 12, **there resulted condemnation to all men** because "all sinned." It is not because Adam did something that was forever going to be forced upon man. Equally, **through the one act of righteousness** (the cross of Christ) **there resulted justification of life to all men**. Paul is speaking of potential. Because of Adam, man has the potential to reign in death; because of Christ man has the potential to reign in life. It is solely his choice. This view allows us to consistently interpret the word **justification** (to mean God's removal of man's sin and giving him the gift of eternal life—6:23). Adam made people potential **sinners**; Jesus makes people potentially **righteous**. If Christ has not been **obedient**, then this discussion would be mute. Fortunately, He gave Himself over to the divine plan (Heb. 5:8). Adam was **disobedient**. Again note the contrast between Adam and Christ.

5:20-21—In 3:20 Paul established that the purpose of the law was to bring the knowledge of sin. Its purpose was not to save or justify (3:31). When God gives more **law**, then naturally there is going to be an **increase** in sin. Yet God had a plan to account for that increased sin: **grace**. He wanted man educated on right and wrong, knowing that the more He revealed about sin the more there would be sin (see 7:7 for an example of this).

Sin has **reigned** because all have sinned. And it only takes one sin for one to experience **death** (separation from God). But thankfully God offered **grace**, through **righteousness** that afforded man the opportunity to enjoy **eternal life**. However, it must be noted that this offer is only **through Jesus Christ**.

ADAM BROUGHT

Death
(vv. 15, 17, 21)

Condemnation
(vv. 16, 18)

Sin
(vv. 19-20)

CHRIST BROUGHT

Justification
(vv. 16, 18, 19)

Grace
(vv. 15, 16, 17, 20)

Life
(vv. 1, 21)

Learning
Romans 6

DENNY PETRILLO

EXEGETICAL NOTES

Chapter Overview: Paul concluded chapter 5 by noting that grace was God's response to increased sin. That might prompt some to live disobediently. In this chapter Paul intends to show that the Christian made a life choice when he united himself with Christ in baptism. That choice was to die to sin and live to God. All men are slaves, and it is essential that we see ourselves as slaves of God and obediently serve Him.

6:1—Paul again uses the Τί οὖν construction (cf. 3:1, 9; 4:1), indicating that he is dealing with another argument or objection. He concluded chapter 5 by saying that increased sin brought increased grace (5:20). As noted in 3:5-8, some took this to mean that we should sin more in order to bring more of God's wonderful grace. Therefore, Paul asks the question on whether it is wise to **continue in sin** in order that **grace might increase**. The use of the word **continue** (ἐπιμένω) indicates that some had already determined that they need not alter their lifestyle of sin for the sake of the Gospel. Their reasoning was "My sin brings more grace."

6:2-3—Paul responds to this in a direct and powerful way: **May it never be!** (μὴ γένοιτο)—a typical response of Paul when he wants to identify the foolishness of an argument (cf. 3:4, 31). Paul has not said anything that would encourage sinfulness. Rather, he has called the Romans to holiness, encouraging them to repent (2:4), to be good examples (2:17-24), and to remember that God will judge the deeds of men (3:6). Here he extends his argument by noting that they had **died to sin**. This death, as will become evident in verse 3, is referring to their baptism (thus a spiritual death).

6:4—It is impossible to read this verse and not appreciate the importance and essentiality of baptism. If one intends to benefit from Christ's death, he is going to have to be united with Christ. The *only way* that this union occurs is through baptism. Our baptism was a death to sin <u>and</u> a resurrection to a new life (one that has died to sin).

THREE QUESTIONS (Romans 6:1-4)

Intro: Sometimes Christians do not act like they should. Sometimes they forget their Christian "roots." Such was the case with the Christians in Rome. Paul asked them three penetrating questions, questions that we should ask ourselves today as well.

1. Are we to continue in sin that grace might increase?
- A. Men are always looking for creative ways to continue in their sinful lifestyles but still have God's forgiveness and still have the promise of eternal life.
- B. This was a fanciful argument (my sin brings in a good thing—grace. Therefore, I should keep sinning. Because if I stop, then I will also stop God from sending His grace!).

2. How shall we who died to sin still live in it?
- A. Referring to their baptism.
- B. Logic would say that one who had died is not going to continue doing that which the living does.

3. Do you not know that all of us who have been baptized into Christ Jesus have been baptized into His death?
- A. Baptism is an act where we unite ourselves with Christ's death.
- B. This was a death to sin.
- C. "There is a definite connection between the death of Christ and man's justification. Paul has said that God set forth Jesus to be a propitiation through faith in his blood (3:25), that we are justified by his blood (5:9), and that we have been reconciled to God through the death of His Son (5:10). The book is written to those who have been reconciled to God by the death of His Son (1:7). Thus, Paul is describing for us how that reconciliation was realized, and how that gift of righteousness was received. It is in baptism that the Christian realizes that mystical union with the death of Christ" (Owen 39).

6:5—How does one become **united with** Christ? When he goes through that act which is **in the likeness of His death**. There is no other act, besides baptism, in which the Christian does this. It is well known that the word for *baptism* (βάπτισμα) means a burial or immersion. This fact alone automatically eliminates infant baptism, sprinkling, pouring and Holy Spirit baptism (because you can't be "raised" out of the Holy Spirit). Immersion in water is the one and only logical explanation of this section. Besides, it is clear that Paul wants our *physical* act of immersion to establish a *spiritual* link to the death, burial, and resurrection of Christ. When one is sprinkled, how is he "dying"? We don't sprinkle a little dirt on the corpse. We <u>bury it</u>! In addition, Paul notes that **if we were united with Him** (through baptism), then we will also be partakers **of His resurrection.**

6:6-7—Christians should know what their baptism meant (see Sermon Seeds). They have **died** (by their baptism) and are thus **freed from sin**. What did baptism do? It **freed** one from sin and its consequences. The word **freed** is actually the word *justified* (δικαιόω). This makes it clear that the Christian is justified *at the point* that he dies to sin. He dies to sin when he is baptized.

6:8-9—Why does one decide to be baptized? It is not only to be freed from sin, but it expresses a hope of a wonderful future where **we shall also live with Him**. One has two choices: life with Christ or death with Satan. It is noteworthy that Jesus, having been raised, is **never to die again**. His experience with death is over—so also, then, should the Christian's death to sin be over. Jesus won't have to die again, so the Christian shouldn't have to die to sin again.

6:10-11—Like Christ, we **die to sin**. The import of this should not be lost. How can a corpse do anything? How can it continue to respond to the commands of its master (in this case, Satan)? It can't! We are **dead to sin**. Yet we still live, but now with a new Master: God. **Even so** (οὕτως) is drawing a comparison: Christ and us.

KNOWING WHAT OUR BAPTISM MEANS (Romans 6:6)

Intro: Apparently the Roman Christians had forgotten what their baptism meant, and how it should have impacted their lives. Paul reminds them that there are three important truths that they should *know* because of their baptism.

1. **We should know that our old self was crucified with Him.**
   A. The old manner of life—the old way of living
   B. Crucified—shows permanence. This was a gesture of finality.
   C. We are happy to have killed that old self—because that was a lifestyle that was opposed to God and to everything good.

2. **We should know that our body of sin was done away with.**
   A. I would rather not keep a dead body around ("Behold it stinketh!")
   B. Why, then, would we want to keep around the old body that lived in contradiction with God? That old body was left in the watery grave. A new body emerged (v. 4; cf. 2 Cor. 5:17).

3. **We should know that we are no longer to be slaves to sin.**
   A. Why return to the old taskmaster? We hated him anyway!
   B. It is important to see that we were, in fact, *slaves*. We obeyed a master that wants only our demise.

Conclusion: It is clear (abundantly clear) from this verse that baptism is the dividing line between salvation and condemnation, serving God and serving Satan.

BAPTISM TERMINATED OUR RELATIONSHIP WITH SIN

1. Where Satan was our spiritual father and master
2. Where we were bondservants to sin
3. Where we were the property of Satan (Lanier 38)

6:12-13—Since we have died to sin, we **must not let sin reign**. This shows that (a) Paul was not expecting perfection. We do still sin—but we don't let it control us; (b) We are the one in control. **In your mortal body**—*mortal* means "subject to death" (cf. 8:11). We must develop a toughness, a determined attitude where we decide who is boss—and it isn't going to be Satan. We must respond to God's gift of grace and salvation by offering ourselves as **instruments** to God, ready to devote the **members** of our body to Him for His use.

6:14—Sin shall not be **master**—this means complete dominion over us. We may occasionally sin, but that doesn't make sin our master. How can this be? Because **you are not under law, but under grace**. Law demands perfect obedience, and those under law have no hope of justification (2:12-15). This verse had been widely misapplied by those who call for a "new hermeneutic." They point to this verse as proof that the NT is not a "law" or have a "pattern" for Christian conduct. God's grace (so they say) allows for flexibility in doctrine and practice. However, to promote this view is to completely miss what Paul means by the word **law**. Throughout Romans Paul is using this term to refer to *a system of justification by law-keeping*. He has made it clear that one cannot be justified through this approach (because it demands perfection, and all have sinned). Instead, we are **under grace** (a system that still demands obedience to the pattern but provides forgiveness when we fall short).

6:15-16—Again using the Τί οὖν terminology, Paul is ready to return to the question of 6:1. Of course one shouldn't sin just because he is **under grace**. The fact is our allegiance is apparent by noting **whom you obey**. In reality, everyone has a master (thus everyone is a slave). Yet a choice needs to be made on who is going to be one's master. Yet one should consider the consequences.

6:17-18—Paul is grateful that they were **obedient from the heart** (true, genuine) to that **form of teaching**. The word **form** (τύπος) has to indicate a pattern—because all the Christians obeyed it.

6:19—Paul is speaking in **human terms** by using slave/master terminology. They need to see that there are *two* masters in view, and they must decide which master they are going to serve. At one time in the past (before they were baptized) they **presented** themselves to (a) **impurity**—ἀκαθαρσία—that which is unclean and defiling; and (b) **lawlessness**—ἀνομία—that which clearly violated the laws laid down by God. Such a choice only leads to deeper depravity (**resulting in further lawlessness**). **So now** (now that they have died to sin) they should present themselves to God as **slaves to righteousness** (subjecting themselves to God's system of justification). This

Learning Romans 6

DO'S AND DON'TS (Romans 6:12-13)

Intro: One might ask: "How can I ever kill the sin in me? I'm not always like a corpse to temptation!" Paul here clarifies by two don'ts and one do.

1. Do not let sin reign.
    A. In your "mortal body." Remember, your body is still subject to the judgment of God. Fear Him for that reason! (Matt. 10:28f).
    B. That you should obey its lusts. Remember that you are still in control. You do not *have* to sin (cf. 1 Cor. 10:13).
    C. *Reign* does not have reference to an occasional sin
    D. On the Day of Judgment we will have no excuse—because we *let* Satan call the shots in our lives.

2. Do not go on presenting yourself…to sin.
    A. The terminology is that of one formally offering himself in service, and swearing allegiance to this master.
    B. Present "the members of your body"—has reference to our hands, eyes, ears, brain, feet, etc. Each part can be used for the benefit of Satan and his kingdom.
    C. As "instruments." Satan can use those body parts to further his evil intentions.

3. Do present yourself to God.
    A. "As those alive from the dead"—God has resurrected us to a new life. We are no longer dead in sin but alive to God.
    B. "Your members as instruments of righteousness." God can use us—all of our "instruments" to build and spread His kingdom.

The word *instrument* (ὅπλον) can have the following meanings: tool, weapon, or medical instrument (Bauer 716).

results in sanctification. One cannot be sanctified until he is justified. Sanctification represents the goal of one saved: to be like Christ.

6:20-21—When they served Satan, they were not expected to serve God. One can only obey one master (Matt. 6:24). We do not expect non-Christians to worship, give, evangelize, etc. They are **free** from the Lord who commands this (because they are obeying their master Satan). Yet, what **benefit** (καρπός—literally "fruit") did that lifestyle provide? Their former lives of sin produced nothing of value and even had some lingering negative affects now. They were **ashamed** of their past (unlike those of Jer. 6:15).

6:22-23—**But now** serves as a contrast to their past life of serving Satan. Paul reminds them that they have been **freed from sin**—again answering the question of verse 1. Also, if verse 14 means that there is nothing we need to do (since we're not under law), then what does being **enslaved to God** mean? What did being "obedient" to doctrine mean (v. 17)? Certainly as slaves of God we are expected to joyfully conform to His doctrine. Paul also notes that we have a **benefit** (fruit) as a result of our obedience: **sanctification** which leads to **eternal life.** This is vitally important, because the **wages of sin** (payment for services rendered) is **death** (God gives men what they have "worked" for). **Eternal life** is a **gift** (but only **in Christ**, and Christ must be **our Lord**—master, ruler, commander.

OBEYING THAT FORM OF DOCTRINE
WHY ONE BECOMES A CHRISTIAN

Intro: All Christians were called by the same message. There was a "form" that each needed to conform to in order to please God and become a child of His (6:17). But the reasons for such a decision are not always apparent—or we just forget about them. In 6:22-23, Paul reflects upon the decision to obey the Gospel.

1. WHY they obeyed
  A. To be "freed from sin"
    1. Law-keeping won't work.
    2. One has to have sin removed in order to stand before God and have any hope of eternal life.
  B. To become "enslaved to God"
    1. Being a slave to God is the only logical choice.
    2. Since men are going to be slaves to someone (v. 16), it only makes since that God be the one we choose to obey.

2. WHAT they received
  A. Their "benefit"—redemption, justification
  B. This benefit (καρπός—literally "fruit") is something that one reaps in this life but also in the life to come.
  C. Two parts of this benefit:
    1. Sanctification
    2. Eternal life
    i. Which is a free gift that God gives to those who make Jesus their "Lord."
    ii. Is the opposite of "death"—spiritual death; eternal separation from God.

WAGES VS. GIFTS (Romans 6:23)

1. Sin gives wages: no fruit, death.
2. God gives gifts: grace, redemption, eternal life.

Learning
Romans 7

DENNY PETRILLO

EXEGETICAL NOTES

Chapter Overview: While Paul had noted that the Law could not save, a critical question remained: How was the Jew to excuse themselves from obedience to the Law, since it was given to them by God Himself? In this chapter Paul will show them how they are released from that Law and free to join themselves to another (7:1-13). The Law revealed man's sinfulness. And, even though man is no longer under the Mosaic Law, he still struggles with sin under the law of Christ (7:14-25). There is only one way to win the battle with sin—through the Lordship of Christ.

The exegete will note that Paul uses the word *law* 23 times in this chapter, and the word *sin* is used 15 times.

7:1—It is clear that Paul is addressing specifically Jews here, those who **know the law**. The Law only has **jurisdiction** over a living person. Logically, we do not expect a dead person to be subject to any law.

7:2-3—Paul here offers an illustration to prove the point of verse 1. The Jew still lives, therefore how can he be released from his obligations to the Law of Moses? This illustration will show how. Paul notes that a woman is **bound** (δέω) by **law** (the law of God) to her **husband** as long as he is alive. However, once he **dies**, she is **released from the law**—she is no longer considered bound to him. However, if she decided to leave him (while he was alive) and marry another, she would be an **adulteress**. But she is not charged with such a sin if she remarries after her first husband died (v. 3).

7:4-6—Paul now gets to the point of this illustration. The Jews were **made to die to the Law**. But how could this be? This was brought about **through the body of Christ**. His death enabled them to **be joined to another**. That "other" was the risen Christ. He reminds them (v. 5) that being under the Law was not a profitable time, only leading them to **death**. But thankfully they have been **released from the Law**—how?—**having died to that by which we were bound** (**bound** here is κατέχω). So the death of Christ enabled them to have a fresh start.

RELEASED FROM THE LAW (Romans 7:1-6)

LAW HUSBAND	For the married woman is bound by law to her husband while he is living (7:2)	SINNER WIFE
LAW (DEAD) HUSBAND	...but if her husband dies, she is free from the law (7:3)	SINNER (FREE) WIFE
CHRIST HUSBAND	Therefore, my brethren, you were also made to die to the Law through the body of Christ, that you might be joined to another, to Him who was raised from the dead (7:4)	BELIEVER WIFE

Paul's illustration demonstrates how the Jew, bound to the old law, could be released from that law. Through the death of Jesus, they died to the Law. That freed them and enabled them to marry another. They joined themselves to Christ.

7:7—Beginning with yet another Τί οὖν Paul is ready to draw a conclusion based on verses 1-6. Might a Jew respond by saying that the **Law** was **sin**? This thought would be logical, because he might reason that since the Law could not justify and since the Law was something they were trying to get out from under, it must be evil. But such is far from the truth (**may it never be!** μὴ γένοιτο—6:1). Paul intends to prove that the law is "holy, righteous and good" (7:12). To do this, he uses himself as an illustration (and will do so through the rest of the chapter). Paul sees good in the law in that it opened his eyes to what was sinful. For example, he would not have known that **coveting** was **sin** until the Law so declared it (Ex. 20:17; Deut. 5:21).

7:8-9—Once God made it known that coveting was a sin, Satan immediately sprang into action and **took opportunity** through God's command to produce coveting **of every kind**. Before the

Learning Romans 7

commandment coveting was not sinful; after the commandment it was sinful. Paul says that he was once **alive apart from the Law**. Since the Law had been in existence 1,400 years before Paul, he must mean he was **alive** as a child—before he reached the age of accountability. Today we build the same case—that children are not charged with sin and do not need to be baptized until "sin becomes alive." Paul is simply saying that he had been covetous before he understood the Law condemned such. The Law did not *make him* more covetous. Once, however, that he became accountable to God's commandment and realized he was in violation of it, he **died** (again this must mean spiritually—as in Ephesians 2:1).

7:10—God gives His commands so that mankind can know wrong and avoid it. It was intended to **result in life** (if obeyed). However, it would be naive for us to assume that Satan would stand by and not use a command for his own evil purposes. Such was the case with coveting. Once Satan succeeded in getting Paul to covet, that command resulted **in death** (cf. 6:23). Death is the consequence when one violates God's laws.

7:11—Once it became a sin (when God revealed it), Satan then tempted man to covet. Thus, **sin** took **opportunity through the commandment**. It also **deceived**. How? (a) By promising more joy from the sin than it can deliver, and (b) by making the sinner think that there are no consequences if he commits the sin. Satan is the great deceiver (Rev. 12:9; cf. Heb. 3:13; Eph. 4:22).

7:12-13—Paul uses the terms **Law** and **commandment** synonymously. He finds no fault with the Law, but instead declares it to be **holy, righteous, and good** (see Sermon Seeds). So it isn't the law's fault that Paul sinned. The problem (weakness) lies solely with Paul. The Law was **good**, but **sin** used it to bring about Paul's **death**. God gives commands so that we might see sin the way He sees it. Such was the case with coveting. It is, in the eyes of God, a repugnant evil with horrifying consequences. But how does **sin become utterly sinful**? When it uses that which is good (the commandment) as a tool for evil (encourage someone to sin).

THE LAW (Romans 7:12)

Intro: Paul did not want to leave the impression that the Law was man's problem—and that he could blame the law for his sinfulness. The problem did not lie with the Law, but with man who is weak. To Paul the Law was...

1. Holy
  A. It originates from the holy God.
  B. It is a law that defines, promotes, and identifies holiness.
2. Righteous
  A. It demonstrates God's righteousness, justice, and equity.
3. Good
  A. It is for the betterment of mankind.
  B. It helps them know how to become better people.

7:14—Paul does not want to leave the impression that the person redeemed no longer struggles with sin. Even when one was under the **law**—a **spiritual** law (because it was God-given), there was still the struggle with **sin**. Again Paul clearly places the blame where it belongs—on him—not on God or His holy Law. Even though we have been "released from the Law" (v. 6), it wasn't because there were inherent flaws with the Law. The problem was with the weakness of man—and Paul is among them. Now that he is a Christian, he still has the same struggles. Removal of the Law did not alter this struggle. Why? Because **I am of the flesh**—I have the desires that are common desires (e.g. "lust of the flesh").

7:15—Paul here details his struggle. He says regarding what he is **doing**: (a) He does not **understand**—knowing his commitment to the Lord, it doesn't make sense that he would have this struggle; (b) he is not **practicing** what he would like to do—the desires of the flesh get in the way of full devotion to the Lord and His will; (c) he is **doing** the very thing that he **hates**—the person truly committed to the Lord is not satisfied with flaws in his character and genuinely despises weaknesses and failings in his character.

7:16—Paul does not like the way this is working out. His own life and actions trouble him greatly. Every true Christian can relate to this struggle. In fact, Paul acknowledges that his desire to do right confirms that the Law is **good** (because if it wasn't, why would one try to live up to its standards?) He is not sinning because he loves to sin, but because he is weak.

7:17-18—As Paul has reasoned through this, he has come to the conclusion that there are *two parts* to his character. The "real" Paul wants to do good and completely obey God. The weak, fleshly Paul represents the **sin that indwells**. The **wishing** to do good is **present**, but the fact is the **doing of the good** is not. This shows an attitude of genuine spirituality—he *wants* to do right. He has not accepted (or justified) sin in his life. This is a genuine struggle.

7:19-20—The words **do** (ποιέω) and **practice** (πράσσω) are admittedly difficult (especially in light of 1 John 3:9). Yet the exegete reminds himself that this is Romans—not 1 John. The context is radically different, and the meaning of *practice* is equally different. Paul here is discouraged by the presence of sin in his life—sins that occur far too frequently for this spiritual man. To him *any* sin in his life is unacceptable. He repeats that this sinful person is not really him, but **sin which dwells** in him.

7:21-23—Paul here shows that he is not really dealing with a battle with the Law of Moses, but a struggle with two laws (the **law of evil** and the **Law of God**). The "real" Paul (what he here calls the **inner man**) **joyfully concurs** with everything God has asked of man to do. He has no problem with God's ordinances and is prepared to obey them all. However, reality sets in and he sees failures in his body, which seems to beckon to the call of a **different law**—one that yields to fleshly desires. This struggle is so great that Paul sees himself as a **prisoner**, being held captive by a body that does things he does not want to do. The goal of Paul (and every Christian) is to allow the spiritual mind (the **law of my mind**) to take over and conquer the fleshly body (the **law of sin**).

PAUL & THE CHRISTIAN'S STRUGGLE (Romans 7)

Intro: Many commentators have argued that Romans 7:14-25 is not to be understood as the struggles Paul had with sin.

1. Interpretations
- A. Paul is detailing his personal battle with sin.
- B. Paul is reflecting on his past battles with sin as one under the Mosaic Law. He now, under the Law of Christ, no longer has these struggles.
- C. Paul is merely using himself as an "example" of the plight of every Christian. He does not personally have these struggles.

2. Evidences in favor of 7:14-25 being a personal treatise of Paul, detailing his personal struggles with sin:
- A. He changes the verb tenses from past tense (7:1-13) to present tense (7:14-25). This clearly puts the context into the present (thus eliminating argument *B* above).
- B. He uses the personal pronoun "I" 24 times, and "me/my/mine" 14 times. The natural understanding, then, would be that Paul is detailing a personal struggle.
- C. There is nothing to indicate that Paul is using a literary technique where he is only using himself as an "example" of the struggle of every Christian.
- D. Uses the word *now* (νυνί) in verse 17, indicating a present situation (cf. 5:9, 11; 6:21; 7:6).

THE JUSTIFIED MAN IN NEED OF SANCTIFICATION

1. This man delights in the Law of God (v. 22).

2. This man serves the Law of God (v. 25).

3. His will is always towards that which is good (vv. 15, 18, 19, 21).

4. There is a war going on in this man who loves and wishes to do good; such is not the case of the unregenerate person

5. The note of hope and triumph of this man proves him to be regenerate (v. 25) (Lanier 49).

But how is this to be done? Paul will answer this in the next two verses.

7:24—Paul concludes that he is a **wretched man** (ταλαίπωρος—despondent, fed-up, and miserable). He continually fights this battle and loses far too frequently. He doesn't see, within himself, the ability to win this war. He is captured by **the body of this death**—not his physical body, but those evil tendencies that he buried with Christ when he was baptized (6:6). Those tendencies are still present, despite his baptism.

7:25—Finally, Paul finds the answer: **Christ Jesus**. His commitment is to Christ and to **serving the law of God**. He knows that the **flesh** still has to deal with the **law of sin**. Yet victory is in Christ. One might conclude that Paul considers himself lost—until he gets to this verse. Paul demonstrates a joy (**thank God**) that there is deliverance. Not deliverance from sin, but from the *consequences* of sin. This verse, then, provides a fitting summation of chapters 1–7: all men have sinned; all men need a Savior; all men need Jesus Christ. He is our one and only hope. It is only through Him that one can receive much needed grace and justification.

THE WRETCHED MAN (THE STRUGGLE WITH SIN)

Intro: Every Christian who struggles with his/her own frailties and weaknesses can relate to Romans 7:14-25. Paul, describing his personal battle with sin, ultimately concludes that he is a "wretched man." Who is this wretched (miserable) man?

1. The one who is justified
   A. We are not here dealing with one who questions his own salvation. He is saved.
   B. A justified person is not a sinless person. He is one who has had the blessing of God's removal of all his sin

2. The one who has not reached the goal of being conformed to the image of Christ (8:29)
   A. He desires to do that which is good and right.
   B. He is justified but not sanctified to the degree he desires.
   C. His goal is to grow stronger spiritually.

3. The one who is not satisfied with sin in his life
   A. He is not going to say, "Oh well, I guess I'll always have this sin problem!"
   B. He hates sin and continually wars against it (7:23).
   C. He intends, with Christ's help, to conquer sin and be "set free" from a body that yields to sin (7:24).

Learning
Romans 8

DENNY PETRILLO

EXEGETICAL NOTES

Chapter Overview: There is an unfortunate break here, because Paul is continuing the thought introduced in 7:24-25. How is he going to be "set free" from a body that continually does evil? The answer is "through Jesus Christ." But what does that mean? Chapter 8 provides the answer—the answer for how the Christian can conquer sin in his life and meet the goal of 8:29. Paul will detail, in a series of points, how the Christian conquers sin. We will call these "God's incentives to holiness."

8:1—The most logical place to start, if you are trying to encourage one to press on and not give up, is to assure him that he is saved. If there is no hope for salvation, why try? Paul states definitively: **there is no condemnation for those who are in Christ Jesus**. When he asked, "Who will set me free" (7:24), the answer is "Christ will."

8:2-4—The **law of the Spirit of life** is the Gospel (cf. 2 Cor. 3:6—"covenant of the Spirit"). The Gospel is the "new law in town" and it says that you are free from the old law **of sin and death** (the law that said "if you violate my precepts you have sinned and deserve to die"). The **law** could not justify or save—because man was **weak** (unable to keep it). Therefore, God took care of the problem by **sending His Son** and **condemned sin in the flesh** (in the flesh of Christ). This enables us to meet the **requirement of the Law** (perfection) through the avenue of grace. What Jesus did on the cross did not automatically save all, but only those who walk **according to the Spirit**.

8:5-8—Paul here contrasts the fleshly **mind** with the spiritual **mind**. The fleshly mind is described in four ways (vv. 7-8), whereas the spiritual mind is **life and peace**.

8:9-11—If one has the **Spirit of God** dwelling in them then they are spiritually **alive**—because of **righteousness** (not because of sinlessness, but because God has justified). It is this indwelling Spirit who will eventually bring about our resurrection.

GOD'S INCENTIVES TO HOLINESS (Romans 8)

Intro: God does not want us to become hopelessly discouraged by our own sinfulness. He challenges us to greater heights, with the ultimate goal of "being conformed to the image of His Son" (v. 29). But how can this be done? This chapter provides God's incentives.

1. **There is no condemnation in Christ (v. 1).**
   A. We have to start here—having the assurance that our sins were not the "deal breaker"—destroying any hope of salvation.
   B. It is essential to note that his assurance is only "in Christ."
2. **We are freed from the law of sin and death (vv. 2-4).**
   A. There would be no value to forgiving our past violations of law, only to return to that law (that allowed NO mistakes).
   B. We are now subject to a new law—one that has grace.
3. **We have divine instructions on how to live spiritually (vv. 5-8).**
   A. We can "walk according to the Spirit."
   B. There is no need for us to be dominated by the fleshly mind.
4. **We have confidence and assurance because of the indwelling Spirit (vv. 9-11).**
   A. Without this Spirit we "do not belong to Him" (v. 9).
   B. This Spirit will raise our bodies like He did the body of Christ.
5. **We have been given a divine mandate (vv. 12-17).**
   A. God has expressed confidence in us that we can be faithful.
   B. He has "adopted us" and now expects us to conduct ourselves as His children.
6. **We have promised blessings if we strive toward holiness (vv. 18-25).**
   A. God puts before us the glorious day we will be revealed to be His children (despite what others may have said about us).
   B. Our bodies will be redeemed (v. 23).
   C. We have our hopes realized (vv. 24-25).
7. **We have the promise that God will help us (vv. 26-30).**
   A. God gives us the Holy Spirit to "help our weaknesses" (v. 26).
   B. We have that same Spirit to "intercede for us" (vv. 26-27).
   C. God promises that ultimately it will all work out for good (v. 28).
   D. As His children we are the "predestined," "called," "justified," and "glorified."
8. **We have confidence that our struggles have nothing to do with God's love for us (vv. 31-39).**
   A. Four great questions designed to provide confidence and assurance:
      i. If God is for us, who can be against us? (v. 31)
      ii. Who will bring a charge against God's elect? (v. 33)
      iii. Who is the one who condemns? (v. 34)
      iv. Who shall separate us from the love of Christ? (v. 35)
   B. Bottom line: Nothing can separate us from God and His love (v. 39).

Learning Romans 8

8:12-13—God's forgiveness does not remove our **obligation** to live holy lives (returning to the thought of 6:1). We have no obligation to the **flesh**—that which wants us to follow our lusts in violation of God's will. The flesh is our enemy because if we yield to it, we **must die**. How does one win the battle against the flesh? Paul says one is able to put to death the deeds of the flesh **by the Spirit**. This refers to the Holy Spirit (because of v. 14, where Paul calls Him the "Spirit of God"). By **live** and **die** Paul must mean spiritual life and death, because all men die physically.

8:14-15—Paul here identifies what we are obligated to do—follow the lead of the **Spirit of God**. When we do this (and only when we do this) can we be identified as **sons of God**. To be **led by the Spirit** is to be guided and directed by the Spirit through the inspired Word (1 Cor. 2:13; Eph. 3:3-5). The Holy Spirit, in the first century, led the apostles to the truth (John 15:26; 16:13). When we follow the Spirit-inspired apostles (through their writings), then we are also being led by the Spirit. The Spirit no longer leads directly. All men are accountable to the written revelation. This text is not talking about how to become a Christian, but how, as Christians, we should live.

Our obligation to God is found in the fact that He has **adopted** us and enabled us to have an intimate relationship with God by which we can say "**Abba! Father!**" We should not have an attitude of a slave (**spirit of slavery**) but the attitude of a **son** (**spirit of adoption**).

8:16-17—How can we *know* that we belong to God and that He considers us His children? The **Spirit Himself** bears **witness** to this fact. He does this through the Word. By studying Scripture, we know exactly who God's children are. And, if we are God's **children**, then we are also **heirs**. But the wonderful inheritance is only for those who are willing to **suffer with Him**. This indicates that suffering is a necessity (2 Tim. 3:12). But what do we receive as heirs? The answer to that is found in verses 18-25.

8:18—This section is based upon the promise of verse 18. The **sufferings** in this life should not be **compared** with the marvels of our inheritance (**glory to be revealed to us**). It is noteworthy that the apostle Paul, who suffered greatly for the sake of Christ, is the one saying this.

8:19-22—This unique section has Paul comparing the desires of the **creation** with our own desires. Our struggle with sin makes us long for the next life. It also makes us long for the day that we will be vindicated for our choice to follow God. We will be universally revealed as being **sons of God**. In this context the **creation** (κτίσις) can only mean the material universe: the land, trees, planets, etc.). It was this material universe that was **subjected to futility**. This happened when Adam and Eve sinned, and the earth was commissioned to produce thorns and thistles and to produce her fruit only with much effort (Gen. 3:17-19). This was not what the creation wanted to do (**not of its own will**), because God had created her to be fruitful and beautiful. But she was **subjected** to God's will but nevertheless **hopes** for the day when she will be **set free**. This freedom, in context, means a day that she will again return to doing what she was originally created to do. For this day the creation **groans**, waiting for the day that she can give birth to the new earth (2 Pet. 3:13; Rev. 21:1).

OUR HOLY OBLIGATION (Romans 8:12-17)

Intro: As a boy I was motivated by my dad saying "Son, I'm counting on you." He entrusted me with a job, and I was obligated to do my very best. I didn't want to let him down. Equally, God has charged us to move toward holiness. This obligation has the following requirements:

1. We are not obligated to the flesh.
- A. We do not have to "live according to the flesh."
- B. Satan is no longer our master. We owe him nothing—no allegiance, no devotion, no obedience. He is our enemy!
- C. If we obligate ourselves to the flesh, we "must die."

2. We are obligated to the spirit.
- A. Through this we "put to death the deeds of the body."
- B. God is now our master, and we have voluntarily put ourselves under His control and direction. Our minds are now given over to spiritual thinking with spiritual commitments.
- C. By making this choice we "will live."

3. We are obligated to live as sons.
- A. God has exalted us from "slave" to "son." This move carries with it even greater obligations.
- B. As sons we are obligated to "suffer with Him." This means to:
  1. Deny self
  2. Take up cross
  3. Follow Him (Matt. 16:24)

Conclusion: Only those who live up to the divine obligation can have any reasonable hope of receiving the inheritance and be glorified with Christ. There is an inheritance waiting, but it will be given only to those to whom God says, "Well done."

8:23—The creation is not the only one that **groans**. Paul says that even **we ourselves** (God's children) groan, those who have the **first fruits of the Spirit**. "First fruits" is terminology that indicates more to follow (cf. 1 Cor. 1:16; 15:20; 16:15). This seems to be saying that we have received only a portion of what the Spirit is going to give us. Christians **wait eagerly** for their **adoption as sons**, which will occur when we are resurrected (**the redemption of our body**).

8:24-25—Our **hope** is not a vain one. It is that desire and expectation that encourages us to "hold the fort" and not give up. By not giving up we will be **saved**. We hope for that which we know by faith.
8:26-27—Paul says **in the same way** (ὡσαύτως) the **Spirit** does the same thing as the creation and

the sons of God do: it **groans** (compare with vv. 22, 23). The sons of God struggle with **weakness**, and Paul says that the **Spirit helps our weakness**. What weakness is he referring to? **We do not know how to pray as we should**. We may struggle with the words and how to express ourselves—but no need to worry. God has even taken care of that concern by letting the indwelling Spirit communicate our feelings. Paul says that the Spirit **intercedes** (ὑπερεντυγχάνω—to petition or plead) for us, with **groanings too deep for words**. What we are not able to put into words the Spirit can. How is he able to do this? It is because He (the Spirit) **searches the hearts** of those He indwells. He knows what the spiritual mind is (not, as in NAS, the mind of the Spirit. The Spirit is the subject, and therefore cannot be said to know His own mind. He knows *our* minds, that we are spiritual people, and is able to **intercede** for us, the **saints**). He only does this for the saints, and He does it because it is God's will for him to do it.

PAULINE COSMOLOGY
WHAT WILL HAPPEN TO THE CREATION (Romans 8:18-25)

Intro: Scholars have long marveled (and struggled) with what Paul says about the creation in this section.

1. The creation is presented as something animate, not inanimate.
- A. The creation has anxious longing (v. 19).
- B. The creation waits eagerly (v. 19).
- C. The creation has a will (v. 20).
- D. The creation hopes (v. 20).
- E. The creation groans (v. 22).
- F. The creation suffers (v. 22).

2. The subjection of the creation
- A. She was originally created to easily produce fruit (Gen. 2:9-17).
- B. She was forced, by God, to be "cursed" (Gen. 3:18) and to produce that which is worthless (Gen. 3:19) and to produce that which is valuable only with much effort (Gen. 3:19).
- C. Paul says that subjection continues "until now" (8:22).

3. The future of the creation
- A. Something will happen to it when the sons of God are revealed (v. 19).
- B. The creation will be set free from its slavery to corruption (v. 21). It is going to be burned up (2 Pet. 3:10-12).
- C. The creation is "pregnant" and is anticipating "childbirth" (v. 22).

Conclusion: This section goes along with 2 Peter 3:13 and Revelation 21:1, where we are told about the "new heavens and new earth," terminology which describes our eternal abode (John 14:1-3).

8:28—The Greek continues to have the Spirit as the subject (not God, as in the NAS). The Spirit here is said to **cause all things to work together for good**. This translation is misleading, suggesting that the Spirit will turn events so that they favor the elect. Such is not at all what the verse is saying. Rather, it is the Spirit who *works in all things for good*. This allows bad things to happen (see vv. 18, 35-36), but there can ultimately be a good result (our "glorification" in the end—v. 30). The foremost concern is that *God's* **purpose** is accomplished. The Spirit uses those who **love God**.

8:29-30—God's ultimate purpose for us is for us to be **glorified**. But this will only happen when we meet the ultimate goal: to be **conformed to the image of His son**. This is what God **predestined** (that He would save those in Christ). This is solely *our choice*. God does not predetermine what you will do, but predetermined what *He will do* to those in Christ: **call, justify, glorify**.

8:31—Paul introduces this section with a preliminary question: **What shall we say to these things?** On the basis of the previous discussion (that God loves us and wants to save us), what conclusions ought to be drawn? In order to answer this, Paul asks four questions, all beginning with the Greek τίς. The first question is a first-class conditional, meaning "since God is for us."

8:32-33—The next question asks a question based upon the sacrifice of Christ. Is it logical to see what happened to Jesus and *still* conclude that God doesn't want to save us? This being the case, there is no **charge** that can legitimately be brought up against **God's elect**—because God has **justified** (meaning, there is no sin left, therefore nothing to charge us with).

8:34—Again the sacrifice of Jesus is in view, detailing four acts that all prove that those in Christ will not be **condemned**. This verse describes the entire redemptive work of Christ.

8:35—The final question has to do with **separation**. Paul is going present a long list of events that have the *potential* to separate us from God. Certainly history will bear out that events like **tribulation, distress, persecution**, etc. have cause Christians to forfeit their faith. The words **tribulation** and **distress** (θλῖψις and στενοχωρία) are words Paul used in 2:9 to describe what evildoers will receive. Sometimes the righteous receive the same as the wicked.

8:36—The OT (Psalm 44:22) confirmed that the lot of God's people would be a difficult one. Therefore, they ought not be surprised when things turn out poorly (again, showing that v. 28 is not promising an easy life).

8:37-39—The key is, no matter what may befall the Christian, that he can **overwhelmingly conquer**. Yet the victory is not because of some mystical inner strength, but because of **Him who loved us**.

Learning Romans 8

ALL THINGS (Romans 8:28)

Intro: This passage has often been misapplied, supposedly offering divine intervention to make life good for Christians. Yet reality teaches us that "all things don't work out for good." It didn't work out for good for Jesus, or Lazarus, or those Christians under the altar in Revelation 6.

1. We must not let the doctrine of predestination color our understanding of this verse.
   A. God has not developed a blueprint or script for your life.
   B. He is not the cause of everything that happens to us in life.

2. We must not understand this verse to be teaching that the Christian will be spared pain and suffering.
   A. These are obviously not "good."
   B. 8:18, 31-39 clearly show that one may have a multitude of troubles—even to the point of death.
   C. Frequently what people think is this: "God promises to make all things good for those who love Him. It hasn't worked out for good for me. Therefore, He must not like me and is trying to get back at me for not loving Him like I should."

3. We must understand this verse to be saying that God loves us, *regardless* of what happens.
   A. There will be ultimately a good result (but not necessarily in this life).
   B. The good mentioned is the "glorified" in v. 30.

GOD'S PREDESTINATION

1. His original plan, before creation, was to save those in Christ.

2. His original plan was for the saved to imitate Christ.

3. Those who follow Christ are considered those who have answered God's call.

4. Those who answered God's call are justified

5. The justified are the ones who will ultimately be glorified.

THE FOUR QUESTIONS: LESSONS ABOUT GOD (Romans 8:31-39)

Intro: The Christians needs to understand exactly where he stands in God's scheme of things—in spite of difficulties, struggles and persecutions. These questions are designed to get us to see the "big picture."

1. If God is for us, who is against us?
   A. God is almighty and all-powerful.
   B. What force, then, would dare stand against us?
   C. Proof: God "delivered" up Jesus for us. This establishes the fact that He is "for us."

2. Who is the one who brings a charge against God's elect?
   A. God stands as the ultimate Judge (James 4:11), and He has made His decision: "Justified!"
   B. Satan would have a legitimate case if our sins were not completely removed (where our slate is clean). But, with *no* sin on our ledger, what can he charge us with?

3. Who is the one who condemns?
   A. Certainly we might anticipate the answer to be "Satan."
   B. Yet, when God has justified, there is no one who can condemn.
   C. On what basis can we bypass condemnation? Paul offers as evidence the redemptive work of Christ:
       (1) Jesus died—emphasizing the importance of His blood.
       (2) Jesus was raised—now serving as our High Priest.
       (3) Jesus is at right hand—position of power and influence.
       (4) Jesus is our intercessor—we have a divine advocate.

4. Who shall separate us from the love of Christ?
   A. Seven (complete number) possibilities are offered—but none can succeed.
   B. OT predicted sufferings—but we conquer because of His love.
   C. Nine other powers listed that might separate—they all fail.
   D. No external force can separate—it has to be *our choice*.

BIBLIOGRAPHY

Aageson, James W. "Scripture and Structure in the Development of the Argument in Romans 9–11." *Catholic Biblical Quarterly* 48:2 (April 1986): 265-89.

Aalen, S. "Glory, Honour." *New International Dictionary of New Testament Theology*. Grand Rapids: Zondervan Publishing House, 1986: 46.

Alford, Henry. *Alford's Greek Testament: An Exegetical and Critical Commentary, Vol IV*. Grand Rapids: Baker Book House, 1857.

Allen, Kenneth. "Justification by Faith." *Bibliotheca Sacra* (April-June 1978):109-16.

Batey, Richard. "'So All Israel Will Be Saved.' An Interpretation of Romans 11:25-32." *Interpretation* 20 (April 1966): 218-28.

Bauer, Walter. *A Greek-English Lexicon of the New Testament and Other Early Christian Literature*. 2nd Edition. Revised by William F. Arndt, F. Wilbur Gingrich, and Frederick W. Danker. Chicago: University of Chicago Press, 1979. (Abbreviated as "BDAG" in the text).

Bromley, Geoffrey W., ed. *Theological Dictionary of the New Testament*. Grand Rapids: Wm. B. Eerdmans, 1985.

Brown, Colin, ed. *New International Dictionary of New Testament Theology*. Grand Rapids: Zondervan, 1975.

Bruce, F.F. *New Testament History*. Garden City: Doubleday and Company, Inc., 1972.

Bruce, F.F. *Romans: An Introduction and Commentary, Vol. 6 of Tyndale New Testament Commentaries*. Downers Grove: InterVarsity Press, 1985.

Büchsel, Friedrich. "Ἐριθεία," *Theological Dictionary of the New Testament*. Grand Rapids: Eerdmans, 1964: 661.

Cranfield, C.E.B. *A Critical and Exegetical Commentary on the Epistle to the Romans*. Edinburgh: T & T Clark, 1975.

Cranfield, C.E.B. "Romans 9:30-10:4." *Interpretation* 34 (1980): 70-74.

Dunn, James D. G. *Romans 1–8, Vol. 38A of Word Biblical Commentary*. Dallas: Word, Incorporated, 1988.

Earle, Ralph. *Word Meanings in the New Testament.* Peabody: Hendrickson Publishers, 1986.

Guthrie, Donald. *New Testament Introduction.* Downers Grove: InterVarsity Press, 1970.

Harrison, Everett F. "Romans" in *The Expositor's Bible Commentary: Romans through Galatians*, ed. Frank E. Gaebelein. Grand Rapids: Zondervan Publishing House, 1976: 29.

Hastings, James. *The Speaker's Bible.* Aberdeen, Scotland: The 'Speaker's Bible' Offices, 1924.

Heil, John Paul. "Christ, the Termination of the Law (Romans 9:30–10:8)." *Catholic Biblical Quarterly* 63:3 (July 2001): 484-98.

Hiebert, D.E. *An Introduction to the Pauline Epistles.* Chicago: Moody Press, 1954.

Hughes Robert B. and Laney, J. Carl. *Tyndale Concise Bible Commentary.* The Tyndale Reference Library. Wheaton: Tyndale House Publishers, 2001.

Jamieson, Robert, Fausset, A. R., and Brown, David. *A Commentary, Critical and Explanatory, on the Old and New Testaments.* Oak Harbor: Logos Research Systems, Inc., 1997.

Keener Craig S. and InterVarsity Press. *The IVP Bible Background Commentary: New Testament.* Downers Grove: InterVarsity Press, 1993.

Kittel, Gerhard and Friedrich, Gerhard, ed. *Theological Dictionary of the New Testament* (10 Volumes). Grand Rapids: Wm. B. Eerdmans Pub. Co., 1967.

Kittell, Gerhard, Bromiley, Geoffrey W. and Gerhard Friedrich, eds. *Theological Dictionary of the New Testament.* Electronic ed. Grand Rapids: Eerdmans, 1964. (Abbreviated as TDNT in the text).

Lanier, Roy H. Sr. *Class Notes on Romans.* Bear Valley Bible Institute. Denver, Co.

Lard, Moses E. *Commentary on Romans.* Delight: Gospel Light Publishing Co., 1875.

Lenski, R.C.H. *The Interpretation of St. Paul's Epistle to the Romans.* Minneapolis: Augsburg Pub. House, 1936.

Louw, Johannes P. and Eugene Albert Nida. *Greek-English Lexicon of the New Testament: Based on Semantic Domains.* New York: United Bible Societies, 1996.

MacArthur, John. *New Testament Commentary: Romans 9–16.* Chicago: Moody Press, 1994.

Metzger, Bruce Manning and United Bible Societies. *A Textual Commentary on the Greek New Testament, Second Edition a Companion Volume to the United Bible Societies' Greek New Testament (4th Rev. Ed.).* London; New York: United Bible Societies, 1994.

Moo, Douglas J. "The Epistle to the Romans," *The New International Commentary on the New Testament*. Grand Rapids: Wm. B. Eerdmans Publishing Co., 1996.

Mounce, Robert H. *Romans, Vol. 27 of The New American Commentary*. Nashville: Broadman & Holman Publishers, 1995.

Morris, Leon. *The Pillar New Testament Commentary: The Epistle to the Romans*. Grand Rapids: Wm. B. Eerdmans Pub. Co., 1988.

Newman, Barclay Moon and Eugene Albert Nida. *A Handbook on Paul's Letter to the Romans, UBS Handbook Series*. New York: United Bible Societies, 1973.

Owen, Dan R. *The Righteousness of God*. Unpublished Commentary, 1984.

Owen, Dan R. *A Teacher's Commentary on Romans*. Murrells Inlet: Covenant Books, 2024.

Paschall Franklin H. and Hobbs, Hershel H. *The Teacher's Bible Commentary: A Concise, Thorough Interpretation of the Entire Bible Designed Especially for Sunday School Teachers*. Nashville: Broadman and Holman Publishers, 1972.

Sanday, W. and Headlam, A.C. *A Critical and Exegetical Commentary on the Epistle to the Romans*. New York: Scribner's, 1896.

Applying
ACKNOWLEDGE THE POWER OF THE GOSPEL

ROMANS 1:16-17

JOE WELLS

"For I am not ashamed of the gospel, for it is the power of God for salvation to everyone who believes, to the Jew first and also to the Greek."

INTRODUCTION

It's been said that it's the most challenging mountain to climb in the world. Ever since the first recorded attempt in 1902, the grim statistic of it claiming 18% of climbers' lives is a strong testimony to the accuracy of such a claim.[1] Located high in the Karakoram range, on the border between Pakistan and China, stands a mountain so brutal it's been nicknamed "Savage Mountain." Officially known as K2, it's the second-highest peak in the world at a staggering 28,251 feet (8,611 meters). But don't let that number fool you. This beast is a different ballgame compared to Everest, the highest mountain. For anyone brave (or crazy) enough to take it on, climbing K2 isn't just about physical strength. It's a mental battle, a test of endurance, and a willingness to face nature's wrath head-on.

K2's slopes are no joke. Unlike Everest that has well-trodden paths and fixed ropes, K2 throws everything at you: sheer rock faces, exposed ridges, and climbs so steep they'll leave your legs screaming. The most common route, the Abruzzi Spur, is a treacherous maze of ice walls, falling rocks, and gut-wrenching angles. You can't afford to make a single mistake. Then there's the Bottleneck, the mountain's most infamous section. I want you to picture yourself at 26,000 feet above sea level, crawling along a narrow path with a massive hanging glacier (known as a "serac") looming over your head. It's like walking through a minefield where one wrong step or an unlucky ice collapse could end it all.

---

1. Loh, Matthew. "What You'll Encounter If You Try to Climb K2, the King of Mountains That Terrifies Even the Most Experienced of Climbers." *Business Insider*, Business Insider, 23 Aug. 2023.

When climbing K2, you're in a place where oxygen levels are so low your body struggles for every inch of progress and every ounce of oxygen. Above 26,247 feet, every breath feels like sucking air through a straw. Walking even a few steps can feel impossible, and your brain starts to get fuzzy from lack of oxygen. Even the most experienced climbers can't escape altitude sickness, pounding headaches, nausea, dizziness, and worse. It's a battle to stay focused and make wise decisions when every bit of energy drains out of you.

If the altitude doesn't wear you down, K2's weather will. This mountain is infamous for its wild storms and extreme, bone-chilling cold. Winds can hit 125 miles per hour, ripping apart tents and knocking climbers off balance. Temperatures regularly drop to -58°F, and frostbite is always lurking. The scariest part? You can spend weeks stuck at base camp, waiting for a brief window of decent weather to make your move. Even then, storms can roll in out of nowhere, trapping climbers high on the mountain with nowhere to hide.[2]

While many claim K2 isn't just a mountain—it's a legend; I want you to consider an even more strenuous and terrifying mountain. Perhaps it's the nature of this mountain that makes it so difficult. You see, this mountain is not a physical obstacle to be conquered. Instead, it's a mountain that stands between you and what God wants to do in your life. It's the mountain of transformation, not merely the hill of behavior modification. It requires every ounce of who you are and will cost you everything you have. Many who stare at this mountain only see the difficulty and challenge. However, once an individual gets past the self-doubt and fear and embraces the one who has overcome the whole world—much less an obstacle like this one—the journey becomes much more peaceful and exciting.

What Is Transformation?

In Romans 12:2, the apostle Paul wrote to the Christians in Rome, *"And do not be conformed to this world, but be transformed by the renewing of your mind, so that you may prove what the will of God is, that which is good and acceptable and perfect."* In this seemingly simple statement, we see a great chasm between what many do and what God demands from those who claim to be up to follow Him. On the one hand, there is the path of conforming. On the other, it is a more arduous journey of being transformed.

In this text, the word *conform(ed)* is the Greek word συσχηματίζω, *suschēmatízō* and means "to form according to a pattern or mold."[3] Peter used this same word when warning Christians against forming to the pattern or mold of their former lusts they once bathed in while in their ignorance (1 Pet. 1:14). Like a baker uses a mold or a form to cut cookie dough into shapes, we have the choice as to what "shape" we will fit our lives in to. The world and its thinking are often very alluring and enticing, being a wide path of easiness and self-indulgence in passions that lead to death (Matt. 7:13; Rom. 7:5; Gal. 5:24). However, not all molds are meant to be chosen; especially by those who have been sanctified, set apart, in faith in Christ Jesus (Acts 26:18).

---

2. Britannica, T. Editors of Encyclopaedia (2024, December 5). K2. *Encyclopaedia Britannica.* https://www.britannica.com/place/K2
3. Arndt, William, et al. *A Greek-English Lexicon of the New Testament and Other Early Christian Literature.* Chicago: University of Chicago Press, 2000, 979.

Acknowledge the Power of the Gospel

In opposition to this, the more rigorous pathway is that of being "transformed." This is the Greek word μεταμορφόω, metamorphóō and means "to change inwardly in fundamental character or condition."[4] Beyond merely altering external behaviors or habits, transformation demands a difficult and consequential alteration. It's difficult because there is a great deal of pain involved in the changes that result. It's consequential because the person who walks this journey is never the same as he once was. That's the very nature of transformation. Just as a butterfly never changes into a caterpillar, the Christian is never to turn back to the world's darkness. Transformation is only for the decisive and requires much more than casual engagement. It demands shining a light into the dark crevasses of our inner beings and allowing for brutal honesty when taking inventory of what must be rooted out and making room for what must be planted. It's only then that a person transitions from being an informal negotiator with God, seeking to do just enough to convince himself he is appeasing Him, and becomes an in-tune, dedicated disciple who is changed from the inside out.

Where Does Transformation Begin?

Simply put, transformation begins internally with being honest with oneself. In the popular business book *Leadership and Self-Deception*, the author highlights a powerful roadblock for companies excelling in their endeavors. For many who are in positions of authority within the company, when problems arise, they have been trained to look for causes and fix them. Often, the entire focus is on external factors such as people, conditions, supplies, finances, and other tangles such as these. However, attention is rarely ever turned inward.

To illustrate this point, the author of *Leadership and Self-Deception* turns the reader's attention to a European obstetrician from the mid-1800s. Dr. Ignaz Semmelweis practiced medicine at the Vienna General Hospital, a valuable research hospital. The dilemma before Dr. Semmelweis was that in the maternity ward where he worked, there was an unusually high mortality rate amongst the patients: 1 out of every 10. Dr. Semmelweis went to great lengths to figure out why his ward had a higher mortality rate than that of others. He tried to equalize the differences between his ward and others, standardizing everything from birthing positions to the way the laundry was washed; however, nothing changed. Finally, to obtain answers, he left on a 4-month trip to study what maternity wards in other hospitals did that resulted in far fewer deaths of their patients.

To his surprise, upon returning home, he was informed that the death rate had vastly improved. With a hopeful and renewed investigative zeal, Dr. Semmelweis was able to tie the reason back to the fact the Vienna General Hospital was a research hospital and that he and other doctors studied cadavers between the time spent with actual patients. In doing so, they transferred germs from the cadavers to the patients, making them deathly sick. He hadn't known before. What would become known as the germ theory was not discovered and accepted until the later part of the 19th century from the work of the French chemist and microbiologist Louis Pasteur, the English surgeon Joseph Lister, and the German physician Robert Koch.[5] However, once he realized that he and the other doctors, due to their lack of proper cleaning and washing after handling the cadavers,

---
4. Arndt, et al. 639.
5. "Germ Theory." *Encyclopedia Britannica*. https://www.britannica.com/facts/germ-theory.

were the source of the problem, he remarked, "Only God knows the number of patients who went prematurely to their graves because of me."[6]

It would be horrific to have to live with the acknowledgment that your lack of understanding had been the foundational reason why others died. However, once Dr. Semmelweis correctly recognized the problem and understood the remedy, adequately washing and sanitizing their hands before moving from cadaver to patient, the results changed. Fewer and fewer patients died.

Before the outcome will ever change, there must be a change in protocol. Before the protocol changes, there must be a better understanding of the problem and what is causing the problem. Before any of that, there must first be an acknowledgment that there is a problem, and the problem, if change is going to occur, must be seen in such a way that stirs and disturbs us to our very core. That's why self-deception is such a dangerous and threatening reality. It tries to lock the door and keep honesty and self-reflection at bay, operating on the idea that if we don't admit a problem exists, it doesn't. The father of lies, the devil (John 8:44), could not be happier than when we allow this detrimental way of thinking to permeate our lives, especially when it comes to the subject of sin and our need for salvation.

STEP #1: THE POWER OF THE GOSPEL

DISCUSSION

In considering real transformation, spiritual transformation, the question lingers, "Where does it begin?" Dr. Semmelweis and the other doctors at Vienna General Hospital began their transformation with a stirring quest for a remedy to a significant problem in the maternity ward. Spiritually speaking, transformation always begins with recognizing the need for a substantial change in our condition because we come face-to-face with the unnerving and terrifying reality of our sinful condition.

In Isaiah 59: 1-2, we are reminded regarding the impact of our sinful choices, *"Behold, the Lord's hand is not so short that it cannot save; nor His ear so dull that it cannot hear, but* **your iniquities have made a separation between you and your God,** *and your sins have hidden His face from you so that He does not hear"* (emphasis added). In writing to the Christians in Rome, the apostle Paul said regarding the result of our sinful life, *"For the wage of sin is* **death** *..."* (Rom. 6:23, emp. added). In 2 Thessalonians 1:6-10, Paul further explains the consequential reality of sin on the day of Jesus return when he writes,

> *For after all it is only just for God to repay with affliction those who afflict you, and to give relief to you who are afflicted and to us as well when the Lord Jesus will be revealed from heaven with His mighty angels in flaming fire, dealing out retribution to those who do not know God and to those who do not obey the gospel of our Lord Jesus.* **These will pay the penalty of eternal destruction, away from the presence of the Lord and from the glory of**

---

6. The Arbinger Institute. "The Problem Beneath Other Problems," *Leadership and Self-Deception, 2nd Edition.* Oakland: Berrett-Koehler Publishers, Inc., 2010, 18–20.

Acknowledge the Power of the Gospel

***His power**, when He comes to be glorified in His saints on that day, and to be marveled at among all who have believed—for our testimony to you was believed* (emp. added).

As we turn our attention to Romans 1, it is noteworthy that the word *sin*, [ἁμαρτία, hamartia], "to miss a mark on the way, not to hit the mark"[7] is not found. As a matter of fact, we don't see this word appear until Romans 2:12; however, that does not mean the footprints of spiritual failure are not present before then. Of the 32 verses in chapter 1, almost half—15 verses—are dedicated to a deathly and dire description of a life lived in complete and utter rebellion against our loving God.

To effectively describe such an unruly life of despair, the Holy Spirit inspires the apostle Paul to use words and phrases that boldly paint a life of darkness, void of any true peace and calm. Instead, the use of these exact words reveals a sin sickness that permeates every aspect of the life of a person who chooses the path of dishonoring God. Consider the following:

- v. 18 – *"ungodliness"*—a lack of reverence for deity[8]
- v. 18 – *"unrighteousness of men"*—the quality of injustice, wickedness[9]
- v. 18 – *"suppress the truth in unrighteousness"*—hold down, stifle[10]
- v. 21 – *"futile in their speculations"*—thoughts became directed to worthless things[11]
- v. 21 – *"foolish heart"*—void of understanding, senseless[12]
- v. 21 – *"darkened"*—figuratively of moral darkness, ignorance[13]
- v. 22 – *"fools"*—to make dull, not acute[14]
- v. 28 – *"did not see fit to acknowledge God any longer"*—accept as proved, approve[15]

In drawing the readers of this letter deeper into a more mature understanding of the gravity of the death spiral of sin, Paul uses the phrase *"God gave them over"* three times (vv. 24, 26, 28). On each occasion, the emphasis is on the impending truth that God will not rescue—He does not protect—those who willingly choose a lifestyle of rebellion in sinful indulgence. Instead, He allows them to pursue the deadly direction of their hearts' desire. That being true, the text says that He hands them over to *"the lusts of their hearts to impurity"* (v. 24), to *"degrading passions"* (v. 26), and to *"a depraved mind"* (v. 28). He further amplifies this terrible condition when he expands on where these desires ultimately take a person.

> ...*Being filled with all unrighteousness, wickedness, greed, evil; full of envy, murder, strife, deceit, malice; they are gossips, slanderers, haters of God, insolent, arrogant, boastful, inventors of evil, disobedient to parents, without understanding, untrustworthy, unloving, unmerciful; and although they know the ordinance of God, that **those who practice such things are worthy of death**, they not only do the same, but also give hearty approval to those who practice them* (Rom. 1:29-32, emp. added).

---

7. Zodhiates, Spiros. *The Complete Word Study Dictionary: New Testament*. Chattanooga: AMG Publishers, 2000.
8. Arndt, et al. 141.
9. Arndt, et al. 20.
10. Arndt, et al. 532.
11. Arndt, et al. 621.
12. Arndt, et al. 146.
13. Zodhiates.
14. Zodhiates.
15. Arndt, et al. 255.

The ultimate outcome of such a baseless life is that the wrath of God will be poured forth on such. The same God who lovingly and sacrificially sent His only begotten Son to redeem mankind will one day shower the rebellious and unrepentant with His indignation and divine judgment. What a terrible and terrifying expectation that exists for those who, as Paul penned, *"do not honor Him as God or give thanks"* (Rom. 1:21)!

With the unmistakable understanding of rebellion against God being laid descriptively bare before the reader, we are reminded that Paul's emphasis on the remedy to man's most considerable predicament has already been revealed. Before Paul ever addresses the Gentiles in Rome who are living such a depraved life of rebellion, we read regarding the topic of salvation,

> *"For I am not ashamed of the gospel, for it is the power of God for salvation to everyone who believes, to the Jew first and also to the Greek. For in it the righteousness of God is revealed from faith to faith; as it is written, 'But the righteous man shall live by faith'"* (Rom. 1:16-17).

In this hopeful and redeeming text, we find confidence and calm. We see the love of God and His unmatched ability to right the wrongs caused by our sinful choices. Here, we learn of the source of hope, His power over sin, and the all-inclusive offer placed before us. As we investigate these components, I invite you to note the first step of transformation that Paul outlines, the acknowledgment of the power of the Gospel.

The Source of Hope—"of God"

The main word occurrs 153 times in the book of Romans—*God* [Θεός, *Theós*] is the main subject. Second to this are the words referring to Jesus: *Christ/Jesus/Lord*, occurring 152 times. What that reveals to us, as we come to a more complete understanding of transformation, is that God is central to this process. Without Him, we are simply floundering in the sea of self-confidence and self-interest while convincing ourselves real change has occurred. The stark reality is that you won't be transformed unless God is central to your transformation. He is the beginning of true transformation and the end. We would do well then to embrace what Paul says about God in Romans 1 when we learn the following attributes of God brought boldly to the surface.

He Is the God of Promise (Rom. 1:2):

When you consider God's desire revealed in the creation account in Genesis 1–2, one factor becomes extraordinarily clear regarding the relationship He intended with mankind. God has always yearned to be in fellowship with humanity for eternity. He created Adam and Eve, placed them in the perfect location, and provided for all their needs. He even demonstrated His tremendous love by giving them the freedom of choice. All they had to do was choose their relationship with Him over the appetites of any other aspect of life. If they did so, they would enjoy the indescribable gift of walking with God for eternity. However, in being omniscient, God knew mankind would fail and need to be redeemed. Therefore, before the foundation of the world was laid, God's perfect plan of redemption was established (Eph. 1:4; 1 Pet. 1:18-20; Titus 1:1-2).

Acknowledge the Power of the Gospel

He Is the God of Proclamation (Rom. 1:2):

Not only is He the God who makes and keeps promises (Heb. 6:18), but the apostle Paul intends for the reader to understand He doesn't keep the promise secret. Instead, He has demonstrated His overwhelming desire to communicate with mankind regarding the good news of restoring fellowship. He has done so throughout the Old Testament as well as the New Testament, which powerfully speaks to the value and importance of the message.

In Luke 24:44, Jesus spoke to this very element of the proclamation when He said, *"These are My words which I spoke to you while I was still with you, that all things which are written about Me in the Law of Moses and the Prophets, and the Psalms must be fulfilled."* From Genesis 3:15 to the promise made to Abraham in Genesis 12:3, the gospel has been proclaimed. The proclamation of the good news has sounded forth through the psalms (110) and continues throughout the major and minor prophets (consider Isaiah 53). Without skipping a beat, the New Testament picks up. It carries the story of redemption through not only telling of the birth, life, death, and resurrection of Jesus Christ but also through the establishment of the church and the letters written to disciples intended to encourage, rebuke, and edify Christians scattered throughout the known world as they continued to look forward to the second coming of the Christ.

He Is the God of Purpose (Rom. 1:5):

Scripture teaches us God's great desire to bless mankind through His Son, Jesus Christ. The eternal nature of God's plan declares the immense significance of this purpose. We read of this purpose in passages such as 2 Peter 3:9 when the apostle wrote, *"The Lord is not slow about His promise, as some count slowness, but is patient toward you, not wishing for any to perish but for all to come to repentance."* Another passage that emphasizes His purpose is in John 3:16-17, *"For God so loved the world, that He gave His only begotten Son, that whoever believes in Him shall not perish, but have eternal life."* Jesus regularly echoed this purpose as He walked with His disciples. Such can be found in Luke 19:10, *"For the Son of Man has come to seek and to save that which was lost."*

In sending Christ, Immanuel (Matt. 1:23), to the earth for the redemptive price to be paid upon the cross, God has done His part as both the just and the justifier (Rom. 3:26). In doing so the way He did, all prophecy was fulfilled regarding Jesus, including Him being a descendent of the lineage of David (Rom. 1:3) and in the fact He was declared *"the Son of God with power by the resurrection from the dead"* (Rom. 1:4). Now, as Romans 1:5 says, the Gospel has been and still is to this day preached to bring about response on the side of the hearer. This response is the "obedience of faith" to present the glorious message of the love of God displayed through His only begotten Son, Jesus, and for that message to stir within those who have open and tender hearts a submissive compliance with the will of God. That's the purpose of God we see revealed in Romans 1.

The Power for Salvation—"the Gospel"

Used 10 times in the book of Romans, the word *Gospel* is likely one of the most well-known words in Christendom, perhaps in all the world. Being a combination of two Greek words, *eu*, "good, well," and *aggéllō*, "to proclaim, tell," εὐαγγελίζω, *euaggelízō*, the good news of salvation offered by God through His Son Jesus Christ has the power, not only to change people but to change entire cultures.[16] Muslims become Christians and preach the good news of the death, burial, and resurrection of Jesus Christ. Faith-based organizations, in the name of the Gospel of Jesus Christ, respond to natural disasters by pouring resources into helping those they don't know find relief in a very trying time. Individuals who once drew lines between people based on the color of their skin now hold hands as they pray and sing praises to God. Some even lay down their very lives in service of others because this is what they have seen and experienced in and through Jesus Christ in their own lives. These examples are but a small taste of the Gospel's transformative power.

More important than all the societal and personal changes toward our fellow man, the very salvation of our souls hinges on this power of God (Rom. 1:16). While there is no insignificant teaching found in Scripture (2 Tim. 3:16-17), it is the Gospel that is said to be the *"power,"* δύναμις *dúnamis*, "functioning in some way, power, might, strength, force, capability" that God has chosen to use as the vehicle for transformation when it comes to bringing back into fellowship those who have been separated from Him because of sin.[17] Perhaps this is why Paul, in other letters including when he wrote to the church in Corinth, emphasizes the premier importance of this eternal, soul-saving message, saying,

> *Now I make known to you, brethren, the gospel which I preached to you, which also you received, in which also you stand, by which also you are saved, if you hold fast the word which I preached to you, unless you believed in vain. For I delivered to you* **as of first importance** *what I also received, that Christ died for our sins according to the Scriptures, and that He was buried, and that He was raised on the third day according to the Scriptures...* (1 Cor. 14: 1-4; emp. added).

The significance of the Gospel is highlighted and brought to the forefront in Romans 1 in that Paul, a Jew (Phil. 3), was *"set apart for the gospel"* (v. 1). In using the phrase *"set apart,"* ἀφορίζω, *aphorízō*—"to select one person out of a group for a purpose, set apart, appoint,"[18] Paul is most likely drawing from his past as a Pharisee and the dedication to the Law of Moses for which he as once set apart. The Pharisees were believed to have derived their name from this same word. Paul may be making a statement of the power of the Gospel in His own transformation and denoting his life's focus on the importance of the Gospel.

Not only does he say he is *"set apart"* for the Gospel, but in his service to God, he preaches the Gospel (1:9). Just as a farmer sows good seed in the ground with the expectation a beautiful crop will come forth, Paul knows that if the power of God for salvation is going to change both Jews and Gentiles (v. 14), it must be planted in their hearts. Before it will ever get into their hearts, it

---

16. Zodhiates.
17. Arndt, et al. 262.
18. Arndt, et al. 158.

must get into their lives through their ears. Someone must preach the Gospel, and Paul makes it clear he will be one of those "someones" who steps up and steps out with the soul-saving message of the power of God. He does so with a sense of obligation (v.14) and an unashamed (v. 16) spirit.

The All-Inclusive Offer—"to Everyone"

Some gatherings in life are by invitation only. If you receive one of these prized invitations, you are in a special category of the honored ones who get to attend. Those who are invited usually have a specific connection to the hosts. For instance, if a wedding is a "by invitation only" event, to receive one of the special tickets, usually the invitee is connected to the bride or the groom in such a way that they want to share their most special day with each guest. It's a very high privilege to be invited, and it reveals the unique and special place one has in the heart of the hosts.

In our acknowledgment of the power of the Gospel, we must never overlook the extraordinary honor bestowed on each of us in that the Gospel's invitation is for everyone. When Paul writes, *"For it is the power of God to salvation to everyone who believes, to the Jew first and also to the Greek"* (v. 16), he is drawing a stark contrast with the belief many Jews held in that day. As the chosen people of God in the days of Moses (Ex. 19:5-6), the Jews seemed to have severely struggled with the idea that the special invitation of fellowship with God could be extended to the Gentiles without them first converting to Judaism. That lingering struggle carries over into the New Testament when Peter in Acts 10 was effectively instructed not to consider Cornelius or any Gentile unclean and unworthy of God's saving grace. Because of what God has accomplished through the resurrection of Jesus from the grave, Gentiles as well as Jews can enter a special covenant relationship with God. The door to that covenant relationship, as God designed it, is through our faithful response to the Gospel's invitation (v. 16). What an honor to be invited into such a relationship with God through the Gospel call (2 Thess. 2:14)!

CONCLUSION

As we close this chapter on transformation and the power of the Gospel, I ask you to imagine a story of a man we'll call Daniel. Raised in a troubled home, Daniel grew up burdened by an ever-present sense of inadequacy. Throughout his teen years, he sought significance and acceptance from his peers, often hanging out with the wrong crowd and participating in behavior he thought would increase his social acceptance. By his early twenties, he had built a life of compromise. The spiral of disappointment and despair pulled him further into darkness. As an adult, he works tirelessly to earn approval but consistently falls short. Bitterness, guilt, and shame shaped every decision he made, and he's turned to the sinful and unhealthy habit of internet pornography as a way of coping.

One day a co-worker invited him to a Bible study. Skeptical but curious, Daniel agreed to go. The group was studying Romans 1, and as the leader read aloud, Daniel was pierced by the words, *"For I am not ashamed of the gospel, for it is the power of God for salvation to everyone who believes, to the Jew first and also to the Greek"* (v. 16). For the first time, Daniel realized this whole time, he had been trying to gain the acceptance and admiration of people. He had rooted his value and worth in what others thought of him or in what he had. As we reflect on where he came from and the troubled home life he grew up in, we can understand that we are privileged to look at Daniel's life from the outside. However, for Daniel, this realization is monumental. For the first time, he understood the mountain of shame and failure he had been climbing wasn't meant to be conquered by his strength. The power to overcome was found not in striving harder but in surrendering to God's power for salvation—the Gospel.

That night, Daniel decided to obey the Gospel in faith (Rom. 1:5). With hopefulness in his heart, he repented of his sins and was immersed for the forgiveness of his sins. From that moment, change began. Daniel threw himself into studying God's Word, surrounded himself with Christians, and replaced the lies he believed about himself with the truth of God's promises. Little by little, bitterness gave way to forgiveness, guilt to freedom, and shame to assurance of God's love. His life is a testament to the power of the Gospel as the catalyst for hope, change, and purpose.

As you reflect on this chapter, remember that transformation begins with acknowledging God is the source of hope in our lives, the Gospel is the power of God for salvation, and that all are blessed because we are invited into a covenant relationship with God through the Gospel. Climbing the mountain of transformation may be steep, but with God, all things are possible, even a transformation in your life (Matthew 19:26). Let the Gospel guide and strengthen you and watch as God works wonders in your life.

Applying
RECOGNIZE YOUR NEED FOR GOD

ROMANS 3:10

JOE WELLS

"As it is written, 'There is none righteous, not even one....'"

INTRODUCTION

It has been said before, in some form or fashion, that sometimes you don't look up until you hit the bottom. I would never wish this statement to be true for anyone; however, in ministry, I have seen this play out more times than I can count. A man who is addicted to work and who puts himself in compromising positions is warned about the dangers of the path he is walking. Instead of heeding those warnings like the young man in Proverbs 7, he continues further down the path, seeking what the darkness has to offer. He stumbles and gives in to a woman at work one night on a business trip.

Both internally and externally, he begins to justify why that happened. His relationship with his wife is brought under much harsher scrutiny as he seeks justification. In the office, he brags about his "manly" escapades without any concern, even for his co-worker with whom he had an affair. The more he justifies and hides, ironically in the open, the deeper he sinks into despair.

This is the same man who comes home and hugs his wife, telling her how much he loves her. He is the one who will be found in a church pew on Sundays, patiently enduring the worship service but looking the part while he's there. The facade of a double life is eating at him, and his excuses no longer ease the wounds he carries. He sees a broken and scared coward whenever he looks at himself in the mirror. He longs for a way out, but the fear is like a prison, keeping him in the pit of despair.

You may have never heard or seen a man walk this road. If it isn't this one, chances are you have seen individuals jolt down pathways of destruction (drugs, alcohol, pornography, etc.), all while making excuses for why they "had to do it" or why they "deserved" to chase after happiness. Of course, it's not true happiness, but they have convinced themselves it is. They have deceived themselves into thinking that they are approved if they continue looking and acting the part if they "talk a good game" in front of those with high morals. The problem is that no manner of further chasing after darkness or lying by living a life of pretense will be the salve to the deep wounds they suffer daily.

In Romans 1:18–3:20, the apostle Paul provides a profound exploration of why all humanity stands in desperate need of God. He is the only One who holds the much-needed grace for which our sin-scarred souls cry out. Through His Son Jesus, we can bask in the healing ointment of forgiveness. In this passage, Paul does not merely highlight human flaws but also exposes the universal nature of sin and the impossibility of achieving righteousness on our own. Through Paul's argument, we see that recognizing our need for God is the second step toward transformation. While the first step is found in the power of the Gospel, knowing the One who is the author of the Gospel is pivotal. After all, the Gospel is only as good as the one who backs the saving message.

Therefore, if transformation is going to happen in our lives, we must not continue believing in our self-sufficiency. We must recognize God in His whole character, which not only involves love but also His perfect and righteous wrath. We must accept into our very being that righteousness belongs to God alone, and if we are going to be righteous, it will only be because He grants that to us. Thus, this chapter is not merely about the entanglement in sin; the above illustration of the man trapped in the consequences of his sin brings it to light. More importantly, through this chapter we will come to clearly see why God is the only source of healing to the despair sin cast upon all those, either Jews and Greeks, who choose to rebel and turn their backs on Him.

STEP #2: RECOGNIZE YOUR NEED FOR GOD

DISCUSSION

1. The Revelation of God's Wrath (Rom. 1:18-32)

The word is ὀργή (*orgē*), and it means a "strong indignation directed at wrongdoing, with a focus on retribution."[1] In our text, the translators concisely used the word *wrath* to summarize the anger aroused by what is unjust and not merited. However, this word is not merely an emotional word expressing grief and hurt because of what has been done. It's also a word of intent. Inherent to the word is the causation of action or retribution. In other words, *orgē* also involves a judicial response that is righteous and deserving. When Paul speaks of the wrath of God, he is declaring a holy reaction to humanity's rejection of God and the actions or motives that display such.

One of the most effective ways to understand this topic more fully is to investigate the wrath of God in the Old Testament. There, we see God's wrath displayed regarding pagan nations, individual

---

1. Arndt, William, Frederick W. Danker, et al. *A Greek-English Lexicon of the New Testament and Other Early Christian Literature.* Chicago: University of Chicago Press, 2000, 720.

sinners, and even with His own covenant people, Israel. In one of the earliest occasions, God's wrath is demonstrated upon Israel for having refused to believe Him when He told them they would enter Canaan, the Promised Land (Num. 11:10). After He rescued them from Egypt and had given them the Ten Commandments, extending the promise of His covenant to them and allowing them to see His glory (Ex. 19–20), with great complaining, they still disbelieved (Num. 14:1-3). Consequently, God in His wrath condemned the Israelites to wander in the wilderness until a generation died and a new generation would arise and enter Canaan (Num. 14:11-38).

In the Old Testament, God's wrath was displayed primarily because His own people constantly broke the covenant. They provoked God through various actions that include:

- their idolatry (Judges 2:14; 1 Kings 11:9; 14:9, 15)
- their mixing paganism with the worship of the Lord (Isa. 1:10-17)
- their frivolous rebellion (1 Kings 8:46)
- their unbelief (Num. 11:33; 14:11, 33; Ps. 95:10–11)
- their disregard for His concern for love, justice, righteousness, and holiness (Isa. 1:15-17; Amos 5:7-12).

The wrath of God extends to all humanity. It's not as if only the Jews of the Old Testament were on the receiving end of God's wrath, or that today only disciples of Jesus Christ must be aware and concerned with the reality of God's wrath. Every individual who sins and remains in that state should live with the fearful expectation of the indignation and retribution of God (Ezek. 18:4; 2 Thess. 1:5-10). This is clearly seen in the concept of the Day of the Lord. With the intent to express that no one who dies in a sinful, rebellious separation from God will ever escape the wrath of God, the prophets of old, by inspiration of the Holy Spirit, wrote of this terrifying day to persuade men to repent and return to God.

> *Alas, you who are longing for the day of the Lord,*
> *For what purpose will the day of the Lord be to you?*
> *It will be darkness and not light;*
> *As when a man flees from a lion*
> *And a bear meets him,*
> *Or goes home, leans his hand against the wall*
> *And a snake bites him.*
> *Will not the day of the Lord be darkness instead of light,*
> *Even gloom with no brightness in it* (Amos 5:18-20)?

> *Near is the great day of the Lord,*
> *Near and coming very quickly;*
> *Listen, the day of the Lord!*
> *In it the warrior cries out bitterly.*
> *A day of wrath is that day,*
> *A day of trouble and distress,*
> *A day of destruction and desolation,*
> *A day of darkness and gloom,*

> *A day of clouds and thick darkness,*
> *A day of trumpet and battle cry*
> *Against the fortified cities*
> *And the high corner towers.*
> *I will bring distress on men*
> *So that they will walk like the blind,*
> *Because they have sinned against the Lord;*
> *And their blood will be poured out like dust*
> *And their flesh like dung.*
> *Neither their silver nor their gold*
> *Will be able to deliver them*
> *On the day of the Lord's wrath;*
> *And all the earth will be devoured*
> *In the fire of His jealousy,*
> *For He will make a complete end,*
> *Indeed a terrifying one,*
> *Of all the inhabitants of the earth* (Zeph. 1:14-18).

In Romans 1, just as the righteousness of God is revealed through the Gospel (v. 17), we see the terrifying wrath of God revealed. This "wrath" is spoken of four times in the text in consideration for this chapter (1:18; 2:5, 8; 3:5), and in each of these passages, we learn it is never in the absence of the righteous judgment of God. Instead, the wrath of God is always in keeping with His righteousness, the "quality or state of juridical correctness with focus on redemptive action."[2]

Because of the connection between the righteousness and wrath of God, we can rest assured of a few things. First, when the wrath of God is poured forth, it's always right and just. Second, God's righteousness is aimed at the redemption of mankind. Therefore, the wrath of God will not come before an opportunity is extended to know God and to have a covenant relationship with Him. Third, those who are on the receiving end of the wrath of God are the most pitied of all because they had an opportunity for a different outcome; however, they chose to rebel against God.

With this fact in mind, let's consider why the wrath of God is revealed from Heaven, and let's consider what constitutes "all ungodliness," "understood vertically as a lack of reverence for deity,"[3] and all "unrighteousness," "the quality of injustice, unrighteousness, wickedness, injustice."[4]

Suppression of Truth

Paul states that sin begins with suppressing the truth about God. The Greek verb for *suppress* (κατέχω, *katéchō*) means *"to suppress, restrain, hinder, withhold."*[5] This implies an active effort to reject or ignore the knowledge of God, which He has supplied in ample amounts. This truth is

---

2. Arndt, Danker, et al. 247.
3. Arndt, Danker, et al. 141.
4. Arndt, Danker, et al. 20.
5. Zodhiates, Spiros. *The Complete Word Study Dictionary: New Testament.* Chattanooga: AMG Publishers, 2000.

evident in creation, as Paul writes, *"For since the creation of the world His invisible attributes, His eternal power and divine nature, have been clearly seen"* (Rom. 1:20).

- "Eternal Power" (δύναμις, *dúnamis*)—"potential for functioning in some way, power, might, strength, force, capability."[6]
- "Divine Nature" (θειότης, *theiótēs*)—"the quality or characteristic(s) pertaining to deity, divinity, divine nature, divineness."[7]

It boggles the mind to think about what can be known about God by looking at the creation. Even without the microscope and the understanding of the minute aspects, detailed processes such as metabolism within the human body or photosynthesis within a plant, the observer of creation can still know of God's "invisible attributes," His power and divineness. In other words, even without knowing all the details, the observer can know God is there, and that alone should drive a person to want to know God and seek to please Him. However, like many today, those described in this text decided to ignore and purposely turn from this straightforward reality. Therefore, the Holy Spirit, by the pen of the apostle Paul, makes it crystal clear that they are "without excuse" with no legal defense that can be made to justify their rebellion.

The Exchange of Glory

> *For even though they knew God, they did not honor Him as God or give thanks, but they became futile in their speculations, and their foolish heart was darkened. Professing to be wise, they became fools, and exchanged the glory of the incorruptible God for an image in the form of corruptible man and of birds and four-footed animals and crawling creatures* (Rom. 1:21-23).

What an insult to God! The very God who has made Himself known through the creation because of His goodness and desire to be a blessing to mankind, now, because of their selfish desire to live a godless life, is pushed to the back burner while they elevate the very beauty He created. Unfortunately, this tragedy is all too common amongst humanity. When faced with the existence of the Creator and thus the submission to the one who has authority over all creation, including mankind, those who seek self-fulfillment and personal happiness above the glory of God find themselves galivanting in the mire of the pigpen of sin with a smile on their faces.

And where did it all begin?

First, by disregarding the truth that God has placed abundantly around them in His creation, and second, by an extremely horrible exchange. The words *corruptible* and *incorruptible* should not be lost here. Paul is driving home the point that a lousy exchange may, for a time, seem meaningless; however, in the long run, it is the difference between life and death. In the temporary, it may allow them to chase after whatever sexual escapades their lusts

---

6. Arndt, Danker, et al. 262.
7. Arndt, Danker, et al. 446.

demand, but it leads to destruction. In choosing to believe a lie of their own heart or others around them instead of the truth of God's existence and his glory, they unquestioningly find themselves in a hole of degradation and a pit of sorrow. Sometimes, this comes through brokenness, lack of fulfillment, or even health issues. Ultimately, this deep despair will be realized in the fact that when God "gives them over" or allows a sinner to go down the path of rebellion they have chosen, He turns them over to the consequence of such a decision as well, including alienation from the only one who can save them from themselves.

2. The Hypocrisy of Moralists (Rom. 2:1-16)

Some will always believe that they are not accountable in the same way as others. Perhaps it's because of where they were born, their economic or social status, or possibly even their sense of superiority that stems from what they know and have studied. A compelling true story that illustrates this point is the case of Lori Loughlin and the 2019 College Admissions Scandal.

Loughlin, a well-known actress, and her husband, Mossimo Giannulli, were among dozens of wealthy parents charged in a scheme to secure their children's admission to elite universities through bribery and fraud. Despite neither daughter participating in the sport, they paid $500,000 to have their daughters falsely designated as recruits for the University of Southern California's rowing team. With the assumption that their economic and social status would shield them from consequences, this scandal highlighted how individuals with wealth and connections attempted to manipulate systems solely based on merit. After first denying wrongdoing, Loughlin and Giannulli eventually pleaded guilty and served prison sentences.[8]

Believing oneself to be above judgment and accountability is dangerous. It not only reveals a high level of arrogance and false confidence in the person, but it places those at tremendous risk who may allow themselves to be influenced and led astray by such a self-righteous individual. Sadly, the reality of those who think highly of themselves doesn't change until they are brought low by a firm reminder that judgment will be rendered against all who transgress the law, even those who may have the "correct" history and knowledge.

In Romans 2, Paul focuses on those who judge others while committing similar sins as the Gentiles in chapter 1. He declares, *"Therefore you have no excuse, everyone of you who passes judgment"* (Rom. 2:1). This change in the usage of the pronoun *you* indicates a shift in the audience. He's no longer talking about the Gentiles of chapter 1. His attention has turned now to those with a Jewish background in the church in Rome. With a dose of reality, he bluntly reminds them that they, just like the Gentiles, are also without excuse before God (see Rom. 1:20).

But why are they without excuse?

In the first three consecutive verses of chapter 2, the writer three times utilizes the word *practice* (πράσσω, *prássō*) "to do, make, perform in general, expressing an action as continued or not

---

8. Byrne, Suzy. "Felicity Huffman and Lori Loughlin Became the Faces of the College Admissions Scandal 5 Years Ago. They Handled It Very Differently." *Yahoo!*, Yahoo!, 12 Mar. 2024.

Recognize Your Need for God

yet completed, what one does repeatedly, continually, habitually"[9] to answer this question. Their failure wasn't because they accidentally stumbled across a sin or made one bad decision. Instead, sinful practices had become a way of life. They had no problem telling the Gentiles where they were wrong in their obedience to God (Rom. 2:1), and they were correct. All the sins listed at the end of chapter 1, God hates and does not want His covenant people to walk in. However, knowing and doing what God desires are two completely different topics. That's why, in three additional verses, we read about the importance of doing good and doing according to the Law (Rom. 2:7, 10, 13). Thus, they are not without excuse because of what they know. Instead, the indefensibility is found in their actions not lining up with the will of God and in their "stubbornness" and "unrepentant heart" as they willingly violate and diminish the kindness, tolerance, and patience of God (Rom. 2:4-5).

God's Impartial Judgment

The Bible consistently emphasizes that God is utterly impartial, treating all people equally regardless of their background, status, or identity (Acts 10:34-35). This truth is foundational to His character and justice. Romans 2:11 plainly states, *"For there is no partiality with God."* The word *partiality* is the Greek word προσωποληψία (*prosōpolēpsía*) and means "a respecting of persons, partiality, favoritism."[10] In other words, while the Jews may have thought that because they were descendants of Abraham and were special because the Mosaic Law was given to them on Mt. Siani (Ex. 20), they were going to be viewed differently by God in judgment, the impartiality of God prohibits Him from doing so. Each soul is evaluated based upon his deeds and not his external circumstances as noted above in this chapter. It doesn't matter if one is a Jew or a Gentile, rich or poor, male or female; all are subject to the standards of God's justice. This fact, as illustrated in Deuteronomy 10:17, is a blessing that guarantees His judgments are always righteous and just.

The Law Written on the Heart

The heart of an individual is crucial to the argument being developed. In pointing to the Jews, those who are advantaged in every way (Rom. 3:1-3), Paul addresses their hearts as "stubborn" and "unrepentant" in chapter 2 verse 5. Then, in pointing to the Gentiles who are not and were never under the Law of Moses, he says,

> *For all who have sinned without the Law will also perish without the Law, and all who have sinned under the Law will be judged by the Law; for it is not the hearers of the Law who are just before God, but the doers of the Law will be justified. For when Gentiles who do not have the Law do instinctively the things of the Law, these, not having the Law, are a law to themselves,* **in that they show the work of the Law written in their hearts, their conscience bearing witness and their thoughts alternately accusing or else defending them**, *on the day when, according to my gospel, God will judge the secrets of men through Christ Jesus* (Rom. 2:12-16, emp. added).

---

9. Zodhiates.
10. Zodhiates

The Greek term for *conscience* is συνείδησις (*suneídēsis*) and means "the inward faculty of distinguishing right and wrong, moral consciousness, conscience."[11] By using this word, the Holy Spirit, through Paul's pen, speaks to an inner awareness of moral accountability. The point is not to emphasize that one's conscience is the guide for his life, and if one lives according to his conscience, he will be good on the day when God judges all mankind. Instead, the point being made is that all people, regardless of whether they are under the Law of Moses or not, will be held accountable in God's righteous judgment.

3. The Universal Guilt of Humanity (Rom. 3:1-20)

Paul concludes this section by declaring the most significant problem every human will face: their own guilt before God due to their sin. Having already addressed the guilt of the Gentiles in chapter 1 and that of the Jews in chapter 2, it should not surprise us to find such a statement as this in chapter 3, *"for we have already charged that both Jews and Greeks are all under sin"* (Rom. 3:9). The word *sin* [ἁμαρτία, *hamartia*] means "a departure from either human or divine standards of uprightness."[12] With the context of the first three chapters being considered, the divine stand of God is what is being referred to in what they, both Jews and Greeks, have departed.

To further develop the depth of this point, the apostle Paul quotes several Old Testament passages and shines a light on the deeper issue that all stand in the same pitifully dreadful condition before God.

> *There is **none** righteous, **not even one**;*
> *There is **none** who understands,*
> *There is **none** who seeks for God;*
> ***All** have turned aside, together they have become useless;*
> *There is **none** who does good,*
> *There is **not even one*** (Rom. 3:10-12, emp. added).

With a brazenness and lack of shamefacedness, their throats, tongues, lips, mouth, and feet all combine in a flippant rebellious manner to reveal what is truly the dark extent of their condition (Rom. 10:13-18). They don't even try to hide it as they openly walk down the road of separation, galivanting in front of others and, most notably, before God. The Gentiles knew God but did not honor Him as such (Rom. 1:21). The Jews can identify the sinful practices of the Gentiles, but then they turn around and practice the very same things (Rom. 2:17-24). The name of God is treated as a doormat in the pursuit of personal fulfillment, and the Holy Spirit, through the apostle Paul, makes it crystal clear that all people are accountable to God and are incapable of fixing the separation caused by their decisions (Rom. 3:20).

Recognizing one's need for God is fundamental to spiritual growth and maturity. Throughout Scripture, we see examples of individuals who came to understand their dependence on God,

---

11. Arndt, Danker, et al. 967.
12. Arndt, Danker, et al. 50.

Recognize Your Need for God

often through highly challenging circumstances. In the Old Testament, King David exemplifies this recognition in Psalm 63:1, where he writes, *"O God, You are my God; I shall seek You earnestly; My soul thirsts for You, my flesh yearns for You, In a dry and weary land where there is no water."* As David is hiding as a fugitive from King Saul, this vivid imagery of thirst and longing underscores the deep-seated human need for sustenance and guidance only God provides.

Another such case where there was a cry to God for deliverance and help is found in Exodus 2:23-24, *"Now it came about in the course of those many days that the king of Egypt died. And the sons of Israel sighed because of the bondage, and they cried out; and their cry for help because of their bondage rose up to God. So God heard their groaning; and God remembered His covenant with Abraham, Isaac, and Jacob."* With the weight of bondage pressing their very souls, the children of Israel turned to the only one who could help. This heart-wrenching plea for redemption highlights the human need for rescue.

The prophet Elijah's experience during a severe drought in 1 Kings 17 provides a powerful example of God's provision for those who recognize their dependence on Him. When faced with a life-threatening famine, Elijah relied entirely on God, and God sent ravens to bring him food and directed him to a widow who, despite her own dire circumstances, could sustain him. In turning the page to chapter 19, this same man who boldly stood before the prophets of Baal on Mount Carmel (1 Kings 18) cries out, asking for escape from what he thought was certain death. Instead, as God answers, provisions are provided, and direction is given. The presence of God was never away from his disciple, which demonstrates His care and compassion regarding man's existence here in this life.

While it doesn't have to be this way, it's usually in the context of turmoil that mankind looks up to God for deliverance. In my time in ministry, I've seen this repeatedly. A loved one is placed in the hospital after a major car accident. A doctor reveals to a loved one that the cancer is back and has spread. There's a complication with a pregnancy. A marriage is on the verge of ending in divorce. A pink slip was placed in a locker this morning. A company has, without warning, been forced to close its doors. All of these and countless other scenarios often cause us to recognize that we cannot control all the situations in life. They bring us to either accept or fight against the simple fact that only God has the power and ability to deal with our plight. That's when we often look up. That's when many seek God.

In Romans 1–3, Paul desperately wants those to whom he is writing to do this regarding their sin. Until sin is recognized for what it is: relationship destroying, eternal life-altering, real happiness stealing, joy robbing, life-crippling infection that we opted for, we will never see our dire situation and cry out to God as we recognize our great need for Him. Once we do that, everything changes. We no longer look for answers within ourselves. We no longer rest on our heritage or our affiliations. Once we cry out to God because we recognize He is the only source of healing, we will find peace amid the storms of life.

CONCLUSION

Let's return to the opening illustration. If that man had chosen to hide his pain and deal with it alone, the pit of despair within him would have only deepened. But his moment of reflection became a turning point. He realized that no amount of success or achievement could ever fill the void in his heart or bring true meaning to his life. His sin weighed heavily on him, and the more he boasted about his affair, the larger and darker the emptiness inside him grew.

In looking for the answer and the way out of this horrible situation he had gotten himself into, he looked up. It was the only place he hadn't looked for fulfillment and healing. Once he did, he began to listen more intently on Sundays. He began to open his Bible at home and search for true healing and peace. Repeatedly, he found that repentance and submission to God through the Gospel was how renewal occurs.

Then, one Sunday, he truly listened instead of merely enduring the sermon. That day's message was drawn from Paul's words in Romans 1:18–3:20—a call to recognize our deep need for God. For the first time, it all clicked. He understood that he could never repair the damage sin had caused in his life alone. The road to recovery would be painful and humbling, possibly even costing him his marriage. Yet he also knew that staying on his current path of sin and destruction would ultimately cost him something more significant—his soul.

This realization eventually led him to confess everything to his wife and sincerely beg for her forgiveness. It was an extremely tumultuous journey for them both; however, his decision to embrace the Gospel, which Paul describes as *"the power of God for salvation"* (Rom. 1:16), changed everything. The transformative power is available to everyone who acknowledges their need for God and turns to Him in obedient faith. Whether it's those once caught in the sins described in Romans 1 or the adulterous man from the opening story, Paul shows us that recognizing our need for God is not a step backward. It's the first step toward the profound transformation only He can bring.

Applying
ACCEPTING JUSTIFICATION BY FAITH

ROMANS 4:3

JOE WELLS

"Abraham believed God, and it was credited to him as righteousness."

INTRODUCTION

The American idea of being a "self-made man" is deeply woven into the fabric of American culture, embodying the ideals of individualism, hard work, and upward mobility. This notion, which has shaped the American Dream for generations, has its roots in the early 19th century and has evolved significantly over time.

The term "self-made man" was first coined by United States Senator Henry Clay on February 2, 1832, during a Senate debate about a protective tariff.[1] Clay used the phrase to describe individuals in the manufacturing sector whose success came from their own efforts rather than external circumstances. This new label emerged during a period of unprecedented economic expansion in America, reflecting the transformation of society and the rise of entrepreneurial culture.[2]

While the term itself was new, the idea it represented had germinated in American society for some time. Benjamin Franklin, one of the Founding Fathers, is often cited as the classic example of a self-made man. His autobiography, which detailed his rise from humble beginnings to prominence, inspired many and helped solidify the concept in the American psyche.

---

1. Admin, RW. "The American Myths of the 'Self-Made Man,' The American Dream and Meritocracy." *Ray Williams*, 15 July 2020.
2. Winkle, Kenneth J. "Abraham Lincoln: Self-Made Man." *Journal of the Abraham Lincoln Association*, Vol. 21, No. 2, 2000, 1-16, http://hdl.handle.net/2027/spo.2629860.0021.203.

The mid-19th century saw a flourishing of the self-made man ideal. It became popular to publish collections of biographies celebrating such figures. Charles C.B. Seymour's *Self-Made Men* (1858) chronicled 60 such individuals, while Harriet Beecher Stowe focused on 19 subjects in her work.[3] These publications helped to popularize and romanticize the notion of the self-made man.

The renowned abolitionist and orator Frederick Douglass further developed the concept through a series of lectures starting in 1859. Douglass defined a self-made man as someone who owes "little or nothing to birth, relationship, friendly surroundings; to wealth inherited or to early approved means of education." His lectures explored what makes a self-made man, the institutions that foster such individuals, and the criticisms they often face.[4]

As the 19th century progressed, particularly during the Gilded Age, figures like Andrew Carnegie, John D. Rockefeller, and J. Pierpont Morgan were seen not just as successful businessmen but as individuals who, through their ingenuity, had tapped into the secrets of material success on such enormous levels that the self-made man idea not only came to mean success and happiness but wealth and power.[5] Those who saw the American Dream ever before them garnered inspiration from men such as these. However, over time, the lack of opportunities, luck, and inherited wealth began to cause some to realize the degree of results behind the "self-made man" concept varied greatly from person to person. Still, the idea of making on one's own and building the life of your pursuits remained ever ingrained in the American spirit.

Sometimes, the concept of the "self-made man" can make it extremely difficult to understand and accept justification by faith, as Paul lays out in Romans 3:21–4:25. Perhaps it's because we, much like the Jews of that time, know that being in covenant with God not only demands a certain belief but also a particular lifestyle where actions and motives come together out of a desire to please God and bring Him honor and glory. If we fail to live up to those standards, we are failures and thus miss the mark or are counted as sinners. In other words, to be right with God, we must live lives that merit such righteousness. At least, that's the way many think.

When it comes to how we walk in this life, we must choose to walk in the light (1 John 1). That said, even if we sought to walk in the light according to the commandments and statutes of God, we would not be able to do so without failure. That's one of the most significant messages we have seen thus far in Romans 1 and 2. Both the Gentiles and the Jews are without excuse, having ventured into a sinful mindset with actions that have followed. On top of that, the Holy Spirit, through the pen of the apostle Paul, emphasized, *"There is **none** righteous, not even one"* (Rom. 3:10, emp. added). As we turn our attention to our text in consideration for this chapter, we see the Spirit doubling down on this concept, *"For **all** have sinned and fall short of the glory of God"* (Rom. 3:23, emp. added).

---

3. Swansburg, John. "The Self-Made Man: The Story of America's Most Pliable, Pernicious, Irrepressible Myth." *Slate Magazine*, 29 Sept. 2014.
4. Douglass, Frederick. "Self-Made Men." Speech, 1872. From Teaching American History. https://teachingamericanhistory.org/document/self-made-men/.
5. Burton, Tara Isabella. "The Making of the Self-Made Man." *Current Affairs*, Current Affairs, 30 May 2024, www.currentaffairs.org/news/2022/03/the-making-of-the-self-made-man.

Accepting Justification By Faith

The self-made man logic says, "Since I got myself into this mess, I will just have to get myself out of it." Like a man caught in quicksand struggles until he's completely exhausted, only to realize that in his current predicament, he can't save himself, we must come to accept that justification in the eyes of God is not going to be given because we pulled ourselves out of the quicksand of sin. It's given as a gift by the one who holds the righteous judgment and extends the righteous branch of redemption, Jesus Christ.

STEP #3: ACCEPT JUSTIFICATION BY FAITH

DISCUSSION

1. The Righteousness of God Apart from the Law (Rom. 3:21-26)

Having already established in Romans 1:17 that the righteousness of God has been revealed through the Gospel of Jesus Christ, Paul now reiterates that *"apart from the Law the righteousness of God has been manifested"* (Rom. 3:21). To the casual reader, this may not stand out as very significant; however, as we leave this statement in context, the meaning begins to swell. The larger the meaning, the sweeter it becomes to those sitting and resting therein.

In chapter 2, Paul made sure to drive home a serious point. By the Jews' own admission, the Gentiles were never under the Law of Moses as a system of justification. They may have abided by portions of the Law; however, since they were never under it, they wouldn't be held accountable according to such. That truth doesn't mean Gentiles wouldn't be held responsible before God. They were, but it was going to be according to the law of conscience, which God, who had made himself known through the creation to the extent the Gentiles could know Him and honor Him as the true God, had instilled within them and was based on the same basic principles of loving God and loving their neighbor (Rom. 1:21; Matt. 22:37-39). There was no law that they love God and love their neighbor; however, the invisible attributes of God, discoverable in creation, were enough for the Gentiles to understand how the Creator functions and thus, how they should function.

Thus, when Paul begins this section with the statement that *"apart from the Law the righteousness of God has been manifested"* (Rom. 3:21), he draws a bold line. As a matter of fact, he will add in verse 21, *"being witnessed by the Law and the Prophets."* The reality is that even the Old Testament spoke to this point, as the Law and the Prophets pointed to the coming of the Messiah and God's redemptive work for all of mankind, including Gentiles (Jer. 31:31-34). Thus, the righteousness of God is not based on keeping the Law of Moses perfectly. Nor is it based on always doing what is right according to the law of conscience under which the Gentiles are said to be. The righteousness of God is only something that belongs to God, and if it's going to be bestowed upon any specific person, it will be a gift that God chooses to give (Rom. 3:24).

Manifestation of Righteousness

In the book of Romans, we see a word group that Dan Owens calls "The Righteous Family." This family of words is used 56 times in the letter to the Romans; however, each of the usages can be broken down into four categories.

- *Dikaios*—This is often translated as "righteous" or "just" and is used by Paul to mean perfect or without sin in God's sight.
- *Dikaioo*—At times, this is translated as "justify" and is used to relay that someone who is not righteous can be made righteous. Only God can do this in the person's life by giving a person His righteousness.
- *Dikaiosune*—This is the quality of perfection a person can have if deemed "righteous." This word is often translated as "righteousness," and humans can only possess this quality through God's redemptive work through Christ Jesus.
- *Dikaioma*—This word refers to the righteous requirement of God's law. No human can ever perfectly keep either the Law of Moses or the law of conscience; therefore, the only way this is attained is through submission to the Gospel.[6]

When taken as a whole, this family of words teaches a profound lesson, and one the apostle Paul desperately wants the Christians in Rome to understand. God has a requirement that no man in and of themselves can reach. The righteous requirement of living perfectly before Him by law keeping is a mountain no man can climb. However, that doesn't mean all hope is lost. That's the point being made here by Paul. The righteousness of God, that quality that only He has and gives to humans through the redemption work of the Gospel, has been *"manifested,"* made known, apart from law keeping. This revelation has happened through the Gospel of Jesus Christ and is available for all who believe (πιστεύω, *pisteúō*)—"to consider something to be true and therefore worthy of one's trust"[7] (Rom. 3:22).

The Work God Accomplishes Through Christ

In our best effort to understand the Gospel of Jesus Christ and the redemption we find only through His blood, we sometimes fail to understand the serious consequence demanded by God's nature when one chooses the path of sin. Not only does God have a righteous requirement for those who sought to be justified by the Law of Moses or even the Gentiles who may have sought to be justified by just being a good person according to the moral law, both of which have never been possible, as His nature, He is righteous. It's not just a standard He arbitrarily puts forth and demands from people. He is the standard, and because of this, sin is not just a bad behavior. It's an action, attitude, thought, or motivation that treats the very nature of God as if it were less than what it is. That's why God's righteousness toward men must be demonstrated through Jesus Christ.

---

6. Owen, Dan. "Chapter 2." *A Teacher's Commentary on Romans*. Murrells Inlet: Covenant Books, 2024, 18.
7. Arndt, William, Frederick W. Danker, et al. *A Greek-English Lexicon of the New Testament and Other Early Christian Literature*. Chicago: University of Chicago Press, 2000, 816.

Accepting Justification By Faith

Romans 3:25 introduces the concept of Christ as a *"propitiation"* (ἱλαστήριος, *hilastérios*)—the propitiatory gift or that which causes God to deal with us mercifully.[8] This term alludes to the mercy seat of the Ark of the Covenant, where the blood of sacrifices was sprinkled to atone for sins. Jesus Christ is designated here, and in Hebrews 9:5, not only is He the place where the sinner lays his sin down but also the means of our amending before God. Unlike the high priest of the Old Testament whose atonement of the people was accomplished through the blood of something other than himself (Heb. 9:25), Jesus' own blood is used to redeem the faithful. The tremendous value of His blood is seen in that it is the only sacrifice that's enough to pay the ransom our sins demand.

Thus, Paul states that Christ's blood satisfies divine justice, allowing God to be both *"just and the justifier"* (Rom. 3:26). *Just* being in "the Righteous Family" as the word δίκαιος (*díkaios*)—"to being in accordance with high standards of rectitude, upright, just, fair,"[9] and "justifier" being δικαιόω (*dikaióō*)—"to render a favorable verdict, vindicate."[10] In other words, justification is God's doing and is unearned. That's the nature of the sacrifice of Jesus. We did not deserve His blood to be shed on the cross, nor did we do anything to deserve to be brought back into covenant with God. We can't get it all right; therefore, any forgiveness we receive is a gift not owed based on merit but given because of God's grace (Rom. 3:24).

2. Justification by Faith, Not Works (Rom. 3:27-31)

What are the dangers of being a "self-made man?"

While many of us may sit around a table and discuss all qualities we think would fall into the positive category of such a concept, have you ever considered the potential dangers? Consider the dangerous subject of pride. If I genuinely believe that I am the reason for my success, I could risk becoming puffed up or conceited. That may cause me to look down on others who have not had the same level of success as I have achieved, and thus, I might be assuming they aren't seeing blessings because they are not working hard enough. I may even conclude that they don't want to succeed and enjoy living at a lower level. Pride has a way of skewing our vision and tainting any success in our lives. If it has this capability when it comes to this fleshly life, think about it when it comes to our spiritual lives. That's precisely why Paul addresses the subject of boasting in Romans 3:27.

"Where then is boasting?" is how Paul bluntly lays it before the readers (Rom. 3:27). This is more than a question. Instead, after developing his point that all are without excuse and have no hope on their own, he makes a profound statement with this question. What could they possibly boast about? Not keeping the Law of Moses and thus earning righteousness. It couldn't be because the Gentiles got everything right and stopped needing the forgiveness that only God offers through His Son. So...where is their boasting?

---

8. Zodhiates, Spiros. *The Complete Word Study Dictionary: New Testament.* Chattanooga: AMG Publishers, 2000.
9. Arndt, Danker, et al. 246.
10. Arndt, Danker, et al. 249.

Paul makes it very clear in Romans 3:27 that their boasting is "excluded." The Greek here is the word ἐκκλείω (*ekkleíō*), and it means "to make no room for, exclude, shut out."[11] There is no room for arrogant boasting in one's works when it comes to salvation because salvation is based upon the law of faith and not works. The "law of faith" says we must trust in God to do for us what we are entirely incapable of doing on our own. We can't undo our sinful past, nor can we do enough good to build the bridge back to God. Instead, God is the only one powerful enough to accomplish this. As Paul states in Romans 3:28, *"For we maintain that a man is justified by faith apart from works of law."*

3. Abraham as the Example of Faith (Rom. 4:1-12)

To persuade any of those in the church in Rome who had a Jewish background and were still putting their confidence in such, Paul, by inspiration of the Holy Spirit, invokes the name of Abraham. To a Jew, this is one of the big names of their heritage. It was to Abraham that the land and seed promises were given (Gen. 12:1-3). The land promise pointed the Hebrews of old to Canaan, while the seed promise pointed to a blessing to all nations that would come through Isaac, Jacob, David, and culminating in Jesus. Abraham was known to be the faithful father of the Hebrews and thus is held in high esteem. So, when Paul brings Abraham into this discussion, he knows exactly what he's doing in making this appeal.

Paul appeals to Abraham as he writes, *"What then shall we say that Abraham, our forefather according to the flesh, has found? For if Abraham was justified by works, he has something to boast about, but not before God"* (Rom. 4:1-2). This directly counters Jewish thought that Abraham's righteousness was due to his obedience. While obedience to God's commandments, statutes, and ordinances is absolutely and without doubt essential to faith and receiving the blessings of God (Deut. 30:15-20), it still doesn't earn any man righteousness. Even on our best days, we don't push God into a corner where He owes us anything. Thus, the phrase *"it was credited to him"* must not be rushed over.

Credited Righteousness

In Romans 4:3, Paul quotes Genesis 15:6: *"Abraham believed God, and it was credited to him as righteousness."* The Greek word is λογίζομαι (*logízomai*)—"to determine by mathematical process, reckon, calculate."[12] It appears not only here in 4:3 but also in verses 4, 5, 8, 9, 10, 22, and 23. Through this word, the Holy Spirit through the apostle Paul's pen is putting an exclamation point on this critical theological concept. If one is working for his salvation, believing his efforts will ever merit such, he is not trusting in the grace of God but in his own abilities (Rom. 4:4). However, once we stop trusting in ourselves and begin entirely relying on what God can only do for us, we start emphasizing salvation in its proper place—from God.

---

11. Arndt, Danker, et al. 303.
12. Arndt, Danker, et al. 597.

Accepting Justification By Faith

That's not to say that obedience is not essential. This point is established in the bookends of Romans (1:5; 16:26) when Paul made it clear the letter intended to bring about the *"obedience of faith."* The lack of submission and obedience of both the Gentiles and Jews have been emphasized in chapters 1 and 2. What has been made clear is that God is displeased when our behavior doesn't align with His nature and His revealed Word. Thus, as we study about transformation, we should not downplay or underemphasize the importance of obeying God's Word. Instead, the message that needs to permeate our minds and hearts is that because of the grace of God poured forth in our lives, we ought to want to give Him every thought, action, and motivation. His goodness compels us to respond as we desire to walk more closely with Him daily.

Circumcision and Faith

In Genesis 15:6, we read about Abraham: *"Then he believed in the Lord; and He reckoned it to him as righteousness."* It wasn't until Genesis 17:10-11 that we read of God instructing Abraham regarding circumcision, *"This is My covenant, which you shall keep, between Me and you and your descendants after you: every male among you shall be circumcised. And you shall be circumcised in the flesh of your foreskin, and it shall be the sign of the covenant between Me and you."* The significance of the timing of these two verses is the crux of the point Paul is making in Romans 4. Before Abraham was ever circumcised, God credited his account with righteousness. According to Paul in Romans 4, this was done so that righteousness would not be tied to being a circumcised Jew, which was a significant point of confusion and false teaching in the New Testament period (Phil. 3).

The importance of Romans 4:16 needs to rise to the surface in our study. *"For this reason it is by faith,* **in order that it may be in accordance with grace,** *so that the promise will be guaranteed to all the descendants, not only to those who are of the Law, but also to those who are of the faith of Abraham, who is the father of us all"* (emp. added). Paul has strongly stressed salvation by grace leading up to chapter 4. In Romans 3:24, he explains that salvation is a gift given to us by God's grace. Thus, when we get to Romans 4, the discussion of Abraham's circumcision must be kept in context. The Jews thought they were saved by law keeping; however, that belief has been defeated numerous times.

This is why Paul's emphasis on the timing of God crediting Abraham with righteousness is such a significant point in this location in the book of Romans. By invoking Abraham's name, Paul is closing the door on the Jewish belief that circumcision merited salvation. He is showing God crediting righteousness was done outside of law keeping, thus impressing upon the readers that all salvation is because of the grace of God and not because of one's Jewish heritage.

CONCLUSION

The American ideal of the self-made man promotes personal achievement and responsibility. While this principle may be admirable in business or academics, it presents a serious challenge when applied to faith. The idea that success comes solely from hard work can lead people to believe that righteousness must be earned rather than received as a gift from God.

Paul addresses this misconception in Romans 3:21–4:25. Just like someone sinking in quicksand cannot escape by struggling harder, we cannot free ourselves from sin through personal effort. The self-made man ideology tells us to pull ourselves up by our bootstraps, but Paul clarifies that justification does not come from works—it comes through faith in Christ. Righteousness is not a reward for good behavior but a gift from God. If salvation were self-made, Christ's sacrifice would be unnecessary. Scripture makes it clear that righteousness is not something we can earn, and any attempt to do so negates the very need for grace.

The Gospel calls for surrender, not self-sufficiency. The self-made man may achieve great success in the world, but before God, he stands empty-handed. Just as no one can pull themselves out of quicksand alone, no one can escape sin without God's intervention. True righteousness is not self-made—it is given by God (Rom. 5:1). By embracing faith rather than works, submitting in obedience to Christ, and trusting in His sacrifice, we find peace with God, resting in His grace rather than our efforts.

Applying

NESTLE INTO PEACE AND HOPE

ROMANS 5:1-12

JOE WELLS

"Therefore, having been justified by faith, we have peace with God through our Lord Jesus Christ, through whom also we have obtained our introduction by faith into this grace in which we stand; and we exult in hope of the glory of God."

INTRODUCTION

Establishing peace and hope after war is a challenging and lengthy endeavor. To do so often requires an acceptance of the cause of the conflict in the beginning. This process can be excruciating and revealing as all sides must come together to reach a different conclusion than continuing the bloodshed. This moment is sometimes reached only when one side has been defeated by force and brought to the table to discuss what will happen moving forward. Other times, this point may be reached when both sides no longer seek retribution and revenge for what the other has done—or at least is perceived to have done—as the aggressor.

One of the most critical early steps is the disarming and demobilization of forces opposed to one other. This vulnerable step is crucial in creating a reintegration phase for ex-combatants, hoping they can transition away from the fighting mindset and into the cooperative frame required to return to civilian life. Also, reconstructing what has been destroyed due to fighting must be considered. To send people back into towns that have been decimated by fighting only serves to further impoverish a nation and illicit ill-will toward those seen as responsible for such destruction. Establishing peace and hope after a physical conflict like war is daunting but possible.

As tricky as establishing peace and hope pertains to warring parties, obtaining such within oneself seems even more laborious. Perhaps it's because we never escape the knowledge we live with regarding our own failures and imperfections. We tend to be our worst enemy when it comes to picking apart every aspect of our daily lives: our appearance, word choices, tones, thoughts, experiences, interactions with others, and a host of other expectorants that can cause the flames of self-loathing, self-hatred, and self-doubt to roar. With every glimpse into the mirror, a person who lives without peace and hope in life feels the physical effects of stress levels being high, often demonstrated in weakened immunity, cardiovascular issues, as well as anxiety disorders.

A study published in *Health Psychology* found that individuals who practice mindfulness and inner peace exhibit lower levels of the stress hormone cortisol, which helps prevent these health risks.[1] Hope, on the other hand, has been linked to resilience and better mental health outcomes. A study by Charles R. Snyder, a pioneering psychologist in "Hope Theory," demonstrated that individuals with high hopes tend to set meaningful goals, develop strategies to achieve them, and maintain motivation even in adversity.[2] This underscores the idea that hope is an anchor, keeping individuals steady during life's storms. Living with peace and hope ultimately allows us to navigate life's difficulties with purpose and assurance.

When considering peace and hope from a secular viewpoint, countless benefits exist. These are seen in both the external (between two people or two countries who were at war) and the internal, and what the anchor within a person is that helps them stay forward with purpose. However, when we turn to peace and hope as a spiritual discussion, the value is amplified in that this area will feed all other external and internal regions of our lives. When we are at peace with God and our hope is firmly rooted in His promises no matter what external circumstances may come our way, we can look to Him for peace and hope as we nestle into His loving hands.

As we turn our attention to the next step in transformation, it is vital to notice how Romans 5 begins, *"Therefore, having been justified by faith, we have peace with God through our Lord Jesus Christ, through whom also we have obtained our introduction by faith into grace in which we stand; and we exult in hope of the glory of God."* With everything Paul has written up to this point, he is now ready to conclude his opening thoughts. The Gentiles are without excuse (Rom. 1:20). The Jews are without excuse (Rom. 2:1). All of mankind who are old enough to choose to sin against God stand in the exact same predicament (Rom. 3:23). If we are going to have peace with God, it will only come because of His grace (Rom. 4:16). We can't achieve peace and hope on our own, no matter how hard we may strive. That's why it's very significant that Paul begins our text with *"Therefore."* We now focus on the only peace and hope that truly matters in our lives.

STEP #4: NESTLE INTO PEACE AND HOPE IN CHRIST JESUS

---

1. Sayadi, Ahmad Reza, et al. "The Effect of Mindfulness-based Stress Reduction (MBSR) Training on Serum Cortisol Levels, Depression, Stress, and Anxiety in Type 2 Diabetic Older Adults During the COVID-19 Outbreak." *Journal of Medicine and Life* Vol. 15, 12/2022, 1493-1501. doi:10.25122/jml-2021-0437.
2. Browne, Sarah Jeanne. "The Psychological Basis of Hope and How It Gets Us through Hard Times." *Forbes*, Forbes Magazine, 4 Nov. 2021, www.forbes.com/sites/womensmedia/2021/11/02/the-psychological-basis-of-hope-and-how-it-gets-us-through-hard-times/.

DISCUSSION

1. Peace with God through Justification (Rom. 5:1-2)

Like Abraham, all those in a covenant relationship with God came into such based upon the work that God has accomplished, not on their own merit. As previously discussed, righteousness is not a trait or quality one can deem upon oneself. Instead, as Paul points out, any righteousness we are blessed with is because we have been *"justified by faith"* (Rom. 5:1). This phrase is the Greek word δικαιόω [dikaioō] and carries the meaning of "be acquitted, be pronounced and treated as righteous."[3] The weight of this phrase is that a wrong sin was committed, and thus, a righteous and just judge must condemn the one who committed such a heinous offense. With such an enormous penalty to be expected, explained in the book of Romans as *"the wrath of God"* (Rom. 1:18), an equally mammoth price must be paid to avoid such terror. Thus, when Paul wrote that all those who are justified by faith can only be so because God displayed Jesus, His only begotten Son (John 3:16), *"publicly as a propitiation in His blood through faith"* (Rom. 3:25), he declared the tremendous cost sin requires. In this statement, he also declared the vastness of God's love for each of us. When Paul writes that we have *"peace with God through our Lord Jesus Christ"* (Rom. 5:1), he is directing the reader into the reflecting pool of salvation so they will not, in any way, be confused about why they can be called righteous and why they have peace and hope.

The Nature of Peace

In the Old Testament, peace extends beyond a simple absence of conflict. It encompasses a state of well-being, security, and divine blessing and was never to be understood as a mere human achievement but rather as a gift from God, contingent upon Israel's faithfulness to the covenant (Lev. 26:6; Job 25:2; Ps. 29:11). Peace is applied in various contexts, some of which include:

- peace within an individual (Ps. 37:37; Isa. 32:17)
- peace in interpersonal relationships (Josh. 9:15)
- national peace (Deut. 2:26; 1 Kings 5:12)
- peace in the covenantal relationship between God and His people (Isa. 54:10).

The future hope of peace was closely linked to the coming of the Messiah, described as the *"Prince of Peace"* in Isaiah 9:6, whose reign would establish lasting justice and extend peace beyond Israel to the entire world (Zech. 9:9-10). The close of the Old Testament did not fully realize this expectation of peace. Instead, those who clung to God looked to the future, believing the Messiah was coming and God's promise of redemption was yet to be fulfilled.

---

3. William Arndt, Frederick W. Danker, et al., *A Greek-English Lexicon of the New Testament and Other Early Christian Literature*. Chicago: University of Chicago Press, 2000, 249.

As we turn the page to the New Testament concept of peace (εἰρήνη, *eirēnē*) is used in various contexts as well. It is used to refer to:

- a common greeting or farewell (Luke 10:5; Gal. 6:16; James 2:16)
- the cessation of conflict between nations (Luke 14:32; Acts 12:20)
- the cessation of conflict between individuals (Rom. 14:19; Eph. 4:3).

In Luke 1:79, we read that the Messiah would *"guide our feet into the way of peace,"* a prophecy fulfilled in Jesus, whose birth was heralded by angels proclaiming peace to all people (Luke 2:14). This promise was not regarding a worldly peace marked by the absence of tension because Jesus' peace often disrupted existing relationships, bringing division between those who accepted and rejected Him (Matt. 10:34-37; Luke 12:51-53). At its core, the peace that Jesus brings is the reconciliation between God and humanity through His atoning sacrifice (Rom. 5:1; Col. 1:20), which in turn establishes a new covenant community bound together by peace.

Jesus is called *"our peace"* (Eph. 2:14), and God is identified as the *"God of peace"* because of His reconciling work in Christ (Phil. 4:9; Col. 3:15). This divine peace also carries an expectation for believers, as peace is both a fruit of the Spirit (Gal. 5:22) and a call to action, requiring Christians to pursue reconciliation and harmony within the church (Rom. 12:18; Heb. 12:14). Thus, peace in the New Testament is both a present experience of divine reconciliation and mandate for Christian living, ultimately pointing toward the full realization of God's kingdom.[4]

Access into Grace

Imagine standing outside a king's court, awaiting your introduction. When the doors open, someone announces your name and welcomes you before the king. You walk as gracefully as possible down a long red carpet, soldiers standing on either side of you. At the end of the carpet, you see the king sitting on the throne adorned in all his royal garments with the most glorious crown you've ever seen. As you take it all in, the only thought that comes to mind is how fortunate you are to have been invited to participate in this extraordinary experience of a lifetime.

If that seems like a dream, open your eyes because, through Jesus Christ, all those justified by faith have *"obtained our introduction"* (Rom. 5:2) into a much more impressive position than standing before a human king. The phrase is simply the Greek word προσαγωγή (*prosagōgḗ*) and means "a way of approach, access."[5] It is a term commonly used for being invited to the audience of a king or someone in high official standing. The word granted a right of approach to the king or high official without the fear of doing so.

---

4. Walter A. Elwell and Philip Wesley Comfort, *Tyndale Bible Dictionary*, Tyndale Reference Library. Wheaton: Tyndale House Publishers, 2001, 1004.
5. Arndt, Danker, et al. 876.

Nestle Into Peace and Hope

As Paul utilizes this phrase by inspiration of the Holy Spirit, the readers would immediately understand the privilege and gravity of such an introduction. Only by faith can one come into this court of *grace* (χάρις, *cháris*), referring to the "favor and goodwill of God and Christ as exercised toward men,"[6] and only because of grace can it be said that we "stand" in such a condition. The word *stand* here means "to be in a condition or state, stand"[7] and carries the idea of something that is not temporary or unstable. Instead, those who by faith have an introduction into grace stand in a stable, continual condition of grace. That doesn't mean that the same person can't turn his back on this condition and fall from grace (Gal. 5:4); however, as Paul is developing his argument, he wants to make sure the recipients of this letter understand that grace is solid and strong as long as they remain faithful.

2. Rejoice in Hope Amid Suffering (Rom. 5:3-5)

Keeping one's focus on the result is a potent motivator. For those who have been captured in war, the dream of one day being reunited with their loved ones back home as they again enjoy the freedom has been said to be a powerful motivation to endure the harsh treatments of a POW. While not as impactful, something similar could be said of those who run in a race. As the starter gun sounds, they burst out of the blocks, keeping their eyes on the finish line. They visualize crossing the finish line first as they break the outstretched tape. The power of focus and being motivated by what has been promised at the "finish line" is what Paul is referring to when he writes, *"and we exult in hope of the glory of God"* (Rom. 5:2).

In Dan Owen's book *A Teacher's Commentary on Romans*, he points out that "Whenever Paul speaks of hope, he is speaking of the reward that awaits us at the end of life's journey (Rom. 5:5; 8:18, 24-25; Eph. 1:17-18; 4:4)."[8] For the Christian, this motivation is powerful and keeps one moving forward, even though *tribulations* (θλίψις, *thlípsis*) "distress, oppression, affliction,"[9] are expected as those who oppose the righteousness of God squeeze those who rest in being justified by faith. The Christians are encouraged to remember that tribulations, while distressing, serve as opportunities for spiritual growth. Thus, the tribulations become a source of exulting or boasting instead of becoming a shame. It's interesting to note that while boasting in self and keeping the Law as a means of righteousness has been dismissed up to this point in the book of Romans, Paul now writes to the Christians to boast in two specific areas: 1) in hope of the glory of God (Rom. 5:2), and 2) in tribulations because they result in spiritual growth (Rom. 5:3-5).

The Refining Process

Growth in our walk with God does not come about because we obey the Gospel. The growth journey begins at that point; however, as our knowledge of God's will is expanded through continual study of His Word, we are confronted with old ways of thinking and conclusions reached in the past. The ongoing transformation in our lives challenges us to put the teachings found in the Word of God into practice, which often requires removing

---

6. Zodhiates, Spiros. *The Complete Word Study Dictionary: New Testament*. Chattanooga: AMG Publishers, 2000.
7. Arndt, Danker, et al. 483.
8. Owen, Dan R. "Romans 5." *A Teacher's Commentary on Romans*. Murrells Inlet: Covenant Books, 2024, 62.
9. Arndt, Danker, et al. 457.

the old thinking and actions detrimental to living faithfully before God. This refining will continue to happen over the lifetime of a Christian as the Word of God becomes more than something to be memorized or casually read. As life circumstances place us at a crossroads where we are forced to answer whether we genuinely believe what we've seen in His Word, we display where we are in the refining process.

The refining process that Paul specifically addresses here points the reader through a progression of:

- ***tribulation*** (θλίψις, *thlípsis*)—"trouble that inflicts distress, oppression, affliction, tribulation."[10]
- ***perseverance*** (ὑπομονή, *hupomoné*)—"the capacity to hold out or bear up in the face of difficulty, patience, endurance, fortitude, steadfastness, perseverance."[11]
- ***proven character*** (δοκιμή, *dokimé*)—"the experience of going through a test with special reference to the result, standing a test, character."[12]
- ***hope*** (ἐλπίς, *elpís*)—"the looking forward to something with some reason for confidence respecting fulfillment, hope, expectation."[13]

There's no short-changing the process. While immature Christians will see tribulations through the lens of self-pity, mature Christians, because they have grown through the initial infancy phase, will learn to see them as opportunities to grow. Perseverance isn't developed in the comfort of a spiritual recliner. Instead, perseverance only comes when one's faith is placed under the weight of tribulation and holds up. Not only does a maturing faith bear the burden of the weight for a short time, but it stays under the weight with great patience, knowing that the result is beneficial. Thus, proven character can only be developed once faith has been pushed beyond what was initially thought possible. That's why the further our faith is pushed or pressed down, the more we lean into the promise of God that hope is in our future. He didn't disappoint or abandon us in the tribulations, and He won't abandon us as we move closer to graduating from this life into eternity.

Hope Does Not Disappoint

There are a lot of things in this life that disappoint us. Our favorite team loses, and we seem to have a miserable day. Our car breaks down, leaving us stranded on the side of the road. The electric bill goes up, and groceries seem to get more expensive. These don't even include the people in our lives who treat us poorly or make promises and never follow through on them.

In Romans 5:5, Paul writes that *"hope does not disappoint."* The word for *disappoint* is καταισχύνω (*kataischúnō*) and carries with it the idea of cause and effect. The effect of hope will never be disappointment because the hope is firmly rooted and grounded in

---

10. Arndt, Danker, et al. 457.
11. Arndt, Danker, et al. 1039.
12. Arndt, Danker, et al. 256.
13. Arndt, Danker, et al. 319.

God's love. According to Paul, the love of God *"has been poured out within our hearts"* and, in this case, means to "cause to fully experience."[14] The abundant and overflowing gift of the entire experience Christians enjoy regarding the love of God is because, through the Holy Spirit, the justified have been given a seal, a divine guarantee, of God's promise of redemption (Eph. 1:14).

Unlike the people and events in this life, God never disappoints. His promises are sure, as He has a perfect record of keeping His promises. Consider the following verses.

- **Numbers 23:19**—*"God is not a man, that He should lie, Nor a son of man, that He should repent; Has He said, and will He not do it? Or has He spoken, and will He not make it good?"*
- **Joshua 21:45**—*"Not one of the good promises which the Lord had made to the house of Israel failed; all came to pass."*
- **2 Corinthians 1:20**—*"For as many as are the promises of God, in Him they are yes; therefore also through Him is our Amen to the glory of God through us."*
- **Hebrews 10:23**—*"Let us hold fast the confession of our hope without wavering, for He who promised is faithful."*
- **Romans 4:20-21**—*"Yet, with respect to the promise of God, he did not waver in unbelief but grew strong in faith, giving glory to God, and being fully assured that what God had promised, He was able also to perform."*

3. The Ultimate Assurance: Christ's Sacrificial Love (Rom. 5:6-11)

In one of the most impactful sections of the book of Romans up to this point, Paul draws the reader into a deeper and more personal understanding regarding the sacrifice that Christ gave for the redeemed. Up to this point, the death of Jesus Christ has been referenced at least three times (Rom. 1:4; 3:25; 4:24-25). In each of these verses, Paul directs the minds of the Christians in Rome to a deeper understanding of the purpose of Christ's death and the blessing of His resurrection. However, it isn't until Romans 5:6-11 that we see a direct connection made in such a personal manner with the plight of the sinner and the timeliness of the death of Christ. It's in this connection that we see in a way that we have yet, up to this point, that God sent His Son, Jesus, to die a cruel death on the cross before man ever said they were sorry or decided to follow Christ.

Why would God do this?

To answer this, we can learn a vast amount by investigating the word *demonstrates* that Paul uses in Romans 5:8. This is the Greek word συνίστημι (*sunístēmi*) and means "to provide evidence of a personal characteristic or claim through action, demonstrate, show, bring out."[15] Let that resonate for a few minutes. God's love is such that He wanted to show the world how deep and wide it reaches. Many believe today that they have moved too far away from God to be redeemed. They can only see their failures as the cloud of sin blurs their understanding. If they would only focus on

---

14. Arndt, Danker, et al. 312.
15. Arndt, Danker, et al. 973.

what God has done through Christ instead of what they have done in sin, then they would begin to see the peace and hope God offers them.

As we consider this section's deep meaning, another word needs to be brought out. It's the simple word *for* ὑπέρ (*hupér*) and is used multiple times to denote one doing something on behalf of or in the place of another. This is such a strong and significant word here because it brings to the surface the substitutionary nature of the sacrifice of Christ. The punishment that belongs to each of us because of our sin is placed on Christ (1 Pet. 2:24). It's not fair for Him. Christ had no sin, but He became sin on our behalf (2 Cor. 5:21). However, while God is just (Rom. 3:26), He is also the one who decided to send His Son Jesus to be the sacrificial Lamb that appeased the punishment that sin carries. So, instead of you bearing the burden of punishment, He demonstrated His love and allowed His Son to bear the burden on your behalf.

The Sinner's Condition Before

From Romans 5:6-11, we see the sinner's condition described in four ways. In these descriptions, the complete picture is painted of the horrible plight in which one who indulges in sin finds themselves. There's nothing about these sinners that deserves anything except severe punishment. These would fall in line with those in chapter 1 who knew God but did not honor Him as such (Rom. 1:21). These would also keep company with the Jews of chapter 2 who bring blasphemy to the name of God with their consistent inconsistency as they say and teach one thing and live in contradictory manner (Rom. 2:17-24). Perhaps that's why they are described as:

- **helpless** (v. 6) (ἀσθενής, *asthenés*)—"to experiencing some incapacity or limitation, weak."[16]
- **ungodly** (v. 6) (ἀσεβής, *asebés*)—"does not mean irreligious, but one who actively practices the opposite of what the fear of God demands."[17]
- **sinners** (v. 8) (ἁμαρτωλός, *hamartōlós*)—"pertaining to behavior or activity that does not measure up to standard moral or cultic expectations."[18]
- **enemies** (v. 10) (ἐχθρός, *echthrós*)—"pertaining to being hostile, hating, hostile."[19]

The Christian's Condition After

In contrast to the sinner's condition before being redeemed, that of the redeemed Christian is far better. Having accepted that salvation is not based upon meritorious work but rather on faithfully surrendering and obeying the Gospel (Rom. 1:5), the Christian has an entirely different outlook on eternity than those who are still *"helpless," "ungodly," "sinners,"* and *"enemies."* One is filled with peace and hope, the other a terrifying expectation of the wrath of God to be revealed at judgment (Rom. 2:5).

---

16. Arndt, Danker, et al. 142.
17. . Zodhiates.
18. . Arndt, Danker, et al. 51.
19. . Arndt, Danker, et al. 419.

So…what is the condition of the Christian? Here's how Paul, by inspiration of the Holy Spirit, describes it.

- ***justified*** (v. 9) (δικαιόω, *dikaióō*)—"be acquitted, be pronounced and treated as righteous."[20]
- ***reconciled*** (v. 10,11) (καταλλάσσω, *katallássō*)—"the exchange of hostility for a friendly relationship."[21]
- ***shall be saved*** (v. 5, 9, 10) (σώζω, *sṓzō*)—"specifically of salvation from eternal death, sin, and the punishment and misery consequent to sin."[22]

Our Boasting Is Solely in God

The difference between the sinner's condition and that of the faithful Christian is striking, raising the question: Why would anyone choose to face eternity apart from God? Just from our study of Romans 1–5, we see that some will always chase after the fleeting pleasures of this world, suppressing the truth in unrighteousness (Rom. 1:18-32). Others will cling to their self-righteousness, believing they can earn salvation through their works, only to find themselves excluded from God's grace (Rom. 2). Both paths lead to destruction—an outcome no one should willingly choose.

But for those who humbly acknowledge their separation from God (Isa. 59:2) and trust in His power to justify them, an incredible reality awaits. They are no longer lost, no longer hopeless. Instead, they are granted peace with God, filled with hope that drives them forward, knowing that eternal life is their reward. That's why Paul triumphantly declares, *"And not only this, but we also exult in God through our Lord Jesus Christ, through whom we have now received the reconciliation"* (Rom. 5:11). Here, Paul reaches the climax of his argument—boasting in the one thing that truly matters: God Himself. Without Him, there is no hope, no perseverance, no peace. But because of Him, everything changes! Like a grand crescendo in a symphony, Paul's words rise to this powerful truth: our confidence, joy, and future are secure—not because of anything we've done, but because of what God has done—and continues to do—through Jesus Christ. Let that truth ignite your faith and inspire your devotion!

---

20. Arndt, Danker, et al. 249.
21. Arndt, Danker, et al. 521.
22. Zodhiates.

CONCLUSION

Throughout history, peace has been hard-won, both in times of war and within the human heart. As we saw in the Introduction, establishing peace after conflict requires surrender, reconciliation, and a willingness to move forward. The same is true in our spiritual lives. Just as nations must lay down their weapons and embrace a new reality, we, too, must lay down our self-righteousness, guilt, fears, and past failures at Christ's feet. Only then can we experience the true and lasting peace that comes from being reconciled with God. This peace is not just a feeling—it is a state of being, anchored in the certainty of God's promises and secured by the sacrifice of Jesus Christ. Through Him, hope is not wishful thinking but a confident expectation that God is faithful to His Word no matter what trials come.

Imagine a person lost in a raging storm at sea. The wind howls, waves crash, and fear grips the heart as darkness closes in. But then, through the chaos, a rescue ship appears. A strong hand reaches down and pulls them to safety, and suddenly, the storm no longer matters because they are secure. This is the peace and hope we have in Christ. Life will have its storms—tribulations, doubts, and struggles—but when we are in the hands of the Savior, we are no longer at the mercy of the waves. Our peace is not found in calm waters but in the one who walks upon them. Our hope is not in what we see but in the promise of what is to come. So let us exult in God, not just in times of ease but even amid life's most significant challenges, knowing that through Christ, we are justified, reconciled, and forever held in the embrace of His unfailing love. Nestle into that peace. Stand firm in that hope. For in Him, we have everything we need.

Applying

STEP INTO YOUR NEW LIFE

ROMANS 6:11

JOE WELLS

"Even so consider yourselves to be dead to sin, but alive to God in Christ Jesus."

INTRODUCTION

Dropping your first child off at college is a defining moment, one that etches itself permanently into a parent's heart. It's a bittersweet blend of pride and sorrow—watching them spread their wings, filled with hope for the future, while also grieving the season that has passed. Life with them will never be quite the same. The days of saying, "Because I said so," are over. Now, you transition into the role of a guide—offering advice when asked, praying they will make wise choices, and realizing whether they return home is in their hands. The relationship changes, but it doesn't have to fade. In fact, its strength is more crucial than ever.

A different kind of transition occurs when you sit beside a hospice bed, watching a father who once carried you in his arms, now too weak to lift his own. His breath is shallow, his body frail, and time seems to slow as you replay the memories of him laughing at the kitchen table, playing catch in the yard, and you feeling safe under his watchful care. Tears blur your vision as the reality settles in: life is shifting once again. The roles are reversing. When he draws his final breath, you will step into a new reality, one where his absence will be deeply felt, but where you must carry forward the strength he once modeled for you.

Life is a series of transitions, each chapter bringing both heartache and hope. Every new beginning requires closing an old chapter, and while change is rarely easy, it holds the promise of transformation. We leave behind what was, sometimes reluctantly, and step forward into what could be. Research affirms that human beings are built for adaptation and growth. Change is not inevitable but necessary.

Both life moments illustrate the reality of transformation. Whether sending a child off into the world or saying a final goodbye to a parent, each shift challenges us to grow. The parent who drops off their child at college may grieve the days of dependency but find joy in seeing their child forge a new path. The son who watches his father slip away reflects on the past but realizes it is now his time to be the rock for his family. Transition invites transformation—requiring us to let go of the past and fully embrace the present.

This truth is at the heart of Romans 6. To become a faithful child of God is to undergo the most significant transition of all, a spiritual transformation that moves us from death to life. No longer enslaved to sin, we step into the freedom of righteousness. This is more than just a behavior change; it is a complete redefinition of identity. Paul makes it clear that the old life must be buried, and a new life must begin. It is not about merely looking the part—it is about being completely renewed.

So, we must ask ourselves, "What does it truly mean to leave sin behind?" "What must I surrender to walk in the newness of Christ fully?" "How does my transformed life fit into God's grand purpose?"

Stepping into our new life in Christ is not a partial shift. It is a total transformation. The chains of sin are broken, and we are bound instead to righteousness. From the moment we obey the Gospel, everything changes. Paul's message in Romans 6 is clear: True transformation means leaving behind the old, stepping forward in faith, and embracing the new life that Christ has secured for us.

STEP #5: STEP INTO YOUR NEW LIFE

DISCUSSION

1. The Death of the Old Self: Freedom from Sin's Power (Rom. 6:1-7)

Paul begins this passage by addressing a critical misunderstanding about grace that, if left unchecked, could lead to a dangerously misguided approach to Christian living. He had just explained in Romans 5:20 that *"where sin increased, grace abounded all the more."* This truth, meant to magnify the overwhelming sufficiency of God's grace, could be twisted into a faulty way of thinking. Those bent on continuing in the same sinful lifestyle might reason that if grace abounds in response to sin, why not continue sinning so that grace may increase even further (Rom. 6:1)?

Paul does not entertain this notion for a moment. His response is swift, direct, and unyielding: *"May it never be!"* (Rom. 6:2; see also 3:4, 31), μή (*mḗ*) – "not" and γίνομαι (*gínomai*) – "to occur as process or result, happen, turn out, take place."[1] This Greek phrase is one of the strongest possible rejections in the language, carrying the force of an emphatic "Absolutely not!" or even

---

1. Arndt, William, Frederick W. Danker, et al. *A Greek-English Lexicon of the New Testament and Other Early Christian Literature.* Chicago: University of Chicago Press, 2000, 197.

"That idea is unthinkable!" It expresses not just disagreement but complete abhorrence at the very suggestion. Paul will not allow grace to be twisted into a license for sin.

He then presses the matter further with a rhetorical question that demands serious reflection: *"How shall we who died to sin still live in it?"* (Rom. 6:2). Here, Paul introduces a powerful concept. Having died to sin is essential for understanding the Christian life. The Greek verb used here is ἀποθνήσκω (*apothnḗskō*), meaning "dead to that which held us captive."[2] In other words, we are separated from its authority when we die to something. A person who has physically died is no longer subject to the laws of the world—they do not respond to commands, obligations, or influences. Likewise, Paul says believers have died to sin. It no longer reigns over them as it once did. Dan Owens summarized this death by writing, "Death to sin is a mental, spiritual, volitional process in which the inside of a person purposely makes a radical, directional change."[3]

To further illustrate this, Paul turns to the subject of baptism, which is no accident since he has just written about having died to sin. He asks, *"Or do you not know that all of us who have been baptized into Christ Jesus have been baptized into His death?"* (Romans 6:3). The Greek word βαπτίζω (*baptízō*) means "to dip, immerse, submerge"[4] and is used here so the reader has a complete picture of what it means to die to sin. When a piece of cloth was dipped into dye, it became permanently identified with the new color—it was no longer what it once was. Paul uses this word to describe the believer's union with Christ as he writes, "baptized into Christ Jesus" and "baptized into His death."

Up to this point, the Holy Spirit has inspired Paul to write a significant amount regarding the blood of Jesus.

- **Romans 3:25** – in His blood, Jesus is the propitiation for us
- **Romans 5:9** – we are justified because of His blood
- **Romans 5:10** – we are reconciled to God through the shedding of Jesus' blood in His death

In these three verses alone, it is clear the connection is made between our salvation and the death of Jesus. Thus, just as Christ died and was buried, so too have believers die to sin's dominion. It is a picture of being fully immersed into Christ's death, an act that is for the forgiveness of sins (Acts 2:28) and results in a fundamental transformation in identity. This is not merely a behavior change but a change in status. It's a shift from being under the rule of sin to being under the authority of grace. We were once not justified, but now we are. Once, righteousness was held back from us because of our sin. Now, we are deemed righteous because of having been washed in the blood of Jesus.

Paul continues to develop this theme in Romans 6:6, reinforcing what this means for the Christians' daily life, *"Knowing this, that our old self was crucified with Him."* The phrase "old self" refers to our former identity, the person we were before Christ transformed us. This old self was not merely

---

2. Arndt, Danker, et al. 111.
3. Owen, Dan R. "Romans 5." *A Teacher's Commentary on Romans*. E-book ed., Murrells Inlet: Covenant Books, 2024.
4. Zodhiates, Spiros. *The Complete Word Study Dictionary: New Testament* Chattanooga: AMG Publishers, 2000.

wounded or weakened; it was crucified with Christ. This is a dramatic image. Crucifixion was a slow, painful, and inescapable death, and Paul uses this picture intentionally. The old self, the version of us that was enslaved to sin, has been put to death through our being united, σύμφυτος (súmphutos)—"being associated in a related experience,"[5] with Christ.

This means that sin's power over us has been broken. We no longer serve it as slaves. Instead, we are "freed from sin," δικαιόω (dikaióō)—"to cause someone to be released from personal or institutional claims that are no longer to be considered pertinent or valid, make free/pure."[6] Before coming to Christ, we lived pursuing the lust of the flesh, the lust of the eyes, and the pride of life. If sin were personified, we could say it had a controlling grip on us. However, once we were freed from the chains of the past, we no longer live the judicial sentence that comes with sin. God's wrath is appeased in Christ's death, and when we surrender to the Gospel, His wrath against us is removed. Through Christ's death, sin's authority over us was shattered.

This does not mean that Christians are no longer tempted to sin. We still live in the world, and the temptations of darkness are rampant. However, it no longer chooses that path. Our sinful past no longer owns us. It no longer dictates our identity, future, or standing before God. As Christians, we have been set free from its mastery.

This is why Paul's question is so crucial: *"How shall we who died to sin still live in it?"* (Rom. 6:2). If we have been freed from sin, why would we continue to live as though we are still its slaves? The idea that a believer could be rescued from sin's grasp and yet willingly remain in it is unthinkable. It would be like a prisoner who has been released from jail choosing to stay locked in his cell.

Paul emphasizes "knowing this" in verse 6. We need to understand what has happened to us in Christ. This is no small change. In Christ, our complete identity has changed. We were once lost. Now we are found. We were sick, and now we've been made well. We were unjustified. Now, we are justified. We were not righteous, and now we are deemed righteous. It's a total 180-degree difference. We aren't anything like we used to be, and we are supposed to live that way. Changed people live changed lives.

2. Raised to Walk in Newness of Life (Rom. 6:8-14)

Paul does not leave the faithful in the despair of death but immediately moves to the triumphant reality of resurrection. *"Now if we have died with Christ, we believe that we shall also live with Him"* (Rom. 6:8). This is not a mere theoretical hope. It is a present and eternal reality. The word *live* is very significant in developing this message. The Greek word is συζάω (suzáō) and is the pairing of two words together. The first is σύν (sún) and means "together, with, together with, implying a near and close connection."[7] The second word is ζάω (záō), meaning "to live in a transcendent sense, live, of the sanctified life of a child of God."[8] For those who will submit to the

---

5. Arndt, Danker, et al. 960.
6. Arndt, Danker, et al. 249.
7. Zodhiates.
8. Arndt, Danker, et al. 425.

will of God and accept the justification God offers on faith, there is a reality that they are not alone in this life. We live now with Christ in a real sense that we are no longer enslaved to sin and freed by grace. We have peace and hope that can only come from God through Christ. However, we also cherish the promise of God that we are saved from the consequences of sins. Thus, we will live in eternity with Christ as well.

This changes everything. Too often, believers live as though eternal life is something in the distant future. If we have truly died with Christ, then our old selves, our past failures, and the chains that once held us are dead and buried. What remains is a new life, one that reflects the resurrection power of Jesus Himself. This is why Paul speaks with such confidence. It is not a mere possibility; it is a certainty.

But how does this impact our daily lives?

The answer begins in verse 11 as a shift in mindset must happen as one steps into their new life, *"Even so consider yourselves to be dead to sin, but alive to God in Christ Jesus."* The word *consider* is the Greek word λογίζομαι (*logízomai*) and means "as a result of a calculation evaluate, estimate, look upon as, consider."[9] It carries with it the idea of an individual who begins to look at themselves in this life through a different pair of glasses. If you've ever worn eyeglasses, you understand the value of updating your prescription when needed. Your vision becomes much clearer once you put those new glasses on with a better prescription. This is how it is when one changes their evaluation of their life after accepting justification from God. When every thought and action is filtered through the new lens of being dead to sin, no single decision or move in life won't be impacted.

Paul continues explaining the impact in verses 12 and 13 when he writes: *"Therefore do not let sin reign in your mortal body so that you obey its lusts, and do not go on presenting the members of your body to sin as instruments of unrighteousness; but present yourselves to God as those alive from the dead, and your members as instruments of righteousness to God."*

I would like to draw your attention to three specific imperatives or commands in this text: 1) *"do not let sin reign,"* 2) *"do not go on presenting,"* and 3) *"present yourselves to God."* The word *reign* is the word βασιλεύω (*basileúō*) and carries with it the idea of a king who rules over subjects. The word *present* or *presenting* is the Greek word παριστάνω (*paristánō*) and means "place beside, put at someone's disposal."[10] It is the same word used to describe a soldier presenting himself for duty, ready to serve his commanding officer. This is not a passive act. It is an intentional, daily surrender—a recognition that our lives no longer belong to us but to the one who purchased us with His blood.

In two of these, there's the negative *do not*. In the other, there's the positive *do*. These three imperatives are worthy of our attention because each demonstrates a choice that every one of us

---

9. Arndt, Danker, et al. 597.
10. Arndt, Danker, et al. 778.

gets to make. The dichotomy could not be more clear. Simply put, you cannot both present yourself to sin and let it reign in your mortal body and present yourself to God at the same time. A choice must be made, and if you understand what being dead to sin means, there is no dabbling in the pool of filth from which you have been freed. What is dead, is dead. However, if it is still a part of one's life, whether he has been baptized or not, he has admitted that sin is not dead in his life. What a horrible and perilous predicament one is in!

In verse 14, Paul amplifies this message by writing, *"For sin shall not be master over you, for you are not under law but under grace."* The word translated as *master* is κυριεύω (*kurieúō*), which means "to have or exercise rule or authority over, lord over."[11] Combined with the word *reign* used in verse 12, this is a powerful image. Before salvation, sin was not just an influence in our lives. It was a tyrant. It whispered lies, trying to convince us that life is best lived in the pursuit of lust, as did the Gentiles in chapter 1, or by self-righteousness, as the Jews did in chapter 2. But it was wrong. That's why the Holy Spirit, through the pen of Paul, emphasizes our freedom under grace.

It is crucial to understand that this new way of life is not based on legalistic adherence to law keeping but on grace that empowers true righteousness. When Paul says that we are no longer under law but under grace, he is not saying that righteousness no longer matters. Quite the opposite. Grace produces a righteousness that law keeping never could. Law can command holiness, but it cannot create it. Grace, however, transforms us from the inside out, giving us not just the command to be righteous but the power to become and live righteously.

Think of it this way: law-keeping would be like if you were drowning and someone stood on the shore, shouting instructions on how to swim. Conversely, grace is like a rescuer diving into the water, pulling you out, and teaching you to breathe again. Law exposes our weakness; grace fills us with strength.

So, as we reflect on Paul's words, let's ask ourselves: Are we living as those who have died with Christ and been raised to new life? Are we walking in the freedom of grace, or are we still listening to the voice of our former master? Have we truly offered ourselves to God, or are we holding something back?

3. Slaves to Righteousness: A New Identity in Christ (Rom. 6:15-23)

In the final section of this chapter, Paul presents a striking contrast: slavery to sin versus slavery to righteousness. He asks a rhetorical question to drive home a strong reality: *"Do you not know that when you present yourselves to someone as slaves for obedience, you are slaves of the one whom you obey, either of sin resulting in death, or of obedience resulting in righteousness?"* (Rom. 6:16). The Greek word for *slave* here is δοῦλος (*doúlos*), a term that signifies much more than just forced servitude. A *doulos* was someone wholly devoted to the will of another, with no claim to personal autonomy. This wasn't just about external service. It was about complete allegiance, a deep and abiding commitment that shaped every aspect of life.

---

11. Zodhiates.

Step Into Your New Life

Paul's wording makes it clear that every human has a choice to make. We all serve something or someone. Whether we acknowledge it or not, our lives are shaped by who or what we choose to obey. At first, that might sound unsettling. In modern culture, we tend to view personal freedom as the ultimate goal, doing what we want, when we want, without answering to anyone. But Paul flips that idea on its head. He insists that every person is either a *doulos* to sin or a *doulos* to righteousness. There is no neutral ground. True freedom, he argues, isn't found in unrestricted autonomy; instead, it's found in submission to God.

That might sound paradoxical, but Paul explains why this is so important when he writes, *"Having been freed from sin, you became slaves of righteousness"* (Rom. 6:18). Notice the structure of that statement. First comes freedom, having been freed from sin. Then comes slavery, you became slaves of righteousness. This relays a crucial fact that freedom from sin isn't an end in itself. We don't just escape sin to live however we please. True freedom comes with a new allegiance and a new purpose. We don't just drift aimlessly once we're freed from sin's hold. Instead, we are called into a new kind of servitude. We are called to a life devoted to righteousness.

The difference between these two forms of slavery, slavery to sin and slavery to righteousness, is staggering. Consider what Paul points out regarding slavery to sin.

- **Romans 6:19** – In this slavery, we present the members as slaves of impurity and lawlessness.
- **Romans 6:19** – The result of such is further lawlessness.
- **Romans 6:20** – As a slave to sin, we are not righteous.
- **Romans 6:21** – The deeds done under this slavery bring shame.
- **Romans 6:21** – The outcome is death, separation from God.

The blessings jump off the page when we compare this list to descriptions of being enslaved to righteousness.

- **Romans 6:19** – The result of this slavery is sanctification.
- **Romans 6:18, 22** – In this, there is no payment you must make for the sins in your past.
- **Romans 6:22** – The outcome is eternal life.

Imagine yourself playing a game where you must pick between two doors. There are prizes behind each. Typically, this game would be played where the doors were both shut, hiding the prizes behind each. You wouldn't know which door would have the new car behind it and which would have the can of peanuts. However, the game you are imagining is different. Both doors are open in this game, and the prizes are revealed. One door leads you to the list above that describes being a slave of sin. The other door opens to the benefits of being a slave of righteousness. Which would you choose? If you have to think too hard, something's wrong. The contrast couldn't be more stark.

Just to help, Paul concludes this discussion with one of the most well-known verses in all of Scripture, *"For the wages of sin is death, but the free gift of God is eternal life in Christ Jesus our Lord."* (Rom. 6:23). This oft-quoted verse is worth slowing down to consider and better understand the depth of its meaning.

The word *wages* in Greek is ὀψώνιον (*opsōnion*). In the ancient world, this word referred to a soldier's payment, a sum of money or rations given in exchange for service. It was something earned.[12] By using this word, Paul paints a vivid picture: Sin is like a cruel master who pays his workers what they have rightfully earned. And that payment is death—spiritual death, separation from God.

But notice the contrast. While sin pays out wages, God offers a gift. The Greek word for "free gift" is χάρισμα (*charisma*) and means "that which is freely and graciously given, *favor bestowed, gift.*"[13] This is the opposite of something earned. We cannot work for, strive for, or achieve eternal life by our merit. God freely gives it through Christ.

Paul is setting up an undeniable contrast:

- Sin pays its wages—death.
- God gives His gift—eternal life.

The difference could not be more profound. Sin is a master that takes everything and gives nothing but death in return. On the other hand, God is a loving Father who gives freely, not because we have earned it but because He is gracious and merciful. All of this is possible only because of Christ Jesus our Lord. There is no eternal life apart from Him. It is not found in human effort, good works, or religious rituals. It is only found in Jesus.

CONCLUSION

As I reflect on everything Paul teaches in Romans 6, I can't help but think about the sheer magnitude of what it means to be transformed by Christ. This is not a minor adjustment but a shift in thinking or behavior. It's a complete overhaul of identity, a leaving behind of the old, and a stepping forward into something entirely new. We are no longer slaves to sin. We are no longer prisoners to our past. We are no longer defined by the chains that once held us. Christ has set us free, and that freedom is not just a distant promise but a present reality.

This is why Paul's words are so urgent. He knows that the greatest danger for a Christian is not external persecution or suffering but the temptation to forget who we are. To walk in the habits of our former selves instead of stepping boldly into the identity Christ has given us.

So, I want to challenge you today. Don't just know this truth. Live it. Wake up every morning and remind yourself that if you've obeyed the Gospel, you are no longer who you once were. That the life of sin is behind you. Grace is not just something that covers you but something that empowers you. That righteousness is not just a destination but a daily calling.

You have been raised to walk in newness of life!

---

12. Zodhiates.
13. Arndt, Danker, et al. 1081.

Applying
FOCUS ON CHRIST FOR DELIVERANCE

ROMANS 7:24-25

JOE WELLS

"Wretched man that I am! Who will set me free from the body of this death? Thanks be to God through Jesus Christ our Lord! So then, on the one hand I myself with my mind am serving the law of God, but on the other, with my flesh the law of sin."

INTRODUCTION

One of the greatest tragedies in American history was set in the brutal winter of 1846–1847 when a group of pioneers known as the Donner Party found themselves ensnared in an unimaginable struggle for survival. They had set out for California, driven by the same hopes and dreams that fueled thousands of others seeking a new life in the West. But what was supposed to be a journey toward prosperity and freedom became a living nightmare. The journey had been fraught with challenges from the beginning—rugged terrain, broken wagons, dwindling supplies—but nothing could have prepared them for what lay ahead.

An early and relentless snowfall sealed their fate as they ascended the Sierra Nevada mountains. Cut off from the rest of the world, the travelers found themselves trapped in one of the most merciless environments on earth. The cold was inescapable, creeping into their bones and sapping the strength from their bodies. Food became scarce. The livestock they had brought for sustenance perished or were slaughtered far too quickly. When there was nothing left, they boiled leather and tree bark, desperately trying to extract whatever nourishment they could. Hunger gnawed at them relentlessly, and the line between survival and despair grew thinner with each passing day.

One by one, the members of the Donner Party began to succumb—not just to the physical toll of starvation and exposure but to the crushing weight of hopelessness. Disease swept through the camp, further thinning their ranks. As the days turned into weeks and then months, desperation forced them into unthinkable decisions. They faced horrors few humans have ever had to contemplate, let alone endure. The ones who survived did so at a terrible cost, resorting to the ultimate act of desperation—cannibalism. It was not a choice made in cruelty, nor even in madness, but in the stark reality of life and death.

Still, their suffering continued. The howling winds and endless snowdrifts made escape impossible. They were utterly powerless, trapped in a frozen prison of ice and rock, with no way out. Hope had become a cruel mirage—something they could almost remember but could no longer grasp. The weight of despair pressed down upon them like the very snow that buried their camps. No amount of determination or willpower could change their situation. They had reached the limits of human endurance.

Then, just when all hope seemed lost, something extraordinary happened. A rescue party arrived.

Help had come—not from within their own strength but from outside forces. Strangers who had braved the same treacherous mountains risked their own lives to save those who could not save themselves. Against all odds, deliverance had arrived.

The surviving members of the Donner Party did not make it through because they were the strongest, the smartest, or the most capable. They survived because someone else intervened. They had exhausted every possible resource and fought every battle they could fight, and still, it had not been enough. In their moment of greatest need, salvation came from beyond themselves.

The Donner Party's story is haunting, but within it lies an undeniable truth: Salvation comes when we recognize our need for it. We cannot always rescue ourselves, but we can accept the help that is offered. Whether that help comes through the hands of others or, in the most incredible sense, through the grace of God Almighty through His Son Jesus, it is there, waiting.

The plight of those pioneers stranded in the Sierra Nevada mirrors a more profound spiritual truth. In Romans 7:1-25, the apostle Paul describes the desperate struggle of humanity against sin—a battle that cannot be won through human effort alone. Just as the Donner Party could not escape their frozen prison without help, so too are people incapable of breaking free from the bondage of sin without Christ Jesus. In Romans 7, Paul vividly illustrates the struggle of trying to do good yet constantly falling into sin. He concludes that deliverance is only found in God.

STEP #6: FOCUS ON CHRIST FOR DELIVERANCE

DISCUSSION

1. The Law and Its Limited Power (Rom. 7:1-6)

Imagine you're in the audience the very first time this letter is being read. If you have a Gentile background, the struggle of the first part of this chapter would not be as prevalent to you as it would

Focus on Christ for Deliverance

to your brothers and sisters in Christ who come from a Jewish background. Their grandparents and parents observed the Law of Moses and taught them to do the same. With the Law of Moses being deeply ingrained in their culture, to hear the words of this letter teaching that righteousness is not possible based upon Law-keeping as a means of justification would be extremely difficult to accept. Now Paul, in what seems like a very understanding and persuasive manner, lays out why those from a Jewish background no longer need to struggle with their relationship with the Law. Even those who were steeped in a culture centered on the Law of Moses, the opening illustration would have been one that would resonate.

The Law's Authority Over the Living as Opposed to the Dead

Paul begins with a principle that his audience, particularly Jewish Christians, would understand. The Law, which was graciously given to the children of Israel (Ex. 20), holds authority over a person only as long as he lives. He illustrates this with an analogy from marriage when he writes:

> *Do you not know, brethren (for I am speaking to those who know the law), that the law has jurisdiction over a person as long as he lives? For the married woman is bound by law to her husband while he is living; but if her husband dies, she is released from the law concerning the husband* (Rom. 7:1-2, NASB).

The word *jurisdiction*, κυριεύω (*kurieúō*) in Greek, means to "be master of, dominate."[1] This is significant because it conveys the idea of being ruled by something. Just as a woman is legally bound to her husband while he is alive but is free from that legal bond upon his death (1 Cor. 7:39), believers are released from the Law's authority through death.

The significance of the physical death of Christ on the cross can't be overstated. As has already been brought to the surface in this letter, the death of Christ is the pivotal turning point in the discussion of righteousness and justification. In His death, not only was the justice that our sin demanded satisfied (Rom. 3:25) but the relationship the Jews had to the Law of Moses was forever altered as well (Rom. 7:4). When we are baptized into His death (Rom. 6:3), having crucified the old man and been buried with Christ (Rom. 6:4, 6), we are then raised to a new life (Rom. 6:4).

Paul makes it clear that Jewish Christians are no longer under the Law's authority because they have, in a spiritual sense, died to it: *"But now we have been released from the Law, having died to that by which we were bound, so that we serve in newness of the Spirit and not in oldness of the letter"* (Rom. 7:6, NASB).

The word *released* (καταργέω, *katargéō*) means "to cause the release of someone from an obligation (one has nothing more to do with it), be discharged, be released."[2] This doesn't

---

1. Arndt, William, Frederick W. Danker, et al. *A Greek-English Lexicon of the New Testament and Other Early Christian Literature.* Chicago: University of Chicago Press, 2000, 576.
2. Arndt, Danker, et al. 526.

mean the Law itself is bad or irrelevant. In fact, Paul later argues in Romans 7:12 that *"the Law is holy, and the commandment is holy and righteous and good."* Instead, Paul emphasizes that the Law's power over these Jewish Christians has ended because they have died with Christ (Rom. 6:8).

By using the phrase *"died to that by which we were bound"* (Rom. 7:6), Paul teaches that just as death severs a legal obligation in marriage, when one dies with Christ it severs his previous obligation to the Law. The Law, which once stood as a binding contract that exposed sin, no longer holds dominion over those in Christ.

The Purpose and Limitations of the Law

While the Law reveals sin, it cannot save from sin. This distinction is crucial because misunderstanding can lead to legalism or, conversely, to lawlessness. The Law was given by God and was not unholy or evil in any way. It was given to show man's need for God (Romans 3:19-20), but its function was never to bring ultimate redemption. The Hebrews echoed this when writing, *"For the Law, since it has only a shadow of the good things to come and not the very form of things, can never, by the same sacrifices which they offer continually year by year, make perfect those who draw near"* (Heb. 10:1). The writer goes one to say, *"For it is impossible for the blood of bulls and goats to take away sins"* (Heb. 10:4).

So, since the Law was not given for the purpose of taking away the sins of the people, all would do well to keep it in its proper and purposed position. Through the Law of Moses, God revealed His covenant with the children of Israel. In proper covenant language, the highest-ranking one in the covenant sets the parameters. The children of Israel were chosen by God (Deut. 7:6-8) to enter this covenant with Him. It was based on the oath He had made with Abram (Gen. 12 and 17) and one that would require the children of Israel to surrender to God and walk in a manner that demonstrated their complete reliance upon Him.

Joshua was instructed to *"Only be strong and very courageous; be careful to do according to all the law which Moses My servant commanded you; do not turn from it to the right or to the left, so that you may have success wherever you go"* (Josh. 1:7). If the children of God walked according to the covenant, they were blessed by God. However, when they failed to keep the Law, death and destruction would often follow because of their transgressions.

While the Law was merely a shadow of what was to come, we can see why Jewish Christians might struggle with what Paul wrote. All their lives, they had been taught they needed to adhere to the Law and keep the commandments of God. That's why Paul contrasts two thought processes that seem to be at war within some of the readers when it comes to serving God. According to Dan Owen, the difference between these is to be understood in this way.

Focus on Christ for Deliverance

- **Oldness of the letter** – "As Paul explains in 2 Corinthians 3:6ff, the 'letter' is the literal keeping of the Law of Moses according to the specifics enumerated in Exodus, Leviticus, and Numbers."[3]

- **Newness of the spirit** – "The 'spirit' is the spiritual fulfillment of that law in Christ. We do not serve with animal sacrifices brought to a literal temple and assisted by human, Levitical priests. We serve with the sinless sacrifice of Christ in a temple of living stones assisted by a perfect, heavenly High Priest. Our circumcision is a circumcision of the heart, not of the fleshly body (Rom. 2:27-28). The spiritual fulfillment of the Law is everything we find in Christ."[4]

> Paul's analogy of marriage illustrates that just as death releases a spouse from a legal bond, so too does our spiritual death with Christ release us from any form of Law-keeping as a means of justification for the sins we've committed. However, this freedom is not a call to lawlessness; instead, it is an invitation to serve God in *"newness of the spirit,"* where obedience is motivated by love and transformation rather than external obligation.
>
> When we were released from the shackles of sin, we took on the shackles of righteousness (Rom. 6:18). We now gladly serve with joy and not fear. We don't have to live with a yearly reminder of the sins we've committed. Because of the blood of Jesus, we've been set free.

2. The War Within: A Struggle for Deliverance (Rom. 7:14-23)

Few passages in Scripture capture the raw internal struggle of the believer like Romans 7:14-23. Here, Paul opens his heart and lays bare the spiritual war within him. His words resonate deeply because they mirror the shared human experience: the desire to do good, yet the frustrating reality of repeatedly falling into sin. While Paul is often viewed as a pillar of faith and strength, this passage reveals a humbling truth—he, too, grappled with the weight of human frailty.

A Tension Unresolved

> *"For we know that the Law is spiritual, but I am of flesh, sold into bondage to sin"* (Romans 7:14).
>
> Paul begins this section with a powerful and profound statement highlighting the passage's primary tension. God's Law is *"holy, and the commandment is holy and righteous and good"* (Rom. 7:12). Paul even goes on to call it *"spiritual"* in Romans 7:14. Here, Paul uses the Greek word πνευματικός (*pneumatikós*), and it means "it is according to the mind and will of the Spirit."[5] With this recognition, Paul is not placing the blame for his struggle on the Law in any way. However, knowing the Law came from God doesn't mean that now he is a disciple of Jesus Christ he doesn't struggle with sin, being in the flesh with the tremendous desires that exist therein.

---

3. Owen, Dan R. "Romans 5." *A Teacher's Commentary on Romans*, Murrells Inlet: Covenant Books, 2024, 87.
4. Owen.
5. Spiros Zodhiates, *The Complete Word Study Dictionary: New Testament* (Chattanooga, TN: AMG Publishers, 2000).

Paul describes himself in multiple ways in verse 14. First, as being *"of flesh,"* (σάρκινος, *sárkinos*) referring to "to being human at a disappointing level of behavior or character, (merely) human, in reference to the state or condition of a human being, with focus on being weak, sinful, or transitory, in contrast to or in opposition to that which is spiritual."[6] Second, he uses the descriptive phrase "sold into bondage to sin" (πιπράσκω, *pipráskō*), which evokes the imagery of slavery. The word *bondage* is the Greek word ὑπό (*hupó*). It means "marker of that which is in a controlling position, under, under the control of, under obligation."[7] With these descriptions, Paul is not blaming the tension between obedience and sin on God or His Law. However, throughout the course of this section, Paul takes personal responsibility for his frailty.

The Battle of Desire and Action

For Jesus's devoted disciple, resisting this fleshly shell's passion is a battle that must be courageously faced every day. As we age and mature in the faith, the goal is that we will have had enough small victories over sinful thoughts, bad attitudes, evil motives, and even lusts brought about by the desires of this flesh that we are able to struggle less and less over time. However, even those who are mature in the faith will tell you they must remain diligent against the schemes of the devil as he doesn't give up just because we age and mature.

Paul attests to this as verses 15-21 bring this struggle to the forefront. Quite honestly, this section of Scripture allows us to see Paul as a real person with real struggles. He deeply desires to be completely obedient to the will of God. He says as much when he writes, *"I am not practicing what I would like to do"* (Rom. 7:15), *"For the good that I want"* (Rom. 7:19), and *"But if I am doing the very thing I do not want"* (Romans 7:20).

The Greek word for *want* (θέλω, *thélō*) means "to will, wish, desire, implying active volition and purpose."[8] It's the same word that Jesus used in Matthew 16:24 when He said, *"If anyone wishes to come after Me, he must deny himself, and take up his cross and follow me."* The words *want* in Romans 7:20 and *wish* in Matthew 16:24 are the same Greek word. Both entail more than a simple desire that is a fairy-tale dream. Instead, it is an inner desire that stirs to the point of action. This demonstrates that the tension within Paul is serious. He has a strong, inner desire to do what God wants; however, the sinful desires are real and are at war within him.

Another key word to which we would do well to pay attention is the word *practice* (πράσσω, *prássō*). It's a word that denotes habitual action, something repeated over time. This reveals a stark contradiction. Paul's mind yearns for righteousness, yet his actions betray him. He is caught in a cycle where his desires and deeds are at odds.

---

6. Arndt, Danker, et al. 914.
7. Arndt, Danker, et al. 1036.
8. Zodhiates.

Focus on Christ for Deliverance

This struggle is not unique to Paul. Everyone who earnestly desires to follow Jesus Christ has felt the weight of this battle, the longing to be submitted to every beautiful aspect of the will of God but the frustration of struggling with sinful desires, which at times culminate in sinful actions. Even when we know what is right, we sometimes fail to act accordingly. This is the battle Paul faced and that we face even today. It's as if there is a daily battle that is fought within, which is why Jesus charged those who wanted to be His disciples with denying self and daily taking up his cross (Matt. 16:24).

A Tension That Is Answered

As a rubber band stretched to the point just before breaking, Paul expresses his inward wrestling with the seeming helplessness of this situation. His frustration climaxes in verse 24 when he cries out, *"Wretched man that I am! Who will set me free from the body of this death?"* (Rom. 7:24). He completely understands the dilemma and wants the readers to understand as well. The answer is not in better Law-keeping because in trying to do so, knowledge of how much failure results is multiplied. So, where is the answer to be found? That's the essential question.

Before jumping straight to the answer, it would have added benefit to our greater understanding of the depth of desperation in Paul's question. Paul uses the term *wretched* (ταλαίπωρος, *talaipōros*) to convey profound misery that stems from a weighty affliction or conflict. By using this word to describe himself, Paul opens the window of his heart and allows us to see how sin impacts him. He explains this glance using the metaphor *"the body of this death."* He's already written regarding the expected outcome of sin—death (Rom. 6:23). By using this phrase, he is telling the reader that he completely understands the wage he and others earn and that truly and deeply disturbs him to his very soul. He is desperate for deliverance.

This outcry is significant because it reflects the moment when a person realizes his inability to overcome sin through human effort. The weight of sin is unbearable, and self-sufficiency is futile. The natural question arises: If I cannot free myself, who can? Paul does not leave us in despair. The answer to his cry comes swiftly when he writes, *"Thanks be to God through Jesus Christ our Lord!"* (Rom. 7:25).

The solution to Paul's struggle and ours is not in striving harder but surrendering to Christ. He alone provides the deliverance we so desperately need. This passage reminds us that the Christian life is not about achieving sinless perfection through personal effort. Instead, it is about relying on Christ, who has already won the victory. Though the battle within persists, our hope rests in the one who conquered sin and death.

Paul's transparency in Romans 7 is a gift to every Christian. It reassures us that even the most faithful followers of Christ wrestle with sin. But this passage also offers several key takeaways:

- **Recognize the reality of the struggle.** If Paul, an apostle of Christ, experienced this battle, we should not be surprised when we do as well. God absolutely expects that you and I would not choose the path of sin; however, even with this expectation, God is gracious to forgive the Christians when they repent and return to Him.

- **Acknowledge the inability of human effort.** No amount of self-discipline or moral striving can free us from the power of sin. You can't sing loud enough to merit salvation. You can't give enough in the collection plate to make up for your sin. You can't even give enough food to the hungry. At times, Christians believe that when they give into sin, they just need to put forth more effort in this and other areas to make up for it. The truth is, you can't do anything other than run back to God and throw yourself down on His mercy as you seek forgiveness.

- **Rest in the victory of Jesus.** Paul's exclamation in verse 25 points us to the ultimate solution—Jesus Christ. We are not left to fight this battle alone. Through Him, we have victory, and that's why when you lay your head down on your pillow at night, if you have surrendered to God through the Gospel of Jesus Christ, the power of God for salvation (Rom. 1:16), if you continue putting your entire confidence in what God has done through Jesus on the cross, and if you seek God's forgiveness by repentance when you fail to sin, you can rest because the victory of Jesus gives you victory as well.

CONCLUSION

The journey of the Donner Party began with hope and great expectations, but unforeseen obstacles turned it into a fight for survival. When the storms halted their progress, some gave in to despair while others endured. Ultimately, their rescue did not come from their efforts; instead, it came from an outside source.

Life, especially our spiritual walk, often mirrors that journey. We may not face physical starvation or freezing temperatures, but we encounter trials that test our faith. Sometimes, no matter how hard we try, we find ourselves stuck, unable to break free. Just as the Donner Party could not save themselves, neither can we.

The apostle Paul expresses this struggle in Romans 7, describing his battle with sin. He longs to do what is right but continually falls short. However, hope still remains. Paul immediately answers his own question regarding the answer to the tension in his soul: *"Thanks be to God through Jesus Christ our Lord!"* (Rom. 7:25). Just as the Donner Party's survival depended on an external rescue, our spiritual survival depends on Christ. He alone provides the salvation we so desperately need.

While many may struggle trying to rely on their strength or good works to be right with God, even though salvation is not something we can earn, Romans 3:23 reminds us, *"For all have sinned and fall short of the glory of God."* No matter how much we strive, we cannot rescue ourselves from sin's grip. Jesus alone is our Rescuer. He is the only way to true freedom (John 14:6). If we surrender to God through Christ, we will be gifted eternal life (Rom. 6:23). So, in your journey of transformation, stay the course, keep the faith, and rest in the promise that deliverance is possible and found only in Christ.

Applying

WALK CONSISTENT WITH YOUR FREEDOM IN CHRIST

ROMANS 8:3-4

JOE WELLS

"For what the Law could not do, weak as it was through the flesh, God did: sending His own Son in the likeness of sinful flesh and as an offering for sin, He condemned sin in the flesh, so that the requirement of the Law might be fulfilled in us, who do not walk according to the flesh but according to the Spirit."

INTRODUCTION

Imagine a climber who has spent years training and preparing for a life-changing ascent. He finally reaches the base of a towering peak equipped with the finest gear, a carefully studied route, and the guidance of an experienced mountaineer. He has been given everything he needs to succeed. Yet, instead of moving forward in confidence, he hesitates. He can't seem to move. He still carries an old, tattered backpack filled with unnecessary weight—past failures, self-doubt, and old ways of thinking that no longer serve him. Though his new equipment is sufficient, he finds himself out of habit reaching back for the old.

Why would he do that?

He may struggle to believe he's ready to take on such a task. Up to this point, he's been comfortable with climbs that were lower in height and less strenuous. Now as he lifts his eyes to view the top of this new peak, it's very likely that he is intimidated. After all, he's developed a certain level of trust in himself, his abilities, and his gear. He believes he knows his limits, and this new climb is genuinely intimidating.

To climb effectively, he must embrace his new identity as a mountaineer. He is no longer the novice who once stumbled over small hills; he is equipped, trained, and ready to ascend. But as long as he clings to the baggage of his past, he will be hindered. Only by shedding the weight of the past and trusting in the tools he has been given can he walk in the reality of who he now is. The climb demands that he walk in a manner consistent with the training and equipment he has now, not what he had in the past.

In Romans 8:1-25, Paul calls Christians to walk in a manner consistent with their new identity in Christ. We have been freed from the burden of sin, adopted as children of God, and given the guidance of the Holy Spirit as revealed through the apostles and passed to us in the written Scriptures. Yet, too often we hesitate, clinging to the old ways of fear, doubt, and fleshly desires. We struggle to let go of our former identity and live fully in the freedom Christ has given us.

Like the climber who must trust in his new equipment and training, believers must trust in their transformation. The struggle is real, and the temptation to carry unnecessary burdens remains strong. But just as a climber must embrace his new role and walk forward confidently, we must fully step into our new identity in Christ, allowing it to shape how we live, move, and press forward in faith. Just as a mountaineer must commit to each step toward the summit, walking according to the Spirit must not be an occasional effort but a daily discipline.

STEP #7: WALK CONSISTENT WITH YOUR FREEDOM IN CHRIST

DISCUSSION

The writer of Proverbs 23 wrote, *"As a man thinks in his heart, so is he"* (v. 7). This ancient wisdom highlights the profound reality that our mindset shapes our actions and responses and thus influences the direction of our lives. Like a soldier on the battlefield, his mindset determines whether he fights with courage or cowers in fear. His training, discipline, and beliefs inform his ability to stand firm in conflict. The same is true regarding the Christian life. We are in a spiritual battle in which the mind plays a central role (Eph. 6:10-17; 2 Cor. 10:3-6). The apostle Paul in Romans 8:1-9 contrasts two opposing mindsets: one governed by the flesh and the other by the Spirit. This passage is foundational to understanding how believers must orient their thoughts and lives per their new identity in Christ. The new mindset of the Christian is not merely a theological concept but a transformative reality that must define the believer's daily walk.

It All Begins with the Mindset (Rom. 8:1-9)

> Paul begins this section with a profound declaration: *"There is therefore now no condemnation for those who are in Christ Jesus."* The Greek word for *condemnation* (κατάκριμα, *katákrima*) signifies a "judicial pronouncement upon a guilty person."[1] This term does not merely indicate guilt but the execution of a sentence. For those who are in Christ Jesus—meaning those who have been baptized into Him (Rom. 6:3-4)—the sentence of eternal death has been lifted.

---

1. William Arndt. Frederick W. Danker, et al., *A Greek-English Lexicon of the New Testament and Other Early Christian Literature*. Chicago: University of Chicago Press, 2000, 518..

Walk Consistent with Your Freedom in Christ

What's the significance of beginning this way?

Remember, an editor put the chapter divisions in the book of Romans there; they were not in the original letter. That being the case, think back to what Paul wrote at the end of chapter 7 because that thought flows into chapter 8. Paul wrote, *"Wretched man that I am! Who will set me free from the body of this death? Thanks be to God through Jesus Christ our Lord! So then, on the one hand I myself with my mind am serving the law of God, but on the other, with my flesh the law of sin"* (Rom. 7:24-25). The tension Paul explains that exists within him and the joy of having an answer, the only answer, for the consequence of sin, spills into Romans 8:1. Thus, the beginning verse declares that in Christ, you don't have to look over your shoulder and wonder if you're going to have to suffer the consequence for sin that has been forgiven. Under the tremendous power and influence of grace, Christians need to be reminded they no longer carry a guilty verdict worthy of death (Rom. 6:23).

The reason for this newfound freedom is found in verse 2: *"For the law of the Spirit of life has set you free in Christ Jesus from the law of sin and death."* The word ἐλευθερόω (*eleutheróō*) translated as "to cause someone to be freed from domination, free, set free,"[2] signifies complete liberation from bondage. In this verse, Paul contrasts two completely different laws that make this possible.

1) The law of the Spirit of life, which grants freedom,
2) The law of sin and death, which enslaves.

The battle for the mind begins with understanding this reality. New Testament Christians are no longer under the jurisdiction of sin and death but are governed by the law of the Spirit of life, the Gospel (Rom. 1:16). To continue living under a mindset of guilt and condemnation is to deny the freedom Christ has provided. It's like knowing your conviction has been thrown out by the judge but refusing to accept the freedom and thus continuing living as a jailed inmate. It falls in the category of spiritual self-harm, and God doesn't want that for His children.

Because the law could not justify man (Rom. 8:3), God provided the solution: *"By sending His own Son in the likeness of sinful flesh and for sin, He condemned sin in the flesh."* Echoing what we read in John 1:14, *"And the Word became flesh and dwelt among us,"* Paul emphasizes the fact that Jesus came in the flesh. The Hebrew writer shared the importance of this when he wrote, *"Therefore, since the children share in flesh and blood, He Himself likewise also partook of the same, that through death He might render powerless him who had the power of death, that is, the devil"* (Heb. 2:14). In rendering the devil powerless, God through Jesus made it possible for you and me to be set free from the bondage of sin. Jesus took on the flesh of humanity but did not sin (2 Cor. 5:21), making Him the perfect high priest to advocate on our behalf (Heb. 4:14-16).

---

2. Arndt, Danker, et al. 317.

With the acceptance of this security and freedom in Christ, Paul delves deeply into the importance of the mindset one lives with regarding the outcome of one's life. In verse 5, Paul states, *"For those who live according to the flesh set their minds on the things of the flesh, but those who live according to the Spirit set their minds on the things of the Spirit."* The key term here is φρονέω (*phronéō*), meaning "To be mindful of, to be devoted to."[3] The clear teaching in this verse is that those who set their minds on fleshly things will inevitably live according to the flesh, whereas those who focus on the things of the Spirit will live according to God's will. This is not merely a matter of external behavior but of internal orientation. The diabolically opposed mindsets, set on the flesh versus set on the Spirit, brought out in this verse highlight two fundamentally opposed pursuits.

Paul further explains the implications of these two mindsets in verses 5-8. In these verses, he points out four realities of living with a mind set on the flesh and pleasing the carnal desires of such.

- First, he says the mind set on the flesh is death (v. 6). This firm and dreadful description is entirely consistent with what Paul said earlier in Romans 6:23 regarding the wages of sin. In Ephesians 2:1-3, Paul pointed out to the church in Ephesus that, while alive in this life, those who live their lives seeking the fulfillment of the lusts of the flesh are "dead," separated from God, in their trespasses and sins.
- Second, he claims the mindset on the flesh is *"hostile toward God"* (ἔχθρα, *échthra*) meaning "enmity, hatred, hostility"[4] (Rom. 8:7). What stands out in this description is that there is no middle ground with God. You're either with Him or against Him.
- Third, Paul describes the mindset on the flesh as one that *"does not subject itself to God, for it is not even able to do so"* (Rom. 8:7). With a dedication to only living for the desires of the flesh, the impossibility of serving two masters is fundamental.
- Fourth, the mindset on the flesh *"cannot please God"* (Rom. 8:8). "This is true because God's righteous requirement is only satisfied by those who 'do not walk according to the flesh but according to the Spirit.'"[5]

In stark contrast to these descriptions, those who set their minds on the Spirit, living according to the will of God as justified people who have obeyed the Gospel, have life and peace before them. Because of Jesus, the redeemed have eternal life before them. However, we also understand that the only possible reason is that through the death, burial, and resurrection of Jesus, we have peace with God (Rom. 5:1). Our faith brought us to complete surrender. Our faith allows us to continue walking in complete surrender as we rest in the redeeming arms of God.

Paul concludes this section with a decisive statement: *"You, however, are not in the flesh but in the Spirit, if in fact the Spirit of God dwells in you."* The verb οἰκέω (*oikéō*), translated as *dwells*, conveys the idea "to reside in a place, live, dwell."[6] This affirms that those in

---

3. Zodhiates, Spiros. *The Complete Word Study Dictionary: New Testament*. Chattanooga: AMG Publishers, 2000.
4. Zodhiates.
5. Owen, Dan R. "Romans 5," *A Teacher's Commentary on Romans*. Murrells Inlet: Covenant Books, 2024, 98.
6. Arndt, Danker, et al. 694.

Walk Consistent with Your Freedom in Christ

Christ don't spend their entire time on this earth jumping in and out of a close relationship with God. Instead, Paul is teaching a stable and consistent dwelling. The Spirit of God is promised to all those who respond to the Gospel and are baptized for the remission of their sins (Acts 2:38). The Spirit of God is given to us as a seal of the salvation we live with in this life. One day, we will fully realize this salvation when Jesus returns (Eph. 1:13). In the book of Romans, we learn that the Spirit of God and the Gospel that reveals justification by faith are so intertwined that to have the Spirit of God dwelling in you means you live in a consistent manner to reflect that justification. Dan Owen pointed out that it's the same meaning as when Paul wrote in verse 10, *"If Christ is in you."* Owen writes, "Christ is obviously in a person who is displaying the attitudes and actions of Christ. Such a person is not being ruled or guided by the carnal body because for such a person, 'the body of sin was done away' (Rom. 6:6)."[7]

Actions Follow the Mindset (Rom. 8:10-13)

People's actions are a visible outworking of their inner thoughts and beliefs. A gardener who carefully cultivates his land expects a harvest that reflects his labor. Likewise, a Christian's life should display the evidence of a renewed mind. In Romans 8:10-14, the apostle Paul argues that the believer's mindset is not merely a private matter but a reality that manifests in their conduct. If the Spirit of God truly dwells within someone, it will be evident in how they live.

Paul begins with a crucial theological truth: *"If Christ is in you, although the body is dead because of sin, the Spirit is life because of righteousness"* (Rom. 8:10). If Christ indeed dwells within a person, then a transformation must follow. He no longer lives pursuing the lusts of the flesh because the body has been put to death (Rom. 6:6). However, when Paul writes, *"the Spirit is life because of righteousness,"* he's referring to the inner desires and motivations behind one's actions being brought to a new life as the person lives in a manner consistent with the new life he now has in Christ. God has justified and made righteous those who surrender to the Gospel. Since that's the case, there is an expectation that the redeemed disciples of Christ will live in a manner consistent with this new identity.

In verses 12-13, Paul stresses the moral obligation that accompanies the Christian life when he writes, *"So then, brethren, we are under obligation, not to the flesh, to live according to the flesh."* The phrase "under obligation" is the Greek term ὀφειλέτης (*opheilétēs*) and is defined as "one who is under obligation in a moral or social sense, one under obligation, one liable for."[8] This specific word relays a strong concept that when one dies to the flesh, they no longer owe the flesh anything. They don't owe it to the flesh to pursue the desires of the flesh, whether good or bad. What they once pursued and were enslaved to no longer is master over them (Rom. 6:18). This change has occurred because of what Paul writes in verse 11, *"But if the Spirit of Him who raised Jesus from the dead dwells in you, He who raised Christ Jesus from the dead will also give life to your mortal bodies through His*

---

7. Owen.
8. Arndt, Danker, et al. 742...
9. Zodhiates.

Spirit who dwells in you." The transformation in the child of God is not merely behavior modification. Any behavior changes that occur do so because there has been an internal change as the Spirit of God now dwells within.

In verse 13, Paul issues a stark warning when he writes, *"for if you are living according to the flesh, you must die; but if by the Spirit you are putting to death the deeds of the body, you will live."* The verb θανατόω (*thanatóō*), translated as "put to death," is in the present active tense, signifying a continuous action. This means that putting to death sinful deeds is not a one-time event. The Christian who accepts a different way of thinking internally also accepts a lifetime battle of pushing aside the continual pull to live according to the flesh.

Paul's words echo Jesus' teaching in Matthew 16:24: *"If anyone wishes to come after Me, he must deny himself, and take up his cross and follow Me."* The Christian life is marked by continual self-denial and submission to the will of God, as they live according to the Spirit.

New Identity, New Expectations in Christ (Rom. 8:14-25)

Identity is powerful. It shapes how we see ourselves, how we interact with the world, and, ultimately, how we live. When a person experiences a radical change in identity, whether by adoption, citizenship, or a life-altering event, it redefines his entire existence. The same is true for Christians. In Romans 8:14-25, Paul presents a vision of the Christian's new identity in Christ, showing that this transformation is revolutionary.

For those in Christ, identity is no longer rooted in sin, fear, or condemnation. Instead, our transformative identity is solidified in adoption, hope, and the future glory promised by God. This passage challenges believers to embrace this identity fully, recognizing that it changes everything: our past, present, and future.

Paul begins by affirming that those who are led by the Spirit are *"sons of God"* (v. 14). The phrase *"led by the Spirit"* (ἄγονται ὑπὸ τοῦ Πνεύματος) conveys an ongoing action. The Spirit leads through the inspired Word of God, and being "led" is not passive but an active submission to the Spirit's guidance. This leading is the evidence of true sonship.

Paul further describes this new relationship with God in verse 15 when he writes, *"For you have not received a spirit of slavery leading to fear again, but you have received a spirit of adoption as sons by which we cry out, "Abba! Father!"* Here, he contrasts two spirits:

- The *"spirit of slavery"* (πνεῦμα δουλείας) leads to fear. This concept of slavery points us back to chapter 6, where Paul references our former manner of life in sin as that which leads to death (v. 16). The fear (φόβος, *phóbos*) being spoken of here is fear of the wrath of God (Romans 1:18) as the just One who punishes those who live contrary to the Gospel and those who seek to be justified in their law keeping (Romans 3:20).

- The *"spirit of adoption"* (πνεῦμα υἱοθεσίας) grants access to God as Father. The term υἱοθεσία (*huiothesia*), meaning "adoption as sons," is rich with first-century legal significance. In Roman culture, "adoption, when thus legally performed, put a man in every respect in the position of a son by birth to him who had adopted him, so that he possessed the same rights and owed the same obligations."⁹ Paul is saying that Christians are not second-class members of God's family. They are full heirs.

The intimacy of this relationship is evident in the cry, *"Abba! Father!"* Abba (ἀββᾶ, *abbá*) is an Aramaic term for *father*, expressing deep personal closeness, and in the New Testament it is always followed by its interpretation, *"Father"* (Mark 14:36; Rom. 8:15; Gal. 4:6). This phrase is always used to refer to God and was a common phrase in the early church. It reinforces the very close relationship personal relationship one enjoys with God. In this text, this phrase stresses the severe change in identity the Christian enjoys in Christ. We are no longer slaves of sin. We are children of God.

This sonship leads to inheritance. Verse 17 proclaims, *"And if children, heirs also, heirs of God and fellow heirs with Christ, if indeed we suffer with Him so that we may also be glorified with Him."* The word *heirs* (κληρονόμος, *klēronómos*) emphasizes that we are not merely recipients of a blessing but rightful beneficiaries of God's promises (Gal. 3:28-29). However, there is a conditional statement, *"if indeed we suffer with Him."* The word *suffer* (συμπάσχω, *sumpáschō*) draws the reader back to the tribulations of Romans 5:3. Those who decide to put their complete faith in God through Jesus Christ have chosen to walk the path of the few (Matt. 7:13-14). Since that is the case, suffering is to be expected, but so is the future glory we will share with Him when He returns (1 Pet. 4:12-14).

As Paul shifts to a discussion of suffering, he acknowledges the reality of present struggles. Still, he offers a profound perspective in verse 18, *"For I consider that the sufferings of this present time are not worthy to be compared with the glory that is to be revealed to us."* The present hardships are not elaborated on in this text; however, at the end of Romans 8, Paul does reference tribulations again and specifically mentions distress, persecution, famine, nakedness, and sword. This could very well be what he was referring to. The emphasis is not on figuring out what the sufferings were but on the contrasts drawn with the *glory* (δόξα, *doxa*) that awaits the Christian.

To the casual reader, verses 19-22 seem to be squeezed in as a sub-topic, but that is not true. Anytime sin is introduced in our lives or the created world, as it was by Adam and Eve in the Garden of Eden (Gen. 3), destruction is left in the wake. Paul is pointing to creation, a creation that was changed from the beauty and innocence God created it to enjoy, as he talks about the consequence of slavery and the freedom that is coming. This hope of the future is one the creation looks to with *"anxious longing"* (v. 19) for the revealing of the sons of God. The term ἀποκαραδοκία (*apokaradokía*) means "attentive or earnest expectation or looking for, as with the neck stretched out and the head thrust forward."¹⁰ This description of an intense expectation, this straining forward in anticipation of redemption, is precisely how the child of God longs for the end of this suffering and the eternal realization of the promises of God.

---

10. Zodhiates.

Paul concludes with a reminder of how followers of Jesus continue in this life while we wait. *"For in hope we have been saved, but hope that is seen is not hope; for who hopes for what he already sees? But if we hope for what we do not see, with perseverance we wait eagerly for it"* (vv. 24-25). In two verses, he uses the word *hope* (ἐλπίς, *elpís*) five times. It means "looking forward to something with some reason for confidence respecting fulfillment."[11] With a new identity in Christ, the disciple of Jesus can continue with patience and endurance through this life because of the confident hope the Christian lives with as he awaits the return of Jesus.

CONCLUSION

The climber stands at the base of the mountain, heart pounding, staring up at the summit before him. He has trained for this. He has the best gear. He has studied the path and received wisdom from seasoned climbers who have gone before him. He is ready. But still, he hesitates. The old, tattered backpack on his shoulders—filled with past failures, self-doubt, and familiar comforts—feels heavier than ever. He knows he doesn't need it anymore. His new equipment is more than sufficient, yet something in him wants to cling to the old.

Can you relate?

God has given you everything you need for this journey. You are no longer who you used to be. You are not bound by your past mistakes, old ways of thinking, or the fears that once held you captive. In Christ, you have been given new life, new strength, and a new identity. You have been set free from the weight of sin and equipped with the truth of His Word to guide you. But the question remains: Will you trust what God has given you or keep reaching for the old?

Paul reminds us in Romans 8 that there is no condemnation for those in Christ Jesus. You don't have to look over your shoulder, wondering if you are good enough or if you will fail again. You have already been justified, redeemed, and set free. The burden of sin and guilt has been lifted from your shoulders. So why would you continue carrying it? Why let fear keep you from the climb God has called you to?

Like the climber, you must embrace your new reality. You are not who you once were. You are a child of God, sealed by His Spirit, and are perfectly equipped to walk in the fullness of His grace. Yes, the path ahead may seem intimidating. It will take endurance, faith, and perseverance. But you are not climbing alone. He who called you is with you every step of the way.

So, let go of the old burdens. Take hold of the life that is truly life. Step forward in faith, trusting in Him who has already secured your victory. The summit is before you, and the journey is worth it. Walk in the freedom and confidence of who you are in Christ.

---

11. Arndt, Danker, et al. 319.

Applying

MORE THAN CONQUERORS THROUGH JESUS CHRIST

ROMANS 8:37

JOE WELLS

"But in all these things we overwhelmingly conquer through Him who loved us."

INTRODUCTION

Mountain climbing is an extremely powerful metaphor for human perseverance and triumph. The historic ascent of Sir Edmund Hillary and Tenzing Norgay to the peak of Mount Everest in 1953 exemplifies this very well as we consider that their journey to the summit was far from easy. It was a grueling test of endurance, skill, and sheer willpower. Mount Everest is the tallest mountain in the world, reaching 29,031.69 feet above sea level, and climbing it had been attempted multiple times before 1953.[1] However, no climber had successfully reached its peak and returned to tell the tale.

Hillary, a beekeeper from New Zealand, and Norgay, a seasoned Sherpa from Nepal, formed an unlikely but formidable team. Their expedition faced extreme cold, the constant threat of avalanches, and the deadly effects of high altitude. As they ascended, every step became a battle against fatigue and oxygen deprivation. The final stretch, known as the "Hillary Step," was a near-vertical rock face at 29,000 feet. One wrong move could mean a fatal fall. Despite their exhaustion, they pressed on, relying not only on their training and equipment but also on their unwavering determination and trust in each other.

Finally, on May 29, 1953, they stood atop Everest, looking down at the world beneath them. The feeling of triumph was unparalleled. Yet, their victory was not simply about reaching the summit—it was about overcoming every obstacle along the way. Their success was a testament to endurance, perseverance, and the power of unwavering resolve.[2]

---

1. Venables, Stephen, Norgay Tenzing, (Henry Cecil) John Hunt, Wilfrid Noyce, Barry C. Bishop. "Mount Everest." *Encyclopedia Britannica*, 13 Mar. 2025, https://www.britannica.com/place/Mount-Everest.
2. The editors of *Encyclopaedia Britannica*. "Edmund Hillary." *Encyclopedia Britannica*, 20 Feb. 2025, https://www.britannica.com/biography/Edmund-Hillary.

When thinking of this monumental moment in history, there are numerous parallels between their climb and the spiritual journey of Christians who face the trials of life yet emerge victorious through the power of Christ. Just as Hillary and Norgay faced extreme fatigue, a variety of dangers, and countless effects of the high altitude, Christians in today's world face the same. The temptation to surrender to the fatigue of the Christian race is ever-present. The deadly dangers that lurk in the snares of Satan are abundant. The disciple's desire to be with the Lord instead of in this temporary tent (2 Cor. 5) is ever-present. That's why in Romans 8:26-39 when Paul speaks of a victory that surpasses any earthly conquest, a triumph that is secured through the unfailing love of Christ, we must take pause and appreciate the spiritual summit promised to those who continually walk in this world, putting their trust in God and His saving grace.

I believe Romans 8:26-39 is one of the most encouraging sections in all of Scripture. It not only speaks of the disciple's assurance but also highlights that we "overwhelmingly conquer" (ὑπερνικάω, *hupernikáō*) "prevail completely,"[3] because of who God is and the fact that He is for us. In our transformation, the goal is to grow into a better understanding of the certainty of our salvation because of God's promises. However, it's also to relax into the hands of God as we trust in those promises more and more every day. So, as we study, remember that because of God's grace and His unswerving love for us, we are more than conquerors through Jesus Christ.

STEP #8: MORE THAN CONQUERORS THROUGH JESUS CHRIST

DISCUSSION

1. God Is for Us

Imagine standing in a courtroom, accused of crimes you cannot deny. The weight of evidence is overwhelming, and the judge's gaze is fixed upon you. Just as the verdict is about to be pronounced, a powerful advocate steps forward—not to plead for mercy but to declare that the penalty has already been paid. The judge leans back in his chair and smiles as he declares you to be justified. As he slams the gavel, you breathe a massive sigh of relief and start sobbing as you rejoice. You knew you were guilty, but because of another, the price for your guilt has been paid.

This image captures the heart of Romans 8:26-39. In this passage, the apostle Paul builds to one of the most triumphant declarations in Scripture when he writes, *"If God is for us, who is against us?"* (Rom. 8:31). Our confidence rests on the firm reality that the Spirit is for us (v. 26), God the Father is for us (v. 31), and Jesus Christ is for us (v. 34). This truth changes everything. No accusation, hardship, or enemy can prevail against the one God defends.

---

3. William Arndt, Frederick W. Danker, et al., *A Greek-English Lexicon of the New Testament and Other Early Christian Literature*. Chicago: University of Chicago Press, 2000, 1034.

More Thank Conquerors Through Jesus Christ

The Spirit Is for Us (Rom. 8:26-27)

"In the same way the Spirit also helps our weakness; for we do not know how to pray as we should, but the Spirit Himself intercedes for us with groanings too deep for words" (Rom. 8:26).

Paul begins by addressing our weakness. The Greek word for *helps*, συναντιλαμβάνομαι (*sunantilambánomai*), is a compound term meaning "to come to the aid of, be of assistance to, help."[4] This is not passive support but an active partnership. The Spirit steps into our struggle and lifts the burden alongside us as, "in the same way," He groans on our behalf before God the Father. This groaning must be understood in reflection of what the creation does (v. 22) and what we do (v. 23). *Groaning* (στεναγμός, *stenagmós*) refers to "prayers to God expressed inarticulately."[5]

Paul further states, *"We do not know how to pray as we should."* This phrase highlights the dilemma. Sometimes, we struggle to find the words to express precisely what we are experiencing, our greatest needs, and even the height of our appreciation for our loving Heavenly Father. That's okay. Paul makes it very clear that the Spirit compensates for our deficiency. The phrase "intercedes for us" (ὑπερεντυγχάνω, *huperentugchánō*) conveys a deep, personal pleading on our behalf.

Like a young child who looks around and tearfully realizes he is lost in a crowd. Being emotionally overcome, he struggles to explain to a stranger where he is supposed to be and who he is to be with. The words fail him as he can't stop crying, but then a loving parent arrives, understanding the child's heart and speaking for him. The Spirit does the same for us as He translates our unspoken groanings into perfect petitions before the Father. Think about this: We never pray alone. Divine advocacy is at work even in moments of confusion and sorrow when words fail us.

God the Father Is for Us (Rom. 8:31-32)

"What then shall we say to these things? If God is for us, who is against us?" (Rom. 8:31).

The phrase "God is for us" is emphatic and carries a profound meaning. The Greek preposition *for* ὑπέρ (*hupér*) is "a marker indicating that an activity or event is in some entity's interest, for, in behalf of, for the sake of someone."[6] It signifies active involvement rather than passive approval, and in this context, it has a specific meaning to "be for someone, be on someone's side."[7] All of this means God is actively pursuing what is in your best eternal interest. He's not opposed to you, waiting on you to blow it, spiritually speaking. No, instead, His very action and motivation are for your benefit. Paul reinforces this truth by pointing to the Father's ultimate act of generosity when he writes, *"He who did not spare His own Son, but delivered Him over for us all, how will He not also with Him freely give us all things?"* (Rom. 8:32).

---

4. Arndt, Danker, et al. 965.
5. Zodhiates, Spiros. *The Complete Word Study Dictionary: New Testament.* Chattanooga, TN: AMG Publishers, 2000.
6. Arndt, Danker, et al. 1030.

When Paul writes that God "did not spare His own Son," he uses the same wording that was used in Genesis 22:16 when God speaks of Abraham's willingness to sacrifice Isaac. Like Jesus, Isaac was a special and unique son in that God promised him, and the circumstances surrounding his conception and birth are beyond human reasoning since Abraham and Sarah were old in age and beyond childbearing years (Gen. 17–18). Being such a special son and the avenue through which God was going to fulfill His promises makes us pause when we consider Abraham's faithfulness in his intent to follow the instructions from God to sacrifice his son. Just as Abraham withheld nothing from God, so God withheld nothing from us, not even His "only begotten Son" (μονογενής, *monogenḗs*)—"the only one of its kind or class, unique (in kind)."[8]

This is the highest proof that God is for us. If He has already given the greatest gift, how can we doubt that He will provide everything else we need? This is like a father who, after donating a kidney to save his child's life, would never withhold food, shelter, or protection. If the greatest need has been met, surely every lesser need is secure.

Jesus Christ Is for Us (Rom. 8:34)

"Who is the one who condemns? Christ Jesus is He who died, yes, rather who was raised, who is at the right hand of God, who also intercedes for us" (Rom. 8:34).

The imagery shifts to a courtroom. Here, Paul asks, "Who is to condemn?" The word *condemn* is the Greek word κατακρίνω (*katakrínō*) and means "pronounce a sentence after determination of guilt."[9] He's not truly asking for an answer. Instead, he is making a strong point. God has justified the Christian, so who can outrank God and change that declaration? The implied answer is no one because Christ Himself stands as our advocate. Four truths about Jesus assure us of this:

- **He died for us**—The phrase *"Christ Jesus is the one who died"* highlights His substitutionary atonement.
- **He was raised for us**—His resurrection is proof that the penalty for sin has been fully paid.
- **He is seated at the right hand of God**—This is a position of power and authority.
- **He intercedes for us**—The Greek word ἐντυγχάνω (*entugchánō*) means to plead on behalf of another, reinforcing the legal imagery of advocacy.

In the ancient world, kings and emperors sometimes granted legal immunity to citizens under their protection. If an enemy sought to accuse or harm them, they could present a royal decree that proclaimed, "This one is under the king's protection." Likewise, we stand under divine protection. The decree has been written in the blood of Christ, sealed by the Spirit, and proclaimed by the Father.

Therefore, we walk boldly, not because of our strength, but because of the one who fights for us. No accusation, enemy, or hardship can separate us from His love. With this truth, we live not as fearful defendants but as beloved children, eternally secure in the arms of our God.

---

7. Arndt, Danker, et al.
8. Arndt, Danker, et al. 658.

2. God Causes All Things to Work Out for Good (Rom. 8:28-30)

A young soldier, wounded in battle, looks up at the medic treating him and asks, "Is it going to be okay?" The medic, knowing the soldier's injuries are severe, does not promise an easy recovery but reassures him, "We're going to take care of you." The soldier still faces pain, surgery, and rehabilitation, but his hope rests in the hands of someone who is working for his good.

This is the reality of Romans 8:28-30. When Paul declares, *"And we know that God causes all things to work together for good to those who love God, to those who are called according to His purpose"* (Rom. 8:28), he is not promising that life on earth will be free from suffering. Instead, he points to a greater reality: God's sovereign plan for salvation is unfolding and for those who love Him, the ultimate outcome is glory. This passage is not about earthly comfort but about God's eternal purpose.

Tribulation and Persecution Are Expected

Paul does not write Romans 8:28 in a vacuum. By this point in the letter, he has already outlined the struggles that Christians will face.

1. In Romans 1, he describes the depravity of the world. People suppress the truth, embrace idolatry, and indulge in sin. The Christian stands in stark contrast to this world and, as a result, will face opposition.

2. In Romans 5:3-5, Paul states plainly, *"And not only this, but we also exult in our tribulations, knowing that tribulation brings about perseverance; and perseverance, proven character; and proven character, hope; and hope does not disappoint, because the love of God has been poured out within our hearts through the Holy Spirit who was given to us."* The Greek word for *tribulations*, (θλίψις, *thlípsis*) refers to crushing pressure, like a heavy stone placed on someone's chest. Paul is not naive about the hardships of life. He expects suffering but sees purpose in it.

3. In Romans 7, Paul reveals his personal struggle when he writes, *"For the good that I want, I do not do, but I practice the very evil that I do not want"* (Rom. 7:19). Even the apostle Paul wrestles with sin. He does not present Christian life as easy but as a battle.

So when we reach Romans 8:28, Paul is not suddenly promising an easy road. He declares that despite these struggles, God is working out His plan for good.

Understanding *"All Things Work Together for Good"*

"And we know that God causes all things to work together for good to those who love God, to those who are called according to His purpose" (Rom. 8:28).

The verb *work* (συνεργέω *sunergéō*) means "assist (or work with) someone to obtain something or bring something about."[10] It implies an active process. This is not a passive

---

9. Arndt, Danker, et al. 519.

hope but an assurance that God the Spirit is actively engaged in assuring His divine purpose for those who are justified, no matter what hardships arise in this life.

Notably, *good* (ἀγαθός, *agathós*) in this context does not mean worldly success or happiness. It refers to God's ultimate good. It specifically refers to our salvation and glorification. The verse does not promise that every individual event in life will be pleasant but that, in the grand design, it serves God's redemptive purpose.

Imagine an artist painting a masterpiece. Up close, the brushstrokes seem chaotic—dark, harsh strokes mix with light ones. But when the painting is complete, every stroke contributes to a breathtaking work of art. Likewise, individual life events may seem meaningless or painful, but God sees the whole picture.

The Plan and Purpose of God for Mankind (Rom. 8:29-30)

"For those whom He foreknew, He also predestined to become conformed to the image of His Son, so that He would be the firstborn among many brethren; and these whom He predestined, He also called; and these whom He called, He also justified; and these whom He justified, He also glorified" (Rom. 8:29-30).

To understand the significance of this passage in the context of the book of Romans, we must not forget who the *"those"* are to which Paul is referring. He's talking about Christians, those who have placed their trust and confidence in God's saving grace. They have an obedient faith (Rom. 1:5) and understand the power of the Gospel to save them (Rom. 1:16). These are the ones who have decided to become enslaved to righteousness, having been baptized into the death and burial of Jesus Christ (Rom. 6:3-4). These are the ones who have been raised from the waters of baptism and understand the old self was crucified, and the old body of sin is gone (Rom. 6:6). In other words, the *"those"* in this passage are Christians who have decided to enter into a covenant with God through Jesus Christ.

With this fundamental understanding, we must understand the overall goal explained in this passage is that humans would be *"conformed to the image of His Son."* The word *conformed* (σύμμορφος, *súmmorphos*) means "to having a similar form, nature, or style, similar in form."[11] The form is that Jesus was the *"firstborn among many brethren"* referring to His resurrection from the tomb to live eternally in Heaven. God's plan is that those deemed righteous by Him will enjoy the same one day. That's the glory spoken of at the end of verse 30.

Consider the plan God displays in carrying this out.

- **Foreknew** (προγινώσκω, *proginóskō*)—God set His love on His people before time began.

---

10. Arndt, Danker, et al. 969.

- **Predestined** (προορίζω, *proorízō*)—This means to determine beforehand. God's plan was not reactive but was established before creation.

- **Called** καλέω [*kaléō*] – This refers to the effectual calling of believers through the Gospel.

- **Justified** (δικαιόω, *dikaióō*)—Declared righteous through Christ's atoning work.

- **Glorified** (δοξάζω, *doxázō*)—Notice the past tense. Though glorification is future, Paul speaks of it as already accomplished. In God's eyes, it is certain.

In returning to the wounded soldier, we see the parallel to our spiritual journey. The soldier's present pain does not negate the certainty of his recovery. Likewise, our present struggles do not negate our future glory. Paul does not downplay suffering. He acknowledges it, but he insists that suffering is not going to win ultimately. God is sovereign, and His plan will not be defeated.

3. The Assurance of Christ's Love (Rom. 8:31-39)

In times of uncertainty, people seek assurance. A child scared of the dark asks his parent, "Will you stay with me?" Before a battle, a soldier asks his fellow soldier, "Will you stand with me?" These are not questions searching for new information. Instead, they are appeals for affirmation. The expected response is obvious, yet hearing the answer still carries weight.

The apostle Paul employs this same technique in Romans 8:31-39. He does not merely state theological truths. He asks pointed questions that demand a response so obvious they become undeniable. These rhetorical questions are not designed to gather information but to emphasize unshakable certainty. They are meant to drive home the fact that God is for us, Christ has secured our victory, and nothing can separate us from His love.

"If God Is for Us, Who Can Be Against Us?" (Rom. 8:31-32)

"What then shall we say to these things? If God is for us, who is against us?" (Rom. 8:31).

The phrase *"If God is for us"* is a first-class conditional statement implying that since God is for us, who can stand against us? God is not a neutral observer. He is actively working for His people. This truth is illustrated by the tremendous gift given for our salvation. Paul identifies this very precious gift when he writes, *"He who did not spare His own Son, but delivered Him over for us all, how will He not also with Him freely give us all things?"* (Rom. 8:32).

This argument is known as *"a fortiori* reasoning," meaning Paul is making a point by establishing the greater point (He did not spare His own Son) to the lesser (will He not also with Him freely give us all things?).[12] If the costliest sacrifice has already been made, the lesser provisions needed to continue faithfully: Grace, strength, and perseverance are guaranteed.

---

11. . Arndt, Danker, et al. 958.

"Who Shall Bring Any Charge Against God's Elect?" (Romans 8:33-34)

"Who will bring a charge against God's elect? God is the one who justifies" (Rom. 8:33).

Paul now shifts to a legal concept. Picture a courtroom scene where Satan, the accuser, attempts to indict God's people (Rev. 12:10). But instead of the accusations sticking, the case is dismissed because *"God is the one who justifies."* The validity of the claims against the sinner is not argued against. Instead, the one who is both just and the justifier (Rom. 4: 26) has already dealt with the consequence as He placed the burden of the sin on His Son, paying the righteous price. What's great about this is that there is no one or group of people who have the power or authority to overturn His verdict.

This leads to another question:

"Who is the one who condemns? Christ Jesus is He who died, yes, rather who was raised, who is at the right hand of God, who also intercedes for us" (Rom. 8:34).

As addressed earlier in this chapter, the verb *condemn* means to "pronounce a sentence after determination of guilt."[13] Yet, in this verse, Paul gives four reasons why condemnation is impossible:

- **Christ died for us**—The penalty has already been paid.

- **Christ was raised**—His resurrection is proof that sin and death have been conquered.

- **Christ is at the right hand of God**—A position of authority and victory.

- **Christ intercedes for us**—He is actively and consistently pleading on our behalf.

Imagine a courtroom where the defense attorney is the judge's beloved son. Not only has he paid the debt, but he continually advocates for the accused. This is the Christian's position before God.

"Who Shall Separate Us from the Love of Christ?" (Rom. 8:35-39)

"Who will separate us from the love of Christ? Will tribulation, or distress, or persecution, or famine, or nakedness, or peril, or sword?" (Rom. 8:35).

Paul's final rhetorical question introduces a list of extreme hardships. The Greek verb χωρίζω (*chorizo*), "to separate," implies a forceful severing. However, none of these trials can cut us off from Christ's love, whether external afflictions (tribulation, distress, or persecution) or physical deprivation (famine, nakedness, peril, or sword).

---

12. "*A fortiori*." Merriam-Webster.com Dictionary, *Merriam-Webster*, https://www.merriam-webster.com/dictionary/a%20fortiori.

Paul strengthens this point by quoting Psalm 44:22:

> *"For Your sake we are being put to death all day long;*
> *We were considered as sheep to be slaughtered"* (Rom. 8:36).

Far from promising an easy life, Paul affirms that suffering is expected. However, he confirms that this does not mean defeat when he encourages the Christian by writing, *"But in all these things we overwhelmingly conquer through Him who loved us"* (Rom. 8:37).

The Greek word ὑπερνικάω (*hupernikáō*) is a compound term meaning "to more than conquer, utterly defeat."[14] This is not mere survival. The Christian who is faithful is not barely holding on. Instead, it is a decisive victory. Because of what God has done in our lives through Christ, we have a precious crown of righteousness awaiting us in eternity (2 Tim. 4:8). If we stand steadfast in the saving message of the Gospel (1 Cor. 15: 1-2), walk in the Light (1 John 1: 7), and make sure to not apathetically drift away from what we have been taught (Heb. 2: 1), we will continue to stand in the love of God. Paul writes that of this, he is *"convinced"* (Rom. 8:38-39).

Imagine a soldier facing an overwhelming enemy. If he stands alone, defeat is inevitable. But his confidence changes if he fights, knowing his king has already secured victory. This is the assurance of Romans 8:31-39. We do not stand in uncertainty, questioning God's commitment. His love is proven, and the victory is secured.

CONCLUSION

Returning to the imagery of mountain climbing, consider the moment Hillary and Norgay reached the summit of Everest. The overwhelming joy, the sense of accomplishment, and the realization that they had conquered the highest peak on earth mirror the Christian's spiritual victory in Christ. However, unlike earthly conquests, which are subject to decay and eventual loss, the triumph Paul describes is eternal.

Too often, we measure our standing before God by our circumstances. We see hardships, suffering, and unanswered prayers as signs of defeat. But Paul reminds us that no tribulation, distress, persecution, famine, danger, or even death can separate us from the love of Christ. Victory is not found in the absence of struggles but in the remarkable presence of our Savior within them.

Transformation means seeing our struggles through the lens of God's eternal plan. It means trusting that He is for us even in our weakest moments. It means understanding that today's trials are preparing us for the triumph of eternity. Like a climber who fixes his eyes on the summit rather than the obstacles before him, we must never take our eyes off Christ, the author and perfecter of our faith (Heb. 12:2). The ascent may be grueling. Still, the reward is beyond anything we could ever imagine.

Stand firm. Keep climbing. Fix your eyes on the summit. For in Christ, the victory is already won!

---

13. Arndt, Danker, et al. 519.
14. Zodhiates.

Building

THE ACKNOWLEDGMENT OF GOD: A PATH TO DIVINE UNDERSTANDING

Romans 1

GARRETT BERNETHY

"For in it the righteousness of God is revealed from faith to faith; as it is written, "But the righteous man shall live by faith." For the wrath of God is revealed from heaven against all ungodliness and unrighteousness of men who suppress the truth in unrighteousness."
Romans 1:17-18

INTRODUCTION

Within the opening chapter of this wonderful book, the apostle Paul begins to lay a firm foundation that would distinguish the difference between the "wise" and the "foolish" in their recognition of the things that had been revealed long ago and now through the prophets of God. Through them, God has revealed knowledge and wisdom that allows us to know all that God has intended for us to know. Paul had great concern for the brethren not only in Rome but in Thessalonica and abroad, as they might not be *"uninformed"* (Rom. 11:25; 1 Thess. 4:13) of the Word of the Lord, which had been given to the people throughout time. Through His prophets, God has revealed His words, which tell of His past work, present expectations, and future judgment. All of which are described as holy and righteous within our present context. In this lesson, we will be examining and working through chapter 1 to identify the things that have been revealed and how they have been revealed from God to man.

FOCUS

Within the opening chapter of Paul's letter to the *"saints at Rome"* (1:7), two things are being brought out, carrying with them a great deal of importance as they have been *"revealed"* (1:17, 18) to man.

1. The righteousness of God… v. 17
2. The wrath of God… v. 18

The words *righteous* and *wrath* both carry with them a great deal of meaning and define your focus in life. You see, righteousness and wrath are not terms that describe a person, but rather, they define an outcome of what you have become and have received as a result.

For instance, a righteous person is one who has lived (past tense) and is currently living (present tense) a life of obedience to the will of the Father. Whereas the term *wrath* is the outcome or result of what a person receives when obedience to the Father is absent from his life.

> God has revealed His method of salvation and warning of wrath, given through the prophets and verified by His creation so that all are without excuse.

Righteousness is seen in the now because of who you have become in the eyes of God. It is brought about because of decision-making, obedience, and faith. It reflects a godly character and focus—an outcome of your obedience to the Gospel of God (1:1, 5; 16:26). To put this simply, righteousness is how God sees you in the now, not in the future. Is there a future home for the righteous? Yes! But only for those who continue to live each day for the Lord.

Wrath, on the other hand, is a consequence that will be rewarded or obtained in the future. It is the outcome of those who have turned from God and have done what is right in their own eyes (e.g., Judg. 17:6; 21:25) or have given into the lust and desires of the flesh (1 John 2:15-17), exchanging all that is right for all that is wrong.

Paul's focus, as well as ours, will remain on how these two things are and have been **revealed** to man through the ages so that we might be aware of the truth of God and not *"suppress or exchange"* it (1:18, 25) for something that will lead us away from glory. Only the truth revealed can lead to the power of God, which brings salvation to everyone who believes.

Jesus stated in the Gospel of John that the *"truth will set you free"* (John 8:32) and that it will *"sanctify you"* (John 17:17) to set you apart and make you holy. Therefore, our interest lies within the words of God as given through the prophets (1:2), which have made known the Word of the Lord, which has given us real insight into the creation of the world, the law of God, the mystery of Christ, the Gospel message, and His final judgment that is to come.

Focus Statement: God has revealed His method of salvation and warning of wrath, given through the prophets and verified by His creation so that all are without excuse.

STUDY KEYS

NOTE: Take some time as you study through chapter 1 to mark each of these words and phrases individually with different color pens, markers, colored pencils, or highlighters of your choice. If

The Acknowledgement of God: A Path to Divine Understanding

possible, make notes in your margins to reflect the meanings of these words or phrases that may help you understand the overall context to a better degree.

WORDS OF IMPORTANCE

- **God** (Θεός)—vv.1, 7, 8, 9, 10, 16, 17, 18, 19, 21, 23, 24, 25, 26, 28, 30, 32
- **Gospel** (εὐαγγέλιον)—vv. 1, 9, 15, 16
- **Faith/Believe** (πίστις)—vv. 5, 8, 12, 16, 17
- **Christ** (Χριστός)—vv. 1, 4, 6, 7, 8
- **Righteousness** (δικαιοσύνη)—v. 17

THEOLOGICALLY SIGNIFICANT

1. **Gospel of God**—God's good news did not originate with Paul but in the mind of God and was initiated by His authority alone. This was His plan before the foundation of the world (cf. Eph. 1:4; 1 Pet. 1:20). It is the news that leads to our salvation from sin, saving us from the *"wrath of God"* (5:9).

2. **Power of God**—Found 13x in the NT. His power knows no limits as we understand it. His power is seen within the creation account (Gen. 1–2), the parting of the Red Sea (Ex. 14:13-21), and the raising of the dead (John 11:1-46), which includes Jesus (Matt. 28:1-8; Mark 16:1-8; Luke 24:1-10; John 20:1-8). The Gospel of God contains the power of God, which can save man from sin and overcome the sting of death (1 Cor. 15:56).

3. **Wrath of God**—Revealed in the text within the writings of the prophets. The wrath of God is equivalent to the anger of God against all unrighteous acts within a person's life. It is the righteous punishment of sin given to the ungodly who disregard God and His commandments.

4. **Revelation/Revealed**—To make fully known or to bring to light something that had not been made known before. The things that have been revealed (1:17,18; 8:18,19) are things that have been made known from God to man. Whether through the prophets (1:2) or from Heaven above (1:18). The realization of understanding our present situation.

5. **Holy Scriptures**—*Holy* (ἅγιος—pure, perfect, words only worthy of God); *Scriptures* (γραφή—The writings; *Script* = writing; *Scripture* = the writings). The holy Scriptures are the original words from the mind and heart of God given through the prophets to man. They are perfect and without error; according to Paul, they are God-breathed (2 Tim. 3:16).

6. **Promised Beforehand**—A discussion of prophecy from the prophets (cf. Heb. 1:1-2) who discussed the coming of the Messiah through the line of David and the events of the future. It is important to note the words of Peter, *"No prophecy of Scripture is a matter of one's own interpretation, for no prophecy was ever made by an act of human will, but men moved by the Holy Spirit spoke from God"* (2 Pet. 1:20-21).

7. **Prophet**—Those who received the Word of the Lord (*diberyhvh*); cf. Acts 8:25—"τὸν λόγος τὸν κύριος." Those who were universally accepted by the people of God as a prophet of God both spoke and wrote His Word to the people and those words were accepted.

8. **Obedience of Faith**—A genuine faith from the heart of a person that leads them to live a life of submission, a theme of the letter which Paul begins and ends with (1:5; 16:26). *Faith* (πίστις, 66x) is a confidence, a conviction of the heart that is not brought about by emotion or personal connection, but rather by reliable truth and fact. True Biblical faith cannot be separated from a life of obedience, as this is the way that we truly show our love to the Lord (1 John 5:1-3).
9. **Servant/Slave**—δοῦλος, (servant or slave) one who is solely committed to another.[1] For a faithful *slave*, his sole purpose for existence is to please his master,[2] a high calling no doubt for those who are obedient to God.
10. **Called Saints**—The term *saints* ἅγιος describes one being dedicated or consecrated to the service of God.[3] Lipscomb writes that this is being "set apart to the service of God,"[4] describing one who strives to grow in both obedience and holiness by the study of His Word and obedience to His will, which drive the increase of one's effort to continually live a life of discipleship.

PAUL'S LISTS

Under Obligation To...1:14-16
1. Greeks and Barbarians
2. Wise and Foolish
    A. The phrase *"Jew and Greek"* (1:16, 2:9, 10) might be a summation of the two previous statements, which would include all. By referring to Denny Petrillo's Sermon Seed: The True Preacher on Romans 1:14-16, you will find that this list describes people of all nations, of every intellectual level, social class, or gender.

Since the Creation of the World...1:20
1. Invisible Attributes—lit. the invisible things of Him or, as the NIV puts it, *"God's invisible qualities."* The word *seen* καθοράω (katharao) combines a preposition κατά meaning to "see" and ὁράω meaning to perceive or discern. Καθοράω is not merely seeing with the eyes but perceiving with the mind to understand.
    A. God's *"invisible attributes"* can be seen first in His **eternal power**, which can be perceived with the mind going back to creation. As God said, *"Let there be light,"* there was then light (Gen. 1:3). The power generated by that statement or those words is both incredible and immeasurable to the human mind.

---

1. Arndt, William, Frederick W. Danker, et al. *A Greek-English Lexicon of the New Testament and Other Early Christian Literature*. Chicago: University of Chicago Press, 2000, 260.
2. Roper, David L. "Romans 1, Depicting the Gentiles, Chapter 1:1-7." *Truth for Today Commentary*. Searcy: Resource Publications, 2013, 28.
3. Arndt, Danker, et al. 10.
4. Lipscomb, David. "Apostolic Greeting, Romans 1:1-7." *A Commentary on the New Testament Epistles, Romans*, Nashville: Gospel Advocate Company, 1943, 33.
5. Arndt, Danker, et al. 446.
6. Vine, W. E. "Divinity, *Theiotes*," *Vine's Concise Dictionary of the Bible*. Nashville: Thomas Nelson, 2005, 101.

The Acknowledgement of God: A Path to Divine Understanding

B. God's *"invisible attributes"* can be seen secondly in His **divine nature**. His nature is also seen within the creation account, showing all the things that make Him God. The term θειότης (*Theiotes*) is the quality or characteristic(s) pert. to deity, divinity, divine nature, and divineness (Rom 1:20)[5]. The KJV translates the term *Godhead*. This word is derived from their distinguished *theotes* in Colossians 2:9. Here in Romans 1:20 Paul is declaring how much of God may be known from the revelation of Himself, which He has made in nature.[6]

Even though they knew God...1:21-23
It is true that the Gentiles *"knew God"* even though Paul has said on numerous occasions that they did not know God (cf. Gal. 4:8; 1 Cor. 1:21; 1 Thess. 4:5). Paul seems to be emphasizing the fact that the Gentiles *"knew of"* God or knew God in the past, however due to their suppression of the truth which was God-given knowledge (1:18) they had become a people ignorant of God.[7]

1. **Did not honor Him**—The Gentiles did not δοξάζω (*doxazo*) give praise or glory to God. While they *"knew"* God, they had no interest in giving Him what was due. How did they know God? We may never know exactly, but we can say that they could know Him in the same way Adam through Noah did, as well as Ninevah and the Babylonians. All were equally Gentile and all aware of God. No man is exempt from giving God the glory for everything he has nor keeping and following His commandments (Eccl. 12:13).

2. **Did not give thanks to Him**—εὐχαριστέω (*eucharisteo*) to be thankful. The Gentile world had become accustomed to ignoring God and, therefore, not being thankful to God for all they had or were given. From the sunrise to the fruitful seasons (Acts 14:17), they enjoyed many gifts from Him but never took the time to thank Him.

3. **Became futile in their speculations**—the term *futile* (ματαιόω, *mataioo*) meaning worthless or stupid. Conceited in their own wisdom, they had rejected their knowledge of God through creation, thus making them fools.

4. **Foolish heart was darkened**—When people "forget" God, they naturally begin to turn to their own ways, thoughts, and imaginations, leading them further away. In turn, their "reasoning was without reasoning." The TEV says that their thoughts became "complete nonsense."

5. **Professing to be wise**—Rome, like many other places, was filled with "worldly knowledge" such as philosophy, scholars, statesmen, and authors who professed their wisdom to the people. However, Paul identified them as *"fools."* Paul likewise would discuss with the Colossian brethren about those who would *"take you captive and delude you with empty deception and delusion"* (cf. Col. 1:22-23). Their *"ways of wisdom"* had nothing to do with education or intelligence but rather attempted to explain the things of the world apart from God's revelation.

6. **Became fools**—Away from God, human reasoning is complete foolishness. Since the beginning of time, as the people of God left Him and lived according to their own wisdom, ultimately they were given into rebellious lives of sin and idolatry that led to their demise in a classic recycled fashion.

7. **Exchanged the glory of an incorruptible God for an image in the form of**...
   A. A massive change in regard to the worship of the people, from the God of creation to the corruptible things of creation. These idolatrous practices, as in the past, would lead to

---

7. Roper, David L. "The Gentiles Subject To God's Wrath (1:18-32)." *Truth For Today Commentary, Romans 1-7, A Doctrinal Study*, Resource Publications, Searcy, Arkansas, 2013, p. 61.

the people's destruction, such as the tribe of Dan, the Assyrians, Egyptians, and more. Here, Paul shows their man-made images of worship, which they viewed to be more than God, a complete showing of their own foolish and moronic understandings of who God is. Here is Paul's list of their gods, which the people had for a time worshipped.

   i. **Corruptible man**—Rome worshipped Caesar, and the Greeks envisioned their many gods in human form. Diana, Zeus, Hera or Juno, Hermes or Mercury are some adopted by the Romans from the Greeks.
   ii. **Birds**—The Egyptians worshipped a variety of birds, including the ibis, which is a long-legged wading bird with a long, curved beak.
   iii. **Four-footed animal**—Israel worshipped the golden calf at Sinai, Egypt worshipped the bull, and in the city of Dan, it is said to have had a large bull or calf at the entrance of the city for all to see as they pass by.
   iv. **Crawling creatures**—Assyrians worshipped reptiles, and the Egyptians worshipped the scarab.

God Gave Them Over...

1. *"Therefore God gave them over in the lusts of their hearts **to impurity**, so that their bodies would be dishonored among them..."* (v. 24, emp. added).
2. *"For this reason God gave them over to **degrading passions**; for their women exchanged the natural function for that which is unnatural..."* (v. 26, emp. added).
3. *"And just as they did not see fit to acknowledge God any longer, God gave them over to a **depraved mind**, to do those things which are not proper..."* (v. 28 emp. added).

A Depraved Mind Does Things Not Properly...1:29-31

1. **Filled with all unrighteousness**—ἀδικία (*adikia*) an act that violates standards of right conduct, *wrongdoing*[8]
2. **Wickedness**—πονηρία (*poneria*) state or condition of a lack of moral or social values, *wickedness, baseness, maliciousness, sinfulness*[9]
3. **Greed**—πλεονεξία (*pleonexia*) the state of desiring to have more than one's due, *greediness, insatiableness, avarice, covetousness*[10]
4. **Evil**—κακία (*kakia*) the quality or state of wickedness, *baseness, depravity, wickedness, vice*. κ. is the opposite of ἀρετή and all virtue and therefore lacking in social value[11]
5. **Full of envy**—Full μεστός (*mestos*) full or filled; Envy φθόνος (*phthonos*) associated with an "evil eye," to be envious or jealous
6. **Murder**— φόνος (*phonos*) murder or killing
7. **Strife**—ἔρις (*eris*) Engagement in rivalry, esp. w. ref. to positions taken in a matter, *strife, discord, contention*[12] also includes quarreling, arguing (CEV), fighting (NCV), and debating (KJV).

---

7. Arndt, Danker, et al. 20.
8. Arndt, Danker, et al. 851.
9. Arndt, Danker, et al. 824.
10. Arndt, Danker, et al. 500.
11. Arndt, Danker, et al. 392.
12. Arndt, Danker, et al. 256.

The Acknowledgement of God: A Path to Divine Understanding

8. **Deceit**—δόλος (*dolos*) taking advantage through craft and underhanded methods, *deceit, cunning, treachery*[13]
9. **Malice**—κακοήθεια (*kakoetheia*) a basic defect in character that leads one to be hurtful to others, *meanspiritedness, malice, malignity, craftiness*[14]
10. **Gossips**—ψιθυριστής (*psithyristes*) *rumormonger, tale-bearer*[15]
11. **Slanderers**—κατάλαλος (*katalalos*) to speaking ill of others, *slanderous*[16]
12. **Haters of God**—θεοστυγής (*theostuges*) meaning God hated
13. **Insolent**—ὑβριστής (*hybristes*) a violent insolent person
14. **Arrogant**—ὑπερήφανος (*hyperphanos*) *arrogant, haughty, proud*
15. **Boastful**—ἀλαζών (*alazon*) *boaster, braggart*
16. **Inventors of evil**—ἐφευρετής κακός (*epheuretos kakos*) people were not satisfied with just being evil; they had to invent new ways of being evil[17]
17. **Disobedient to parents**—ἀπειθής γονεύς (*apeithḗs goneús*), meaning unwilling to be pursued by their fathers and mothers. Lipscomb writes this is common amongst the heathen as they cast off their parents only to take on the reckless nature of the natural authority of their mind.
18. **Without understanding**—ἀσύνετος (*asynetos*) void of understanding, *senseless, foolish,* implying also a lack of high moral quality[18]
19. **Untrustworthy**—ἀσύνθετος (*asynthetos*) one who does not keep an agreement, untrustworthy[19]
20. **Unloving**—ἄστοργος (*astorgos*) *hardhearted, unfeeling, without regard for others.* Barclay writes, "This was an age in which family love was dying. A child's life was a precarious time as children were considered a misfortune. When a child was born, it was taken and laid at the father's feet. If the father lifted it up, that meant that he acknowledged it. If he turned away and left it, the child would be literally thrown out."[20]
21. **Unmerciful**—ἀνελεήμων (*aneleemon*) Barclay would again say, "There was never a time when life was so cheap, a slave could be killed or tortured by his master, for the slave was only a thing, and the law gave the master unlimited power over him…It was a pitiless age within its pleasures, for it was the great age of the gladiatorial games where people found their delight in seeing men kill each other. It was an age when the quality of mercy was gone."[21]

STUDY

A major part of our study within this building session, as well as our study of Romans itself, has to begin with the *"prophetic word promised beforehand."* All men will always have the

---

13. Arndt, Danker, et al. 500.
14. Arndt, Danker, et al. 1098.
15. Arndt, Danker, et al. 519.
16. Roper. "Rejection of God Through a Catalogue of Sins, Romans 1:28-32." *Truth for Today Commentary, Romans 1–7, A Doctrinal Study*, Searcy: Resource Publications, 2013, 81.
17. Arndt, Danker, et al. 146.
18. Arndt, Danker, et al. 146.
19. Barclay, William. "The Life Which Has Left God out of the Reckoning, Romans 1:28-32." *The Daily Study Bible*. Philadelphia: The Westminster Press, 1957, 32-33.
20. Barclay.

opportunity to know God as He has made Himself available to be known by man. He is no secret! His Word is no secret! His way is no secret! It has been widely known since creation what the will of the Father for man is. He has made it both clear and understandable for us to comprehend.

Let's look at the opening verses of the book.

> *Paul, a bond-servant of Christ Jesus, called as an apostle, set apart for the gospel of God,* **which He promised beforehand through His prophets in the holy Scriptures**, *concerning His Son, who was born of a descendant of David according to the flesh, who was declared the Son of God with power by the resurrection from the dead, according to the Spirit of holiness, Jesus Christ our Lord, through whom we have received grace and apostleship to bring about the obedience of faith among all the Gentiles for His name's sake, among whom you also are the called of Jesus Christ; to all who are beloved of God in Rome, called as saints: Grace to you and peace from God our Father and the Lord Jesus Christ* (emp. added).

Underline in your Bible this section: *"Which He promised beforehand through His prophets in the holy Scriptures."*

It really is amazing how God has, throughout time, given us His message and kept it so completely consistent within each word, message, prophecy, story, and doctrine. What a great God we have!

For our study, let's begin looking at the idea of prophecy and just how much it means to the opening chapter, as well as the epistle that Paul wrote to the church at Rome. As Denny wrote in his opening statement of Romans 1:2, "The Gospel is not an afterthought of God." It is very important that we have a firm grasp of this within our minds. Why? Because there are so many teachings, philosophies, and naturalistic ideas that surround us from every direction that if we do not understand the importance of prophecy from a Biblical perspective, we too might be persuaded to *"exchange the truth of God for a lie"* (1:25), and that is not something that we should be willing to allow ourselves to take part in.

To begin our study of **prophecy** and the **prophets,** let's mark our place in Romans 1, but then turn to Hebrews 1:1-2: *"God, after He spoke long ago to the fathers in the prophets in many portions and in many ways, in these last days has spoken to us in His Son, whom He appointed heir of all things, through whom also He made the world."*

Throughout the history of creation, we have never been without God. He did not, as some may like to believe, "make the world and leave," which is a ridiculous idea to say the least. While there may have been a time of "quietness" from the mouth of God in what we call the intertestamental period (Note: 1 Maccabees 4:46; 9:27; 14:41) where there were no prophets and God did not speak to man, that does not mean that He was absent in and with His creation.

God has sustained all of His creation since the beginning (cf. Eccl. 1:4-9; Ps. 104:5; 119:90) and will continue to do so until the time that He is ready to destroy it all and bring all of the faithful into

The Acknowledgement of God: A Path to Divine Understanding

glory with Him (1 Thess. 4:13-17; 2 Pet. 3:3-13; cf. John 14:1-6). Until this time which has been promised to come, He will forever be with us, watching, working, and waiting for us to be built up in the faith, added to the church (Acts 2:38-42,47; Col. 1:13,18), and living a faith-filled life.

Within our Hebrews passage first, we need to note that within the context, it was and is God who *"spoke"* and has *"spoken,"* but what else does it tell us?

In verse 1, the writer states:
1. **The When:** God spoke *"long ago…"*
2. **To Whom:** God spoke *"to the fathers…"*
3. **The How:** God spoke *"in the prophets in many portions and in many ways…"*

What is this referring to? The process of inspiration.

Some critics throughout history and even in our day refuse to believe in the influence of God. In other words, they do not believe in "supernatural influence." Rather, they believe in the naturalistic assumption that all the text had to have come together naturally and NOT supernaturally. Many problems exist within this theory that, in many ways, go against the text.

For instance, one argument is that there would be no way that a writer could write about something that was in the future, such as the 70 years of captivity Jeremiah wrote about (Jer. 25:11-12), the destruction of Jerusalem that would occur in 70 A.D. (Matt. 24), or even Jesus foretelling His death (John 14:1-6).

To have a naturalistic view of the text really doesn't make sense, mainly because the text is in discussion of the supernatural from beginning to end. Think about it.
- God at creation made all things from NOTHING! Is that not supernatural?
- As Moses held his staff in the air, God parted the Red Sea, allowing Israel to walk across dry land (Ex. 14:22)! Is that not supernatural?
- When Gideon led his 300 men into battle against the thousands of soldiers in the valley, defeating them all (Judg. 7)! Is that not supernatural?
- What about when the man was let through the ceiling to be laid before Jesus? Jesus then told him to *"get up, pick up your bed, and go home"* (Matt. 9:6). As all watched this man who had been paralyzed throughout his life stand, pick his bed up, and walk out the door, did they not think there was something supernatural going on?
- Or how about when Mary went to the grave only to find Jesus not there in His tomb (John 20:1). Later Peter and several other apostles, including John, go fishing and see Jesus—the same Jesus who had just been murdered—sitting on the side of the sea waiting for them to bring Him their catch (John 21). Paul also records in 1 Corinthians 15 that He showed Himself to numerous other people, including Peter, Paul, James, the 12, and 500 others. Is that not supernatural?

To have a naturalistic view of anything surrounding the text doesn't seem to be sensible if you have any faith at all. A naturalistic view would make sense for a person who doesn't have faith due to his unbelief, but remember, those who believe and yet have not seen are truly blessed (John 20:29)!

To understand **inspiration,** you must believe in the supernatural, which the Bible claims is true. Therefore, God spoke. When? *"Long ago, to the fathers in the prophets."* What is this referring to?

It seems that we are referring to both prophecy and the very principle that put all things together, referenced as the *"holy Scriptures"* (1:2). Prophets throughout the Bible were given the Word of the Lord and wrote as they were inspired to do so. Within these writings and through their sayings, prophecy was given. *Prophecy* (προφητεία, prŏphēteĭa) is the ability to receive direct revelations from God and communicate them to others.[21] Prophets have always been key players in the revelations of God and are known through four different terms as they have different abilities. **Prophets** received the Word of the Lord. **Seers** saw apocalyptic visions. **Visionaries** saw visions. The **man of God** was another name or phrase for a prophet. Prophets or men of God received the Word of the Lord, the *diberyhwh*, and gave it to the people.

The apostle Peter wrote in 2 Peter 1:20-21, *"But know this first of all, that no prophecy of Scripture is a matter of one's own interpretation, for no prophecy was ever made by an act of human will, but men moved by the Holy Spirit spoke from God."* So, as the text says, all Scripture has come *from God.* Not from man. Knowing this is very important, as it suggests that all Scripture was given to man from the Creator through men who were moved *"by the Holy Spirit."* Thus when men were given what to write, they wrote, and when men were given what to say, they spoke, and the people lived by those words, allowing them an understanding of how one might be faithfully obedient to God.

When we study the history of the Bible and how it was accepted as Scripture, it seems that this was the process for acceptance. Some believe that how we got the Bible is a great conspiracy. Through the decisions of a Jewish council for the Old Testament and a Catholic council for the New Testament, these people decided upon what should and should not be in the Scriptures. Nothing could be further from the truth.

Upon a good study of the text, we find many claims, patterns, and actions taken that explain to us just how the Bible came together throughout time, thus allowing people through the generations to be both acquainted and familiar with His holy Word.

So let's start with this: **The Principle of Canon.**

The **Canonical Principle** says that when the people of God **universally accepted** a person as a prophet of God, the writing of that person was **immediately** and **automatically** accepted by the people of God as **holy Scripture**.

Here are some examples:
- Since he had been in the presence of the Lord (cf. Ex. 33:11), the people could not look at the face of Moses as the righteousness of God literally shown through him to the degree that it was blinding (Ex. 34:29-35). As Moses and God spoke, God gave Moses the **word of the Lord** and had him write down (Ex. 34) all that he had originally received on the mountain and more.

---
21. Owen, Dan R. *How We Got the Bible.* Unpublished Commentary, 1985, 6.

The Acknowledgement of God: A Path to Divine Understanding

When the people heard, saw, and read the words of Moses, the people **accepted** them, not as the words of men, but for what it really was: **the Word of God**.

- Towards the end of the Babylonian captivity in the book of Daniel, we see the result of another prophet's writing. In Daniel 9:1-2, which was in the *"first year of Darius, the son of Ahasuerus,"* we find Daniel observing in the books *"the number of years which was **revealed as the Word of the Lord** to Jeremiah the prophet for the completion of the desolations of Jerusalem, namely, seventy years"* (emp. added). This tells us that the writings of the prophet Jeremiah were already **accepted** as the **Word of the Lord** and were already in circulation. It also tells us that Daniel was searching the Scriptures to find out how long the captivity was to last.

Remember what Paul wrote in 2 Timothy 3:16, *"All Scripture is inspired by God and profitable for teaching, for reproof, for correction, for training in righteousness; so that the man of God may be adequate, equipped for every good work."* The phrase πᾶσα γραφὴ θεόπνευστος or *"all Scripture is inspired by God"* translates as we well know that all Scripture is God-breathed. But what exactly does that mean? It simply means that God, through the various writers of the Bible, asserted His supernatural influence over the writer so that his writing would be exactly as God desired it to be as it was completed.[22] While each writer could write in his own way, the influence of God guided them to write His message without their own interpretation or influence upon the message being written.

As they wrote, as we have found with both Moses and Jeremiah, their writings were automatically added to "the Scrolls" or "the Scriptures" as they were automatically counted as "Bible" within the people of God. No council voted on this process. **This was God's process**. He spoke to a prophet, the prophet heard His Word, he wrote it down as he was commanded to do, and the people accepted the prophet's writings as the *diberyhwh,* the Word of the Lord.

So, within our Old Testaments, God spoke long ago to the fathers in the prophets in many portions and in many ways. Then the Hebrew writer states, *"In these last days has spoken to us in His Son, whom He appointed heir of all things, through whom also He made the world."*

In verse 2, the writer states…
1. **The When:** *"In these last days…"*
2. **The Who:** *"Has spoken to us…"*
3. **The How:** *"In His Son, whom He appointed heir of all things…"*

Remember, God is still the one speaking within our context, as God inspires all Scripture. Here, the principle of canon is **still in play**, as nothing has changed. When the people accept a person as a prophet **universally**, his writings are **immediately** and **automatically** accepted as Scripture.

Here is our context. *"These last days"* are in reference to the days that you are in. The days of the church, the days after Christ's ascension (Acts 1:9) as we are in the last dispensation, before the coming of Jesus (1 Thess. 4:13-17). It is in these last days that God has spoken to us (the apostle, the prophet, the people) *"in His Son,"* Jesus. But were there prophets in the New Testament? Yes!

---

22. Owen 1.

Paul wrote in Ephesians 3:3-5,

> *That by revelation there was made known to me the mystery, as I wrote before in brief. By referring to this, when you read you can understand my insight into the mystery of Christ, which in other generations was not made known to the sons of men, as it has now been revealed to His holy apostles and prophets in the Spirit.*

What is Paul claiming to be here? A prophet. But how? I mean, prophets are only in the Old Testament, right? Unfortunately, I think that to a degree we have unintentionally led people away from this idea as we focus on the word *apostle* so much (and rightfully so). However, Jesus explains in the Gospel of John that as He leaves, the Holy Spirit will be with them, which is vital as Jesus defines what He will do for them, not just the 12, but all who would possess a spiritual gift (grace), particularly the gift of prophecy.

Jesus says....
- **John 14:26**—*"But the Helper, the Holy Spirit, whom the Father will send in My name, **He will teach you all things, and bring to your remembrance all that I said to you**"* (emp. added).
- **John 15:26**—*"When the Helper comes, whom I will send to you from the Father, that is the Spirit of truth who proceeds from the Father, **He will testify about Me**"* (emp. added).
- **John 16:13**—*"But when He, the Spirit of truth, comes, **He will guide you into all the truth**; for He will not speak on His own initiative, but whatever He hears, He will speak; and **He will disclose to you what is to come**"* (emp. added).

This shows us that the Holy Spirit would help them to remember the things said in the **past**, testify about Him in the spirit of truth in the **present**, and guide them and disclose to them what would be in the **future**. This is a fundamental part of being a prophet, being able to speak and write down the Word of the Lord from the past, in the present, and about the future.

He also wrote in Galatians 1:11-12, *"For I would have you know, brethren, that the gospel which was preached by me is not according to man. For I neither received it from man, nor was I taught it, but I received it through a **revelation of Jesus Christ**"* (emp. added). This proves what we read in Hebrews 1:2. That God has spoken to us in these last days in His Son, Jesus Christ. Whom did He speak through? The prophets. Ephesians 4:11-12 states: *"And He gave some as **apostles**, and some as **prophets**, and some as **evangelists**, and some as **pastors** and **teachers**, for the equipping of the saints for the work of service, to the building up of the body of Christ"* (emp. added).

So, let's put this into play here in Romans 1.

> *Paul, a bond-servant of Christ Jesus, called as an apostle, set apart for the gospel of God, **which He promised beforehand through His prophets in the holy Scriptures, concerning His Son**, who was **born of a descendant of David** according to the flesh, who was declared the Son of God with power by the resurrection from the dead, according to the Spirit of holiness, Jesus Christ our Lord, through whom we have received grace and apostleship to bring about the obedience of faith among all the Gentiles for His name's sake, among whom you also are the called of Jesus Christ...* (emp. added).

The Acknowledgement of God: A Path to Divine Understanding

In the opening words of Paul, what is of main interest here are the things that were *"promised beforehand through His prophets in the holy Scriptures,"* which has to do with both inspiration (God inspired the prophet to write down the revelation) and revelation (God speaks to the prophet directly). These are both pointing in one direction—Jesus and the Gospel of God. This is in reference to the fulfillment of the plan that He established before the foundation of the world (Eph. 1:4-6) and promised through His prophets as it had been put into action.

It was this good news that was revealed through the prophets and accepted by the people of God through the generations. Did the Jews initially reject this during the life of Jesus? Yes, but ultimately, a number did come to believe. What the book of Romans teaches us right here in chapter 1 is that the Gospel of God, promised beforehand, prophesied by the prophets, carried out in Jesus, and spoken of by the apostles (also prophets) is good news. And this good news **is not** for one people—it is for all people—people of every class, every ethnicity, background, social status, sex, and age!

This message is for all, and through it, the power of God is seen. It is seen within His Scriptures, within the resurrected Christ, within the creation of all things. What this means is that God is shown in two ways, first through the accepted Word and second through His creation, which encompasses the inspired and revealed words of God, His prophets, and the world in which we live, which the prophet Moses was inspired to write about within the Torah. This means that there is an extreme amount of proof that God is the ultimate deity. The God of all gods should never be turned away from or exchanged for anyone or anything. He is God because our world shows He is, and His Word tells us He is. All things correctly point to this fact.

RIGHTEOUSNESS AND WRATH

Within the main focus of our study, there are essentially two things that are revealed as a result of both the writings and creation.
1. The righteousness of God... v. 17
2. The wrath of God... v. 18

RIGHTEOUSNESS

A character or quality of being right or just is used to denote an attribute of God. Romans 3:25 demonstrates that His righteousness is exhibited in the death of Christ, which demonstrates His holiness as He works to condemn sin.[23] Therefore, His righteousness is **revealed** from faith to faith, meaning that all groups, despite their imperfections and sins, could now move toward God **not** through the Law of Moses but through the Gospel of God.

It is the righteousness of God because it is from Him and revealed to you and me through what was spoken of beforehand through the prophets. The Gospel of God has now been preached to the people, allowing them to build and grow in their faith. Encouraged by His words of fulfillment

---

23. Vine. "Righteousness." 320.

and eternally cleansed to now be called a saint (1:7). This comes, of course, by the hearing of the good news of Jesus as faith is produced within the heart of man (Rom. 10:17). It is in this way that God's righteousness is made known "from faith to faith" (cf. Hab. 2:4). What Paul seems to have in mind here is to live a "faith-based lifestyle" with a continual focus on the Word of the Lord, the blessings of life, and thankfulness within his heart.

Barclay writes that within Pauline's writing, his use of faith means total acceptance and absolute trust and betting your life that there is a God.[24] Faith has to do with receptivity as a man is willing to listen and be open to the fact that he may be right or he may be wrong and submit his life to the foundation of His will. This is a complete surrender of life. Righteousness is gained for mankind because God spoke to the prophets and through His Son both long ago and in these last days through the holy Scriptures.

This means that God has carried out His plan through time to allow us to obtain His righteousness through the faith that we possess. The ability to see what we cannot and believe in it anyway because of all the living proof that His Word is true. We will never be righteous on our own because it is not something that we can physically gain. Rather, it is a way that we are seen. Mainly the way we are seen "in Christ" as a result of our cleansed state, bringing us spiritually to a point where we have no spot or wrinkle. John calls it *cleansed* (1 John 1:7).

For us as people, we can only be given, or be seen, or be rendered the righteousness of God when our heart connects to His, when our mind lines up with His, and when our actions line up with His teachings as a result of faithful obedience. This is how righteousness is—through your faith (cf. Heb. 11:1-2).

WRATH

As stated before, the wrath of God is equivalent to the anger of God. His anger is not toward all of mankind but is stored up for those who have devoted themselves to the absence of Him in their life. Thus, they deny the existence of Him, the workings of Him, the reliability of Him, and His design of how life and choice work. Those who pursue unrighteous acts for adultery, homosexuality, slander, deceit, etc., are essentially pursuing God's wrath unto all of eternity. Remember, while the righteousness of God has been revealed within the Gospel message, the wrath of God is equally revealed in Scripture. It is revealed within their history.

It was not a hard thing to know about the destruction of Sodom and Gomorrah. It was known how Israel had come into the land of Canaan with God leading their way, destroying those who had defiled the land. The history books would have recalled the destruction of Ninevah and Jerusalem, along with countless other times that people had witnessed His wrath. It isn't spent easily, but at the time that God decides it is time to release it, it is for good reason.

God's wrath is reserved for sin. In fact, that is the very thing that we are saved from—the *"wrath of God"* (Rom. 5:9). What Paul is teaching here by way of this epistle is that God's wrath is *"revealed*

---

24. Barclay, "Good News of Which to Be Proud, Romans 1:16-17." *The Daily Study Bible, Romans*. Philadelphia: The Westminster Presses, 1957, 12-13.

The Acknowledgement of God: A Path to Divine Understanding

from Heaven," a teaching from the Word of the Lord that sin must be done away with. These were not the words of the prophet Paul but of God Himself. Where sin grows, so does the anger of the Lord. The term *wrath* ὀργή (*orge*) is a divine reaction toward evil.

The holy and righteous nature of God both determines and demands that He punish sin. One writer called it a holy response to the unholy, a reaction to the unjust, and a pure rejection of the impure.[25] Have we come up with this concept all on our own? Or is there some Scriptural basis here? Remember that all things have been revealed to man and essentially proven through creation. So we must go back to the prophetical writing of what Paul identifies as the holy Scriptures to understand.

In the early stages of the Old Testament, God's main dealings were with His covenant people after the time of Abraham, Isaac, and Jacob, to which the nation of Israel was born through the promise that began with Abraham. The nation of Israel was a covenant people to God who had a special relationship with Him as His chosen people. As long as they kept His Law, the condition of that relationship would be right. If they broke His Law, it would provoke the **wrath of God** and break the relationship they had with Him (cf. Num. 16:43; 25:3).

The prophets would echo the idea of how the wrath of God occurs. Sometimes, we find the wrath of God being discussed as a future event; however, for the prophets, it seems to be an ongoing occurrence, a continuous action. When Israel strayed away from God and was rebellious against Him, His wrath was sent to ruin her and give her into the hands of another. These events were all brought about by anger as it burned against them (cf. Isa. 5:25).

Paul, while only speaking of His wrath three times (Rom. 1:18; Eph. 5:6; Col. 3:6), insists that man will not be able to plead ignorance during the Day of Judgment and to follow Jesus that salvation might be obtained as Jesus can deliver us from the wrath to come (1 Thess. 1:10). Only those who deny His existence and place of God amongst all creation including our lives will see the anger and wrath of God. The Gentiles were no exception to this.

God has been proven to all of creation by His creation, and all that was known about God within the day and even in previous days had been made evident to them. While God may have chosen to make a covenant with the nation of Israel, He certainly didn't forget about the rest of the world. Paul states that *"God gave them over"* (1:24), an interesting statement, don't you think? I thought God only watched Israel. That was not the case here. If God gave them over, what was given is what was deserved.

Three times, Paul says, *"God gave them over"* (1:24, 26, 28), what does that mean? Roper writes, "When God gave sinners over, He was still concerned about them (2 Pet. 3:9); He still hoped they would return to Him...Instead of restraining mankind in its downward spiral in sin, God let people do as they wished (Compare Gen. 6:3).... Further, instead of protecting people from the consequences of their actions, God allowed them to suffer the full penalty of their chosen lifestyles."

---

25. Roper. "The Gentiles Subject to God's Wrath, Romans 1:18-32." *Truth for Today Commentary, Romans 1–7, A Doctrinal Study*. Searcy: Recourse Publications, 2013, 54-55.

J.D. Thomas said, "If you decide to depart from God, He is not going to send a league of angels to stop you. It will break His heart, but He will let you go." Richard Rogers put it this way: "When you give yourself up to something, God will give you over to that thing. It isn't because He is angry, although He may be. It is because He is loving, which He must be."

All of this shows us that God did love the Gentile people, but just as He was willing to give over the nation of Israel to the hands of other nations and sin, He also treated the Gentiles in the same way. God certainly was not going to force them to be obedient, and He doesn't do that to us today. Why? Because if we were forced to love Him, would it be love? If we were forced to serve Him, would it be true service? God isn't looking for that which pleases Him; He is looking for those who love Him. Those who love Him truly will serve because they love Him. Those who serve Him do so because they love Him. Therefore, for those who turn their hearts from Him, God allows them to do so, with the understanding that if they continue on the path of destruction, that is what they will reap.

ACTIVITY

Gather into groups around the room. Make sure that at least one person has a copy of the worksheet and that everyone else has a piece of paper, pen or pencil, and their Bibles. During this activity, your job is to identify as a group the main principles of Romans 1 and how they connect back to the writings of the prophets beforehand.

Pick one person at the table to be a spokesperson. At the end of your time, they will be responsible for sharing with the rest of the groups the answers that you as a group came up with and why you came up with them. (This helps us to see different perspectives).

THREE EXERCISES

1. As a group, pick one of the **Theologically Significant** phrases or words and explain why and how that statement is significant to our congregations and personal lives today. Give three reasons.

2. Then, pick three subjects from Paul's list within verses 29-31 that may connect with your statement and show how the Holy Scriptures:

   A. Teach against it.
   B. Give an example of someone or a group of people who participated in it.
   C. Tell what happened because of their actions.

3. Give two takeaways that you can apply to your everyday life as a child of God and to the church that will both benefit and bless you so that you might stay free from the wrath of God.

The Acknowledgement of God: A Path to Divine Understanding

WORKSHEET

Name Your Group Leader and Spokesman: _____

What **Theologically Significant** phrase would you as a group like to choose?
_____
_____

Why is this phrase or word significant to you and the church today? Explain.

Reason 1:
_____
_____

Reason 2:
_____
_____

Reason 3:
_____
_____

Pick three subjects in Paul's list in verses 29-31:
1. _____
2. _____
3. _____

As a group, it shows how the holy Scriptures:

Teach against it:
_____
_____
_____

Building

Example of person:

Give the result of their actions:

Come up with two takeaways that will help you as an individual and the church benefit from your knowledge of God's Word that will continue to keep you safe from the wrath of God.

Takeaway #1:

Takeaway #2:

Building

THE TRUTH OF WHO YOU SHOULD BE!

Romans 2

GARRETT BERNETHY

"For he is not a Jew who is one outwardly, nor is circumcision that which is outward in the flesh. But he is a Jew who is one inwardly; and circumcision is that which is of the heart, by the Spirit, not by the letter; and his praise is not from men, but from God."
- Romans 2:28-29 -

INTRODUCTION

The opening words of Romans 2 are, *"Therefore, you have no excuse."* An interesting way to start, right? Or is it a start at all? The answer is no; this is not the beginning of a different chapter but rather a continuation of the thought that Paul is making. However, the apostle changes his direction from speaking about the Gentiles to speaking to the Jew himself. Remember, the church in Rome consisted of both Jews and Gentiles, once again showing that the gospel of God is for all people of every kind and that no person—whether they are Greek, Barbarian, Jew, or Gentile—is exempt from sin nor glory. All are equal in the sight of God, who shows no partiality (2:11). As chapter 2 progresses, the "inner man" becomes a major focus of his point. The internal vs. the external. The Law written on stones vs. the law written in the heart. The inner man is often the focus of the transformative message of the Gospel mainly because internal change brings eternal glory. However, we find within Romans 2 the internal struggle resulting from improperly understanding what the holy Scriptures should have taught them. The Jew essentially was against the Gentile, and later in the book, we will find the same in reverse. From the judgments made to the unrepentant hearts, all men will perish or be blessed due to their obedience to the will of the Father.

FOCUS

The Jewish mind during this time relied on the historical context of who the nation of Israel had been in the past. Therefore, the chosen people of God believed that they would be held to a different standard than what everyone else would be held to, which means that they would be saved because they were Jews. Paul, however, begins to dismiss this idea. Something that he could do very quickly, being a Jew himself.

This, unfortunately, can become a bad habit for all of us if we are not careful. Thinking that because we "wear a name" or "belong to a group of people," we are somehow grouped into a blessed eternal reward based on association or title. Remember, a name/title or association is not equivalent to salvation. Only obedience is. That is what "law" requires: obedience no matter who you are. In this case, obedience to the Law of Moses (historically speaking) and to the law of conscience (historically speaking).

For our purposes, we are going to separate this chapter into three sections:

1. Hypocritical practices
2. The laws of man
3. Unfaithful failures

> Our decision to walk according to His law will allow God the ability to judge each person according to his deeds. Will our actions and decision-making reflect His way or our own.

Hypocritical practices are a turn-off to both God and man. Nobody likes it when someone claims to be something and then acts as if he is another. Jesus Himself gave eight woes to the Pharisees, saying, *"But woe to you, scribes and Pharisees, hypocrites, because you..."* (Matt. 23:13-29). Here, Paul exclaims the same thing in verse 1 as he states, *"Therefore you have no excuse, every one of you who passes judgment, for in that which you judge another, you condemn yourself; for you who judge practice the same things."* They had no right to judge the practices of the Gentiles; their actions were **the same**. This shows the upside-down mindset of the Jewish mind that says, "I am a Jew, and God will save me," not because of obedience but because of nationality and historical religious beliefs. This mindset would not have been reached if they had been paying attention to the holy Scriptures of which the prophets wrote.

The Laws of Man references, within our present context, basically three laws in particular. **First**, you have the Law of Moses, which Paul states in 2 Corinthians 3:7 is *"engraved on stones."* **Second**, you have the law of conscience, which has to do with an inner awareness of what is right and wrong. **Thirdly**, you have the law of Christ, which is in reference to the Gospel of God or, according to what Paul also calls it in 2:16, *"my gospel."* In most cases, the term *law* does not possess a definite article; therefore, it can discuss any law, or law in general, even though there is a definite contextual flow of the Law of Moses. More will be said about this in our study.

The Truth of Who You Should Be!

Unfaithful failures seem defined by Paul here by writing, *"Having in the Law the embodiment of knowledge and of the truth, you, therefore, who teach another, do you not teach yourself?"* A direct tie back to the beginning of chapter 2: *"You judge, yet you do the same thing."* The failure is seen very clearly here. The people knew the Law of God; they knew the prophecies of Jesus; they knew now the Gospel message that had been taught but could not let go of the idea that they were still "Jews," the chosen people of God, and therefore no matter what they did, that was enough. However, Paul states that their failure to uphold the Law meant they had no law at all. Only ***doers of the law will be justified***, as God will judge their actions based upon it.

Focus Statement: Our decision to walk according to His law will allow God the ability to judge each person according to his deeds. Will our actions and decision-making reflect His way or our own?

STUDY KEYS

Note: Take some time as you study through chapter 2 to mark each of these words and phrases individually with different color pens, markers, colored pencils, or highlighters of your choice. If possible, make notes in your margins to reflect the meanings of these words or phrases that may help you understand the overall context to a better degree.

WORDS OF IMPORTANCE

- **God** (θεός)—vv. 3, 4, 5, 11, 13, 16, 17, 23, 24, 29
- **Law** (νόμος)—vv. 12, 13, 14, 15, 17, 18, 20, 23, 25, 26, 27
- **Judge/Judgment** (κρίνω)—vv. 1, 3, 12, 16, 27
- **Wrath** (ὀργή)—vv. 5, 8
- **Circumcision** (περιτομή)—vv. 25, 26, 27, 28, 29
- **Jew** (Ἰουδαῖος)—vv. 9, 10, 17, 28, 29

PAUL'S LISTS

Do you think lightly of the riches of His...2:4

1. Kindness
2. Tolerance
3. Patience
   - A. A list of three attributes of God which were directed towards them (the Jews) with the purpose and hope that these three things would bring them to repentance.[1] It is these three things that allowed God to hold back from punishing them for their sins, giving

---

1. Roper, David L. "The Jews Exposed, Romans 2:1-11." *Truth for Today Commentary, Romans 1–7, A Doctrinal Study*. Searcy: Resource Publications, 2013, 140.

them an opportunity to repent. Sadly, they had taken God's goodness as a sign that He had **overlooked** their sins because they were His covenant people. Instead of becoming penitent, they had become increasingly rebellious.

Who by perseverance in doing good seek for...2:7

1. **Glory** (δόξα)[2]—Lipscomb writes that *glory* denotes the highest happiness and distinction that the saved will attain. Essentially, this means that Paul is not discussing one's own glory but rather the glory that one obtains in Christ as he/she is obedient to God. This is an adherence to God's glory as they long to see the glory of God that is to come at the final judgment. This is because glory is a result of the inner transformation of the believer who conforms to the image of God's Son (5:2; 8:18, 21, 30; 9:23; cf. 1 Cor. 2:7; 15:43; 2 Cor. 4:17; Col. 3:4).
2. **Honor** (τιμή)—Closely related to the word δόξα (cf. Heb. 2:7; 1 Pet.:7; 2 Pet. 1:17; Rev. 4:9), *honor* is the value or esteem to which one is held. To seek honor is from the believer to the Father Himself. It, too, is the result of the transformative process of the inner man, resulting from the *"renewal of the mind"* (Rom. 12:1-2). As one conforms to the law of God within his heart, he/she will be held in honor as his faith has produced obedience within his life. Driving outward actions from the inner man.
3. **Immortality** (ἀφθαρσία)—Also translated as *incorruptible,* immortality can be connected to 1 Corinthians 15:53-54 as the *"perishable must put on the imperishable, and this mortal must put on immortality."* Paul seems to be referencing the corruptibility of the flesh, meaning freedom from suffering from decay and an absolute exemption from sin and impurity. God only has incorruption and immortality. Man is eternal in existence but will be given immortality as a reward for his seeking it from the Father.
4. **Eternal Life** (ζωή αἰώνιος)—A life in the presence of God, dwelling and walking with Him as His child, and Him as your God in our eternal home. Peter references this as the new Heaven and new earth where righteousness dwells (2 Pet. 3:13), Paul says it will be with the Lord (1 Thess. 4:17), John says it will be a place of eternal bliss (Rev. 21:1-4), a place for the family of God (Rev. 21:7). It is the bride of Christ (Eph. 5:27), a destination in the home of God (John 14:2-3). Eternal life is never-ending within the spirit realm of the afterlife, where the soul goes on to live forever in the reward of their faithfulness.

Do not obey the truth but obey...2:8

1. **Unrighteousness** (ἀδικία)—An act that violates standards of right conduct, *wrongdoing*[4]
2. **Wrath** (ὀργή)—A state of relatively strong displeasure, with focus on the emotional aspect, *anger*[5]
3. **Indignation** (θυμός)—An intense expression of the inner self, frequently expressed as a strong desire, *passion, passionate longing*[6]

---

2. Lipscomb, David. "Romans 2:1-16." *A Commentary of the New Testament Epistles, Romans*. Nashville: Gospel Advocate, 1967, 51.
3. Lipscomb 51.
4. Arndt, William, Frederick W. Danker, et al., *A Greek-English Lexicon of the New Testament and Other Early Christian Literature*. Chicago: University of Chicago Press, 2000, 20.
5. Arndt, Danker, et al. 720.
6. Arndt, Danker, et al. 461.

The Truth of Who You Should Be!

A. Note that these three things contrast with the four blessings mentioned in verse 7 (glory, honor, immortality, and eternal life). For more, please see Denny's notes in chapter 2:7-13.

A Repeat and Addition of Blessings...2:10

1. **Glory** (δόξα)—The condition of being bright or shining, *brightness, splendor, radiance*[7]
2. **Honor** (τιμή)—The amount at which something is valued, *price*[8]
3. **Peace** (εἰρήνη)—A state of concord, *peace, and harmony*.[9] This peace, not referenced in the previous list of blessings, refers to peace with God and man, the ultimate and complete peace that will only be realized in Heaven.[10]

Confident That You Yourself Are A...2:19-20

1. **Guide to the blind**—Not being the first time the Jews had been identified as *blind guides* (Matt. 23:16, 24), Jesus identified His people similarly. Remember, they *had in the law the embodiment of knowledge and of the truth* (v. 20). The word *embodiment* (μόρφωσις, *morphosis*) is in reference to "formation, the appearance of semblance." While they were confident in their knowledge and even their ability to teach the Gentiles, their lives did not revolve around that which they had come to know, but rather tradition, sinful actions, and indecent behaviors. Thus, being a people to guide others away from the Gospel and not towards salvation.
2. **Light to those who are in darkness**—Rabbis often identified themself as the "light of the word," and all Jews who knew the Law considered themselves within this very light. But instead of bringing people out of the dungeon of darkness, they seemed to be leading people into it. The major issue here seems to be that not only can the blind lead others who are blind (an absence of direction), but one cannot guide others to the light if he is seemingly living in the darkness. Thus, the pride of the Jews was in the way of their ability to conform to their responsibilities, which they should have been indulging.
3. **Corrector of the foolish**—The Jews looked at themselves as "correctors," meaning that they believed they were teachers. A *corrector* (παιδευτής, *paiduetes*) means instructor or teacher. The word *foolish* (ἄφρων, *aphron*) is in discussion of those who "lack judgment or prudence" due to their own foolishness. This means they saw themselves as having the ability to teach those who were ignorant and lacked good judgment; all the while, they (the Jews) were not practicing good judgment.
4. **Teacher of the immature**—Here, Paul uses the word *teacher* (διδάσκαλος, *didaskalos*), which refers to an instructor, and the word *immature* (νήπιος, *nappies)*, which refers to an infant or a child. This is a reference to the **spiritually immature**, a group the Jews should have focused on helping. However, as Paul states, they were **blind guides** leading away from light. Their hypocritical actions, traditional concepts, and historical connections would not allow them to step outside the lines of their mind, live as God's people in Christ,

---

7. Arndt, Danker, et al. 257.
8. Arndt, Danker, et al. 1005.
9. Arndt, Danker, et al. 287.
10. Roper 144.

and live a life of obedience. Remember, they (the Jews) were doing the **same things** the Gentiles were. Thus, they were most likely, on some level, as immature as the Gentiles were.

    A.   These were responsibilities that the Jews should have assumed due to the knowledge they had been blessed with, referenced as the holy Scriptures (1:2). However, even with the knowledge they had obtained through the prophets about Jesus as well as their knowledge of God Himself, their failure was that they did not accept the responsibility of using that knowledge for the betterment of God's people nor their own life. Lipscomb would write, "They had the form or letter of knowledge and truth in the law, but did not perceive or drink of the true spirit of the law; did not take into their heart so that it might become a power to mold their hearts and lives."[11]

If You...

1. **Bear the name Jew**—A designation that we first find in 2 Kings 16:6 referencing the people of Judah who were a part of the southern kingdom. After the Babylonian captivity, this term was applied to the Israelite nation as a whole (cf. Ezra 5:1; Neh. 13:23) as they returned to Jerusalem to rebuild after their seventy years of captivity. It then became the name of the chosen people of God.

2. **Rely upon the Law**—Referring to the Law of Moses (due to context as there is no definite article), the Jews took great pride in the fact that they, of all of the nations on Earth, had been given the Word of the Lord (the *diberyhvh*) which Paul refers to as the (ἐν γραφαῖς ἁγίαις) the holy Scriptures. The Jews depended on this Law to know and discern the will of God and took pride in the fact that it was something they had no one else did (Roper 152).

3. **Boast in God**—The word *boasting* (καυχάομαι, *kauchaomia*) means to take pride in something., *boast, glory, pride oneself, and brag*.[12] Their boasting was in the fact that they had the Law. Denny wrote in his Sermon Seeds: Advantages and Responsibilities that "The Jews claimed a special relationship with God—one that was not shared with the world. Their boasting was that they were in favor of God as if He were their soul guardians, per Lipscomb. While to a degree, this may be true from a personal standpoint as God is "my Savior" from a personal perspective, on the other hand, their boasting was not God-centered; it was self-centered. The NIV may understand this in good terms: "You...brag about your relationship with God."

4. **Know His will**—*"His will,"* in this case contextually, is referencing the will of God. For the Jews, the "Old Testament," which they would have possessed, consisted of three parts: the Law, the prophets, and the writings. In the case of Luke 24:44, Jesus would call these three sections *"The of Moses and the Prophets and the Psalms."* Luke would also record that Jesus stated in Luke 11:50-51 that He accepted each of these "books" as the Word of the Lord, stating a timeline from the blood of Abel to the blood of Zechariah. Of interest, Josephus would also write of these as the accepted works of the Scriptures (the *graphe*). However, as has been pointed out by many commentators, it isn't about knowing His will; it is about **knowing** and **doing** that brings about the blessings of God. The Jews knew His will as it was instructed to them by mouth; it was spoken to them. While the Scriptures were

---

11. Lipscomb 58–59.
12. Arndt, Danker, et al. 536.

The Truth of Who You Should Be!

copied and reproduced by hand, most did not have their own personal copies. However they did learn the Word by having it read to them.

5. **Approve the things that are essential**—*Approve* (δοκιμάζω, *dokimazo*) means to examine, test, or approve. *Essential* (διαφέρω, *diaphero*) means "that which is different or that which is best" either can be referred to. Roper defines this as "the ability to test things that are different."[13] The Law taught that which was important and non-important, right and wrong.

Series of Questions…

1. **Do you not teach yourself?** You hold on to the truth, brag about the truth, claim to know the truth, but refuse to live by it? Refuse to internalize it? Refuse to be transformed by it? It seems their only interest was in telling others what they should do without any interest in how the message would affect their own lives.
2. **Do you steal?** The Law stated, *"You shall not steal"* (Ex. 20:15); however, just as they had not applied the law to themselves, they continued to find ways to "workaround" it in order that they may take what rightfully belonged to others. Prior to Jesus' death, He found that the Jewish leaders had made the Temple *"a robbers' den"* (Mark 11:17). Matthew 12:40 says the Pharisees were *"full of robbery"* as they *"devour widows' houses."* Even grown Jews were robbing their parents of the help and support they should have been given.[14]
3. **Do you commit adultery?** Adultery had become a common practice of the Jews which had corrupted the teaching amongst their people, permitting divorce without reasonable cause. Moses wrote within the Law, *"You shall not commit adultery"* (Ex. 20:14). During the days of Moses, he permitted or allowed them to put away their wives for any cause due to their hardness of hearts (Matt. 19:8). According to J.W. McGarvey, the Jewish Talmud charged some of the celebrated rabbis (teachers) with adultery.[15] This was not an accepted practice or teaching according to Jesus, as stated in Matthew 19:9.
4. **Do you rob temples?**—While it may not be clear how the Jews robbed temples, it seems clear that they were (cf. Acts 19:37). Pagan temples, while storing idols, were also used to store the possessions of the wealthy. Some have proposed that those were some of the treasures which they stole. According to some Jewish writings, some of the idols kept in the temples were stolen by the Jews and stolen for a hefty price to Gentile worshippers (Morris 137). While many scenarios seem to exist, I believe Denny makes it clear to us that this term probably means that they had no problem stealing from pagan temples, thinking it was acceptable since God disapproved of these temples in the first place.
5. **Do you dishonor God?** Denny's opening thought on verse 24 states, "The conduct of the Jews was a horrible reflection upon the character of the God whom they claimed to serve." The inconsistencies of the Jews affected both the vertical and horizontal relationships of their lives. In one minute, we find them boasting about the Law and their connection to it, but then, in the very next minute, we find them breaking unapologetically. Note the entirety of the question, *"Through your breaking the Law, do you dishonor God?"* The simple answer is

---

13. Roper. "The Disobedience of The Jews, Romans 2:17-24." *Truth for Today Commentary, Romans 1–7, A Doctrinal Study.* Searcy: Resource Publications, 2013, 153.
14. Roper 153.
15. McGarvey, J.W., and Philip Y. Pendleton. *Thessalonians, Corinthians, Galatians, and Romans, The Standard Bible Commentary.* Cincinnati: Standard Publishing, n.d., 314; quoted by David Roper, *Truth for Today,* "Romans 1–7," 155-156.

yes! The reality of the situation within the Rome church of Christ was that Jews, in all of their knowledge of the holy Scriptures, should have been teaching and leading the Gentiles closer to God. Instead, they were doing a great job of driving them away.

6. **If the uncircumcised man keeps the requirements of the Law, will not his uncircumcision be regarded as circumcision?** Circumcision is only of value when one **follows the law**. This takes us back to the *"obedience of faith"* that Paul began within 1:5. Physical circumcision was not enough by itself, even under the Law. If you were not living as one obedient in the faith, were you seen as faithful? If one was circumcised but wasn't obedient, they would then be seen as if they weren't circumcised at all. If one, therefore, was circumcised and was obedient, then one could be "seen" as if they were circumcised. This was about the change and obedience of the inner man, not the removal of skin.

7. **He who is physically uncircumcised, if he keeps the Law, will he not judge you who though having the letter of the Law and circumcision are a transgressor of the Law?** Thomas B. Warren wrote regarding this section, "The Jews acted so inconsistently that they caused the holy name of God to be blasphemed (2:24-29). The people of various nations observed the sinful conduct of the Jews and, as a result, blasphemed the true God whom the Jews claimed to serve. The Jews had so many wonderful blessings, but they were neither thankful for those blessings nor active in the life that they should have inferred from those blessings."[16] Again, as in the previous question, obedience to the law of God is the primary objective that the apostle Paul is trying to bring to the forefront of our minds.

STUDY

How do you want to be seen by God? That is the main question that Paul is underscoring here to the Jewish brethren. Let's think back on our **focus statement** for this lesson.

Our decision to walk according to His law will allow God the ability to judge each person according to his deeds. Will our actions and decision-making reflect His way or our own?

We must know and pursue the correct answer to this statement. Throughout time, mankind has done *"what is right in their own eyes"* (cf. Deut. 12:18; Judg. 17:6; 21:25; Prov. 12:15; 21:2), essentially leading his way into trouble. What is right in one's own eye is the way of a fool (Prov. 12:15) and cannot be the desire of a true disciple's life. It just isn't right. When Jesus said, *"Go therefore and make disciples,"* He was telling them to go and find those who are willing to listen and teach them so that they might be taught and grow so that they may teach others. This was the will of a rabbi for a disciple.

A rabbi or teacher dedicates his time to training, teaching, and developing students or disciples to grow into exemplary teachers of the law. However, every rabbi was governed by life. A life that required a beginning and end, a birth and a death—meaning the rabbis didn't live forever. Their disciples would replace them as they grew to a point where they could.

---

16. Warren, Thomas B. "The Need for The Gospel and Its Power, Romans 1:18-3:20." *The Getwell Lectures, The Book of Romans*. Ramar: National Christian Press, 1983, 62.

The Truth of Who You Should Be!

Some may believe unintentionally that the first rabbi was Jesus. After all, the disciples called Him "Rabbi" (cf. Mark 11:21). But this was not the case. Many rabbis existed during, before, and after the days of Jesus. Their purpose was to bring their students along so they, too, would grow to be teachers. This was the effort of Jesus with the twelve He chose. From Peter to Judas, Jesus was interested in their potential.

During the apostles' time with Jesus, He taught, led, encouraged, and was an example for them to follow. Mainly, Jesus showed them how to **walk with God**, for God, and lead others to God through His message, which was revealed to them by the Holy Spirit (John 14:26; 15:26; 16:13; Acts 2:2-4).

Paul wrote in Romans 6:4, *"Therefore we have been buried with Him through baptism into death, so that as Christ was raised from the dead through the glory of the Father, so we too might **walk in newness of life**."* He would later say to the church at Corinth, *"For we **walk by faith**, not by sight"* (2 Cor. 5:7). He wrote to the churches of Galatia and said, *"But I say, **walk by the Spirit**, and you will not carry out the desire of the flesh"* (Gal. 5:16). Then to the Ephesians brethren, he said, *"Therefore I, the prisoner of the Lord, implore you **to walk in a manner worthy of the calling** with which you have been called"* (Eph. 4:1).

The word *walk* is translated as such in the NASB 498x in the NT and is used in several different ways. One is the word στοιχέω (*stoicheo*), which means to hold on, to agree with, or to conform to. It is used in Galatians 5:25 in this way, *"If we live by the Spirit, let us also **walk by the Spirit**."* A second word we find is περιπατέω (*peripateo*) which means to go about, walk around, to behave. Paul used this word in Romans 8:4 saying, *"So that the requirement of the Law might be fulfilled in us, who do not **walk** according to the flesh but according to the Spirit."* A third term that we can find in our New Testaments is the word καταπατέω (*katapateo*), meaning to trample underfoot, as used by Jesus in His Sermon on the Mount. He said in Matthew 5:13, *"You are the salt of the earth; but if the salt has become tasteless, how can it be made salty again? It is no longer good for anything except to be thrown out and **trampled underfoot** by men."* No, we don't see the word *walk* here, but we are able to understand the concept of "walking on" something. Within the context of walking or trampling on the salt, however, this concept can be applied to many things, including Jesus (Heb. 10:29).

Through each of these, we find that there are several ways that one can walk. We can conform to something that brings **transformation**. We can walk according to something, which is a showing of **obedience**. And we can trample over something, which is a blatant **disregard**, in this case, to the teachings of God.

The apostle Peter wrote in 1 Peter 2:21, *"For you have been called for this purpose, since Christ also suffered for you, leaving you an example for you to **follow in His steps**"* (emp. added). The phrase, ἐπακολουθέω ἴχνος, literally means to "follow in steps." According to Peter, contextually, this is a reference to the steps of Jesus. His steps of purpose become your steps of purpose. His steps of suffering become your steps of suffering. His steps as an example become your steps to become an example. All of which leads to the righteous destiny that awaits those who are baptized in Him: His children. **Make no mistake about it:** the walk of a disciple may start as you hear the Word, but your walk doesn't begin until you obey it.

OUR THREE SECTIONS

Section 1: Hypocritical Practices

It seems clear as we look at chapter 2 that Paul is driving home a message of obedience. However, the Jews are anything but. They have become people who look the part but are anything but obedient because of their **hypocritical practices** that we identified within the first section of chapter 2 (vv. 1-10). However, "looking the part" and "living the part" are two very different things. The word ὑποκριτής (*hypokrites*), as you may have heard or read before, carries with it the meaning of an actor or pretender. This is what the Jews had become. They were pretending to be God's chosen people who obeyed the Law to the fullest and, in some sense, on some level, believed it.

It isn't until Paul begins to offend them deep within their core that they even begin to bring down their noses in order to listen to the message he has sent to them. A message from God. Let's connect the dots that Paul is laying out here.
- *"for you who judge, practice the **same things**..."* (2:1)
- *"the judgment of God rightly falls upon those who practice **such things**..."* (2:2)
- *"when you pass judgment on those who practice **such things** and do the **same** yourself..."* (2:3)

Now, let's connect them to chapter 1:
- 1:28—*"And just **as they did not see fit to acknowledge God any longer**, God gave them over to a depraved mind, to do those things which are not proper"* (emp. added).
- 1:32—*"...and **although they know the ordinance of God**, that those who practice such things are worthy of death, they not only do the same, but **also give hearty approval to those who practice them**"* (emp. added).

While we may have gone to the next chapter, we surely have not escaped the context of the letter. Paul charged the Gentiles of being guilty of three types of sins in this order: **idolatry**, **immorality**, and **iniquity**. Now, he is beginning to accuse the Jews of the **same things,** just in the opposite order.[17] A major problem was that the Jews apparently were not taking this judgment on them very seriously, according to verse 4, as they were seemingly taking advantage of God's kindness, tolerance, and patience. It was their own hypocritical actions that were driving the anger of God towards them and their unrepentant hearts. Instead of storing up treasures in Heaven (Matt. 6:20), they were storing up for themselves the wrath of God, which will be righteously given on the day of reckoning.

There are great dangers with this type of behavior, not just for the Jews in Rome but for us today. It is one thing to look the part, but it is also another thing to be the part. Can God see through us like He saw through them? Yes. Does He see if we are doing the **same things** as the people around us who live in the world? Yes. Are the people of chapter 2 any different from our people today? Maybe not as much as we would like to think.

---

17. Roper 155.

The Truth of Who You Should Be!

If we act godly but then live worldly, does the world not see who we really are? Does it drive them away from God like the Jews seemed to do to the Gentiles? God isn't looking for hypocritical people; He desires authentic people who strive to serve Him in a manner of obedience from the heart due to a changed inner man. Saying one thing and doing another is a sure way to place you in the line of danger.

Section 2: The Laws of Man

Let's remember that there are three laws to reference here: the Law of Moses, the law of conscience, and the law of Christ. These are discussed in this section (vv. 11-16). The **laws of man** is a significant topic because they are what a man is to live by (understand *man* as all people or mankind).

While reading this section, it might become confusing as to what Paul is discussing. Many have argued whether this is all about the Law of Moses or not, mainly because when we see the term *Law* or *the Law*, we mainly think about the Law of Moses, which in many cases would be correct. However, here, that isn't always the case.

We must remember that while a word may have a particular definition, that doesn't always mean a particular word will always have that same definition. A word's meaning is defined by its context ALWAYS. Here, this concept is the same way. While the term *the Law* or *Law* in many cases might be referencing the Law of Moses, that doesn't mean that it is always the case here. The context and meaning here are defined in two ways: first, the overall context of the passage, and second, the people who are discussed within the passage.

Romans 2:12 says, *"For all who have sinned without the Law will also perish without the Law, and all who have sinned under the Law will be judged by the Law."* The first thing we need to note is the absence of a definite article within the Greek text, which is the word *the*. The NASB, which is quoted above, translates the definite article in front of the word *Law*.

The Greek reads, Ὅσοι γὰρ **ἀνόμως** ἥμαρτον, **ἀνόμως** καὶ ἀπολοῦνται· καὶ ὅσοι ἐν νόμῳ ἥμαρτον, διὰ **νόμου** κριθήσονται" (Rom. 2:12, SBLGNT). *"For all who have sinned without Law will also perish without Law, and all who have sinned under Law will be judged by Law."*
Reading it from this perspective might allow us to open our minds a little more to the possibility of understanding the immediate and cultural context of the text.

To the Jew, the term *Law* meant the Torah (Genesis–Deuteronomy), which Moses was instructed to write down and was placed by the Ark of the Covenant to remain as a witness against the nation of Israel. The same law that Ezra set his heart to study and teach the people (Ezra 7:10) was a very important part of the Jews' lives.

To a Gentile, the term *law* would have meant something else because they did not keep the Mosaic Law because they were not under it. However, they were to keep the law of conscience or, as some have deemed it, the moral law. While they may not have kept the Sabbath day, they did live by a law of morality that was directed at being honest, caring for other people, and not doing another person wrong. How? The conscience that governs your mind. C.K. Barrett said, "The Gentile is not really outside the sphere of law, though he is, of course, outside the sphere of the law of Moses."[18]

Paul goes on to say in 2:13-14, *"For it is not the hearers of ~~the~~ Law who are just before God, but the doers of ~~the~~ Law will be justified. For when Gentiles who do not have ~~the~~ Law do instinctively the things of **the Law** (of Moses), these, not having the **Law**, are a **law** to themselves"* (strikethroughs mine).

In these verses above, notice that some definite articles are marked out and some are not. The point that Paul is making is this. The Jews were living lives that were a strict, harsh judgment of the Gentiles, but they themselves were guilty of walking down the same path. The Gentiles, Paul says, *"sinned without law"* (i.e., the Law of Moses), and the Jews *"sinned in the law"* (i.e., having the Law of Moses) (2:12). This is why they needed the Gospel message so much. They were the same type of people under two different laws.[19]

THE "UNGODLY" GENTILES	THE "UNRIGHTEOUS" JEWS
They had no excuse for their "ungodliness"...1:20	They had no excuse for their "unrighteousness"...2:1
They were self-deceived in their idolatry...2:21-22	They were self-deceived in their impudence...2:2-3
They ignored God's glory...1:23	They ignored God's goodness...2:4
They had impure hearts...1:24-25	The had impenitent hearts...2:5
They were to be judged unfavorably unless they obeyed the Gospel...1:26-32	They were to be judged unfavorably unless they obeyed the Gospel...2:5b-10

Again, the Gentiles were not under the Law of Moses; rather, they were under the law of morality or conscience. However, they were still under a **law**. The Jews, on the other hand, were not under the law of conscience but rather the Law of Moses, and like the Gentiles while not under a particular law, they were still under **law**. Paul said in regard to the particular law one might be under that they were to be *"doers of the law"* and *"doers of the law will be justified"* (2:13).

Because Gentiles did not have *"the Law,"* Paul says they were a *"law to themselves,"* meaning they **were** under a different law, much like Melchizedek or Jethro. It was this law that was *"written in their hearts,"* as God had instilled attitudes in all men such as honesty, kindness, and integrity (see Denny's notes on 2:14-16). It was in this that they would bring judgment upon themselves as their conscience would bear witness against them, while the Law of Moses would bear witness against its followers (Deut. 31:24-26).

This section ends, however, with a valid point that all need to be aware of and reminded of. The Jew and the Gentile were both in great need of the Gospel of God equally, as they had both

---

18. . Barrett, C.K. *A Commentary on the Epistle to the Romans, Harper's New Testament Commentaries* (N.p.: Harper & Row, 1957; reprint, Peabody: Hendrickson Publishers, 1987, 51; Roper, David. "The Righteous Judgment of God, Romans 2:12-16" *Truth for Today Commentary, Romans 1–7, A Doctrinal Study*. Searcy: Resource Publications, 2013, 145.
19. Winkler, Dan. "Just-If-Ied Never Sinned Despite My Past, Romans 1:18-3:20." *Life-Changing Studies with an Open Bible, Just-If-Ied Never Sinned, A Study of Romans*. Madison: Winkler Publications, 2005, 15.

The Truth of Who You Should Be!

indulged in sinful behavior, which required something more than either of their laws could give them. Salvation. No advantage could be gained by being a Gentile or a Jew for that matter (3:1, 3).

Dan Winkler writes,

> God accepting Gentiles and rejecting Jews generated two potential questions: (a) "Is there any advantage in being a Jew?" and (b) "Has God been unfaithful to His promises relative to the Jews?" (3:1, 3). In responding to the first of these questions, Paul reminded his brethren that they had been the ones to receive "the oracles [lit. "words"] of God" (3:1-2). In responding to the second, Paul reminded them that "unrighteousness demonstrates the righteous of God" in that He has always functioned from the same principle: "Doers of the law will be justified" (2:13). He is, therefore, "righteous" in inflicting His wrath on the Gentiles who violated the written *Code of Morality* (cf. 1:18-32) and on the Jews who violated the written *Commands of Moses* (3:5-6). These Jews were not any "better" than the Gentiles. Both needed the Gospel's redemptive message.[20]

Section 3: Unfaithful Failures

No particular people had possessed the *"oracles of God"* (3:2) like the nation of Israel had. Paul began with the fact they even had the Holy Scriptures, which possessed the message of the Gospel of God, which was promised beforehand. If any people **knew** what the *"will of God"* was, it should have been the Jews. These **unfaithful failures** are in our last section (vv. 17-29).

Every advantage was given to the Jew, five of them listed here (vv. 17-18). They had the name, the law, God, and His Will and could know and understand the things that were essential. This led to the four responsibilities they should have taken on: to guide, be light, correct, and teach. After all, it was the Jews who had the Law (of Moses), which was *"the embodiment of knowledge and of the truth."*

Unfortunately, like so many, while you may be blessed with every opportunity unless you are willing to use the advantages you have, they are nothing more than a waste. In this case, they blew it. They were not focused on who they should be. They were focused on what the Gentiles should be. They were focused on what they should be. They were focused on what the world saw them as—a Jew. The major issue that we see on this side of the paper is this: It no longer mattered if you were a Jew or not. All are one in the eyes of God, for He shows no partiality (2:11). There is no difference.

As a result of the actions and pridefulness of the Jews, the Gentiles regarded Judaism as a "barbarous superstition." They regarded the Jews as the "most disgusting of races" and as "a most contemptible company of slaves."

According to Barclay, the Jews were accused of two special things:

---
20. Winkler 115-16.

First, they were accused of atheism (*atheotes*). It was an odd fact that the ancient world had great difficulty in conceiving of the possibility of any religion without any visible images of worship. Pliny called them "a race distinguished by their contempt for all deities." Tacitus said, "The Jews conceive of their deity as one, by mind alone...Hence, no images are erected in their cities or even in their temples. This reverence is not paid to kings, nor this honor to the Caesars." Juvenal said, "They venerate nothing but the clouds and the deity of the sky." But the truth is that what really moved the Gentile to such dislike was not so much the image worship of the Jews, as the cold contempt in which the Jews held all other religions.

He goes on to say,

Second, they are accused of hatred of their fellow men and complete unsociability. Tacitus said of them, "Among themselves, their honesty is inflexible, their compassion quick to move, but to all other persons, they show the hatred of antagonism." In Alexandria, the story was that the Jews had taken an oath never to show kindness to a Gentile and that they even offered a Greek in sacrifice to their God every year. Tacitus said that the first thing that Gentiles who had been converted to Judaism were taught to do was "to despise the gods, to repudiate their nationality, and to disparage parents, children, and brothers."[21]

Due to their own hypocrisy, pride, and ignorance, Paul asks them a series of questions (reference back to the Series of Questions), which lead them to the point that Paul makes in verse 25. *"For indeed circumcision is of value if you practice the Law; but if you are a transgressor of the Law, your circumcision has become uncircumcision."*

True obedience is not established by physical differences that the Law may have brought about. Rather, it is from the heart of a person as he is led to obey due to his faith.

Let's let Paul close: *"For he is not a Jew who is one outwardly, nor is circumcision that which is outward in the flesh. But he is a Jew who is one inwardly; and circumcision is that which is of the heart, by the Spirit, not by the letter; and his praise is not from men, but from God."*

Let's not allow ourselves to repeat this type of behavior that no doubt leads to the wrath of God. We also, like the Jews, have the Word of God, His will for all people. Let's take advantage of the blessings He had laid before us and live a life of obedience to His will.

---

21. Barclay, William. "The Real Jew, Romans 2:17-29." *The Daily Study Bible, The Letter to the Romans*. Philadelphia: Westminster Press, 1957, 43-45.

The Truth of Who You Should Be!

ACTIVITY

Gather into equal groups where you can sit in a circle, perhaps at a table. Ensure that at least one person has a copy of the worksheet and that everyone else has a piece of paper, pen or pencil, and their Bibles.

During this exercise, each group will be identified as an eldership. It is important that all, no matter male or female, be able to participate in this exercise. This is a pretend eldership to allow everyone to grow as we move through this exercise. Remember, we are simply trying to grow together.

For the activity, you will need to identify one of your group as the spokesperson, as he will be presenting both your findings and results of the case study or studies the "eldership" works through.

Depending on your time and purpose for this exercise, determine how many case studies and which ones each eldership will need to work through. Each case study will have a different situation that will connect with what we have studied thus far in the book of Romans.

Once you have identified which case studies and how many you would like to work through, set an allotted time that the elderships will have to work through the issue.

Eldership Objectives:

1) Read the case study.

2) Discuss the situation as a group to understand it fully.

3) Work to identify Scriptural teachings that either support or go against the situation at hand.

4) You must use at least three principles from the study keys that play a role in the situation.

5) Identify which of the three sections identified in chapter 2 this situation may fall under.

   A. Hypocritical practices—Acting one way and behaving another

   B. Laws of man—Obeying the laws of God or another

   C. Unfaithful failures—Living up to their potential or leading others away from God

4) Identify at least three principles from your study keys which show you as an eldership how to help the situation and the souls of the individuals involved.

5) Name five steps that you will take as an eldership to rectify the problem.

May God bless you in your efforts to grow in this regard!

WORKSHEET

Case Study #1—You have noticed that some people have been uncomfortable around two people whom you have always thought to be very good friends. One day, three families approach another elder and you and ask for a meeting as soon as possible with the eldership. You agree and set the meeting. At the meeting, you learn that these two friends are not just friends. They have been living in a homosexual relationship, which one of the husbands in the room found out by accident through a social media post that was made and a comment that was attached. Through some investigation, he confirmed this was true and now isn't sure what to do. Two of the three families in the room are very angry and want something done right away, and one family isn't sure of what should be done and is fearful of what may happen when they are approached. As of now you are the only group that knows of the situation at hand.

Case Study #2—Tom, one of the men in the congregation, worked hard to convert one of his good friends named Sam. Through a series of studies, answering many questions, and prayer, Sam was successfully converted, baptized into Christ, and is now a member of the church. The following year, Sam became overjoyed by his newfound faith and wanted to know and do more. Tom and Sam took several classes together throughout the year at church and other institutions, conferences, and workshops. While Tom was very knowledgeable in the text, Sam continued to grow excessively, not only in what he came to know but also in his ability to share what he had learned. Same spent many hours studying his Bible every day, grasping for more and more knowledge, until one day he was asked to preach. While nervous, he accepted. When the day came, with the help of Tom, he did very well—so well that he was asked to preach again very soon. Tom eventually found that Sam was gaining opportunities to preach and teach not only in his congregation but also in others, gaining the praise of some very respected people. Tom became very jealous of Sam, saying, "I have been a church member and here for the last 16 years, and I have not been given any of these opportunities! I have been a Christian longer than he has, and I should be looked at first for things like this!" Not only does Tom feel this way, but he also begins telling others, which destroys the relationship between Tom and Sam and leads to Sam's spiritual discouragement.

Case Study #3—One of the families in the congregation is becoming more of a problem with their actions both inside the church and outside. Through a series of events, they begin to attach themselves to certain people in the congregation who are typically more negative than positive. Over time, this group became larger, and you began to hear negative things about the preacher. Eventually, the group became so contentious about the preacher that they began to formulate a plan of how to get him fired. As they begin to build their case, they begin to recruit other individuals and families to join them in their quest. You, as an eldership, are not really seeing what is going on other than a few things you have heard, and you notice that certain people are closer than they once were. You take it as a good thing until the group approaches you. In their meeting with the elders, they bring up a number of false accusations against the preacher, calling for his immediate dismissal with the threat, "If he isn't fired, we are leaving!" You immediately see what has happened here and the division that this family has caused.

The Truth of Who You Should Be!

Case Study #4—A deacon in your congregation has been assigned to be over the worship service to handle the schedule, participants, assignments, etc. He has been doing an excellent job keeping everything in order and ensuring people know what they are doing and when. One day, he calls a meeting with all of the men who have signed up to help for the year to hand out his schedules and other information he might have concerning the worship service itself as they all prepare for the new year. During this time, he begins to talk more and more about how we do things. Such as—the dress attire for each person when serving **must** be a suit and tie; the plate with the bread and tray with the cups must be handed out first to the left and then to the right, the Scripture reading must only be read from one single version and never another, the songs before and after the sermon must be three and two and only a certain number of verses led, the sermon will be 25 minutes exactly, and the closing prayer should be very discrete. As you can imagine, this begins to cause all types of conversations among the men. Some are happy, some are angry, some are not sure of what to think, and a few really don't care. However, it is enough that you are approached by several men who are greatly concerned about his directives.

Keep in mind the Eldership Objectives:

1) Read the case study.
2) Discuss the situation as a group to understand it fully.
3) Work to identify Scriptural teachings that either support or go against the situation at hand.
4) You must use at least three principles from the study keys that play a role in the situation.
5) Identify which of the three sections identified in chapter 2 this situation may fall under.

   A. **Hypocritical practices**—Acting one way and behaving another

   B. **Laws of man**—Obeying the laws of God or another

   C. **Unfaithful failures**—Living up to their potential or leading others away from God

4) Identify at least three principles from your study keys which show you as an eldership how to help the situation and the souls of the individuals involved.
5) Name five steps that you will take as an eldership to rectify the problem.

May God bless you in your efforts to grow in this regard!

Excel Still More Bible Workshop

ANSWER KEY

1) Identify which case study or studies: _____

2) Discuss the situation as a group to understand it fully. Notes:
   _____
   _____
   _____

3) Identify Scriptural teachings that either support or go against the situation at hand.
   _____
   _____
   _____

4) What three principles from the study keys may play a role in the situation and why?
   a) _____
   b) _____
   c) _____

5) Identify which of the three sections identified in chapter 2 this situation may fall under and why.
   _____
   _____
   _____

6) Identify at least three principles from your study keys that will help you as an elder in the situation and the souls of the individuals involved.
   a) _____
   b) _____
   c) _____
   d) _____
   e) _____

7) Name Five Steps that you will take as an eldership to rectify the problem.
   a) Step 1: _____
   b) Step 2: _____
   c) Step 3: _____
   d) Step 4: _____
   e) Step 5: _____

Building
WHAT WE ALL HAVE IN COMMON!

Romans 3

BILLY CLABAUGH

""For all have sinned and fallen short of the glory of God, being justified as a gift by His grace through the redemption which is in Christ Jesus."
- Romans 3:23-24 -

INTRODUCTION

Every person who has reached the stage of accountability in their life has something in common—all have sinned against God. The only exception to that is when God became flesh. The Hebrew writer teaches us that although Jesus was tempted just like any other man, He did not sin: *"For we do not have a high priest who cannot sympathize with our weaknesses, but one who has been tempted in all things as we are, yet without sin"* (Heb. 4:15).

Regardless of religious background or nationality, or whether Jew or Gentile, all people are faced with the same dilemma caused by sin. Every man or woman must come to the proper understanding that that they are under the penalty of sin and in desperate need of salvation.

FOCUS

All the world is accountable to God and there is no reason to boast in law-keeping or in good works. A person can try to earn his way to God, but it will never be enough and will always leave doubt in that person's mind about where he really stands with God. It's not about just doing good works, or a person trying to make himself righteous. Since all have sinned, all are in desperate need of a Savior! Just as Jesus said to His disciples in John 14:6, *"No one comes to the Father, but through Me,"* salvation and righteousness can only come through Jesus. Only by the grace of God is it possible for any person to find salvation and justification from his sins. E.M. Zerr says this about God's grace, "His grace means the grace of God that was offered the world through Christ. The deeds of man could not save upon their virtue, but the favor made possible by the sacrifice of God's Son brought free justification to all who accepted the terms."[1]

Grace is freely given by God through His Son Jesus, but it must be accepted on God's terms. Grace can't be earned, but it cannot be received without devoting oneself to the service of God either. God's grace is accepted by trusting that His Son Jesus is the only solution to the consequences of sin and therefore live a life that honors and pleases the giver of that grace!

Focus Statement: Sin is a real problem for all people, but all people can find victory and hope over their sin through the death, burial, and resurrection of Jesus Christ.

STUDY KEYS

Note: Take some time as you study through chapter 3 to mark each of these words and phrases individually with different color pens, markers, colored pencils, or highlighters of your choice. If possible make notes in your margins to reflect the meanings of these words or phrases that may help you understand the overall context to a better degree.

WORDS OR PHRASES OF IMPORTANCE

- **None righteous**…v. 10
- **All under sin**…vv. 9, 10, 23
- **Justified by faith**…v. 26
- **Righteousness**…vv. 5, 21, 22, 25, 26
- **Faith**…vv. 22, 25, 26, 27, 28, 30, 31
- **Propitiation**…v. 25
- **God is the God of Jews and Gentiles**…v. 29
- **Redemption which is in Christ Jesus**…v. 24

---

1. Zerr, E.M. *Bible Commentary Volume V, Matthew–Romans*. Bowling Green: Guardian of Truth Foundation, 2006, 354.

What We All Have In Common!

STUDY

The apostle Paul in Romans 1 brought out the sin and unrighteousness of the Gentiles and then in chapter 2 he lays the truth before the Jews that some of the same things they were condemning the Gentiles for, they were guilty of themselves. Now in chapter 3, Paul makes it very clear that all, whether Jew or Gentile, are under sin and there is none righteous, no not one (v. 10). Man is unable to justify himself through his works or through the law, but justification only comes through genuine faith in Jesus Christ. He is the justifier of the one who has faith in Him (v. 26b).

God is holy and just and must punish sin, but He has also made it possible for sin to be forgiven. The apostle Paul in Romans 3:25 refers to Jesus as a *"propitiation in His blood through faith."* Jesus was the atonement or the appeasement for the wrath of God against sin. His body that was nailed to the cross and His blood that flowed from His body was the ultimate payment for the sins of the world. Those who believe this great truth and entrust their lives to Jesus by obeying the Gospel no longer need to worry about suffering the eternal punishment they deserve. That's why a person can't afford to place his faith in anyone else other than Jesus. His sacrifice is the one and only sacrifice that God accepted to appease His wrath against the sins of the world. God's grace was given when He sent His own Son to take His wrath for sin that mankind deserved. R.C. Lenski explains it this way, "But how can the just Judge of heaven and earth, without becoming unjust and destroying all justice, follow grace and declare righteous any sinner whose sin cries to heaven for just punishment? Only by one means, the one that perfectly satisfies God's justice and opens the way for His grace: 'through the ransoming, the one connected with Christ Jesus.'"[2]

Connection to Christ or being united with Him in His death is essential to receiving the grace that God has poured out through Jesus. All those who have put on Christ have been ransomed from the despair and the hopelessness of sin. Later in chapter 8 of Romans, Paul would say in verse 1, *"Therefore there is now no condemnation for those who are in Christ Jesus."* It is true that all have sinned and fallen short of the glory of God, but because of the sacrifice freely given on Calvary, all those who are in Christ avoid that condemnation. Instead of condemnation, they find justification by faith in Jesus Christ!

For many Jews in the first century, it may have been difficult for them to believe that a Gentile could be just as much a child of God as they were, but Jesus had broken down all barriers for those who belong to Him.

> *But now in Christ Jesus you who formerly were far off have been brought near by the blood of Christ. For He Himself is our peace, who made both groups into one and broke down the barrier of the dividing wall, by abolishing in His flesh the enmity, which is the Law of commandments contained in ordinances, so that in Himself He might make the two into one new man, thus establishing peace, and might reconcile them both in one body to God through the cross, by it having put to death the enmity* (Eph. 2:13-16).

---

2. Lenski, R.C.H. *Interpretation of St. Paul's Epistle to the Romans.* Minneapolis: Augsburg Publishing House, 1961, 251.

By the blood of Jesus, both Jew and Gentile were made into one new man. He brought peace and reconciled them together into His body! Jesus is the great reconciler and makes it possible for God to be God of all those in Christ. Paul would say He is both the God of the Jews and the God of the Gentiles! Since every man has the same deadly sin problem, regardless of nationality or race, our confidence and boasting must always remain in our God and in His Son Jesus Christ!

Gratitude and thankfulness should be the response to the amazing gift God has given to all men. Paul reminds the saints at Ephesus of their condition before and after Christ:

> *And you were dead in your trespasses and sins, in which you formerly walked according to the course of this world, according to the prince of the power of the air, of the spirit that is now working in the sons of disobedience. Among them we too all formerly lived in the lusts of our flesh, indulging the desires of the flesh and of the mind, and were by nature children of wrath, even as the rest. But God being rich in mercy, because of His great love with which He loved us, even when we were dead in our transgressions, made us alive together with Christ (by grace you have been saved)... (Eph. 2:1-5).*

Being dead or alive spiritually is determined by whether or not a person belongs to Christ. Paul reminds those Ephesian Christians that because God is rich in mercy they had been made alive together with Christ. Although every man has sinned and fallen short of the glory of God, every man has the opportunity to find forgiveness and victory over sin through Jesus! Paul states it as well as anyone could when he says in 1 Corinthians 15:57, *"But thanks be to God, who gives us the victory through our Lord Jesus Christ."*

So even though every man has sin in common, every man as been given a way to conquer that sin, but only through Jesus Christ our Lord and Savior!

What We All Have In Common!

ACTIVITY

1. What does it mean for a person to be under sin? Who is under sin?

2. What are some ways that sin can show up in a person's life?

3. What are some things you are doing to watch for sin in your own life and to not take redemption in Christ for granted?

4. This passage talks about the Jew and Gentile relationship and the fact they both have a sin problem. How does this help us in dealing with sinners or those we are sharing the Gospel with?

5. What is the difference in a life that relies on God's grace and forgiveness and a life that relies on works and trying to earn forgiveness?

6. How can understanding our justification help us have a deeper appreciation for what God has done?

7. What are some ways a person can demonstrate his love and appreciation for justification from his sins?

Building

WHERE DOES RIGHTEOUSNESS COME FROM?

Romans 4

BILLY CLABAUGH

"Without becoming weak in faith he contemplated his own body, now as good as dead since he was about a hundred years old, and the deadness of Sarah's womb; yet, with respect to the promise of God, he did not waver in unbelief but grew strong in faith, giving glory to God, and being fully assured that what God had promised, He was able also to perform. Therefore it was also credited to Him as righteousness."

- Romans 4:19-22 -

INTRODUCTION

Over the last 20 years or so, I have sat at the bedside of many who were nearing the end of their lives. It's always a tremendous comfort when you see people who know their time on this earth is coming to an end and they are looking forward with great hope and an assurance of what is coming. Unfortunately, I've also sat beside those who were worried that they hadn't done enough to go to Heaven. It wasn't that they had been terrible sinners who had lived all their lives for themselves. In fact, it was quite the opposite, some of these people had been members of the church for decades, even leaders in the church who rarely missed a Bible class or worship time, and yet they doubted where they stood with God. Sadly, this can be the case for far too many people who know about Jesus and what He's done. Maybe without even realizing it, they are trusting in their own works for their salvation instead of Jesus Christ and His sacrifice on the cross. Justification from our sins is one of the great blessings of Christianity, but it's not something that any of us can do for ourselves. In Romans 4 Paul is continuing his thought that he started towards the end of chapter 3, that regardless of whether a person was a Jew or Gentile, all people are justified by faith: *"For we maintain that a man is justified by faith apart from works of the Law"* (Rom. 3:28).

FOCUS

In a similar way that Christians today must be careful not to trust in their good works for justification, a Christian with a Jewish background in the days of the apostle Paul needed to be careful not to trust in the Law to be right with God. To get the attention of the Christians in Rome, Paul brings up two of the most revered or admired figures in Jewish religious history to teach from where justification from sins really comes. *Justification* means we are declared righteous, or that we are made right with God.[1] We can now stand right before God because we've been forgiven of our sins and set free from the sin that has separated us from Him. To further make the point that justification is not by our own doing or by observing the Law, beginning in chapter 4 Paul uses Abraham as an example. Most Jews who knew their history would have looked up to Abraham and considered him a great example to follow and a great man of God! But Paul makes the point that Abraham was not justified by the Law. Believe it or not, he was justified before the Law or *"while uncircumcised"* (Rom. 4:10b). Because he believed God, it was credited to him as righteousness (Rom. 4:3, 9). Righteousness was credited to Abraham by faith, long before God ever gave the old Law! Abraham's decision to trust what God said made it possible for God to count Him as righteous. It was Abraham's faith—his complete trust in God and His promises—that led to God counting him as righteous. That means that a Jew couldn't just count on the fact that he was born a Jew or a descendant of Abraham to make him right with God. Just like with Abraham, righteousness comes by faith. The Hebrew writer defines faith by saying: *"Now faith is the assurance of things hoped for, the conviction of things not seen"* (Heb. 11:1).

One of the great examples of Abraham's faith is found in Genesis 22 when God tells Abraham to take his son Isaac up on the mountain to sacrifice him. Even though Abraham may have not understood why God instructed him to kill his promised son, he was committed to obeying God and carrying out God's plan, because of his trust in God. *"By faith Abraham, when he was tested, offered up Isaac, and he who had received the promises was offering up his only begotten son; it was he to whom it was said, 'In Isaac your descendants shall be called.' He considered that God is able to raise people even from the dead, from which he also received him back as a type"* (Heb. 11:17-19).

> Righteousness was credited to Abraham by faith, long before God ever gave the old Law. David also spoke of being credited with righteousness and the blessing of God not counting our sins against us. These two men were certainly not perfect, but both illustrate righteousness comes through a sincere faith in God.

---

1 https://biblehub.com/greek/1344.htm.

Where Does Righteousness Come From?

If Abraham would have had to sacrifice his son Isaac, he had reasoned in his own mind that God could raise him up from the dead. But God stopped Abraham before he had to go through with sacrificing his son, and He provided a ram caught in a thicket to be sacrificed instead of Isaac (Gen. 22:13). One of the most important things about faith is that it will allow us to continue to trust God and believe on His instructions and promises, even if we don't completely understand.

Paul also refers to David, who would have been another important figure in the history of Israel and another man that the Jews would have held in high esteem. David spoke of the blessing it is for a man to whom God credits or imputes righteousness apart from works (Rom. 4:6). David understood that justification had nothing to do with works or a man's merit. Not even the greatest of Jews could earn justification or righteousness before God. But now, anyone—including the Gentile—could be credited with righteousness through faith.

Focus Statement: Righteousness was credited to Abraham by faith, long before God ever gave the old Law. David also spoke of being credited with righteousness and the blessing of God not counting our sins against us (Rom. 4:8; Ps. 32:1-2). These two men were certainly not perfect, but both illustrate righteousness comes through a sincere faith in God.

STUDY KEYS

Note: Take some time as you study through chapter 4 to mark each of these words and phrases individually with different color pens, markers, colored pencils, or highlighters of your choice. If possible make notes in your margins to reflect the meanings of these words or phrases that may help you understand the overall context to a better degree.

WORDS OR PHRASES OF IMPORTANCE

- **Abraham**...vv. 1, 2, 3, 9, 12, 13, 16
- **David**...v. 6
- **Righteousness**...vv. 3, 5, 6, 9, 11, 13, 22,
- **Credited/credits**...vv. 3, 4, 5, 6, 9, 10, 11, 22, 23, 24
- **Believe/believed/believes**...vv. 3, 5, 11, 17, 18, 24
- **Faith**...vv. 5, 9, 11, 12, 13, 14, 16, 19, 20,
- **Blessing**...vv. 6, 8, 9,

---

2 Vine, W.E. "Righteousness." *Vine's Complete Expository Dictionary of New Testament Words*. Nashville: Thomas Nelson Inc, 1996, 535.
3 Vine "Credited." 322.

STUDY

Paul uses Abraham and David in this chapter to illustrate that righteousness cannot be earned, it can only be credited or imputed. In the NASB95 the word *righteousness* is used seven times in Romans 4. *Righteousness* means "the character or quality of being right or just." If a person has been made righteous, they have been made right with God. They are found not guilty of sin and approved in the eyes of God. But it's impossible for us to make ourselves righteous. That can only come through the working power of God. As Paul teaches in Romans 4, righteousness is credited. In the NASB the word *credited* or a form of that word is used at least 10 times in Romans 4. *Credited* means "to reckon, take into account" or metaphorically, "to put down to a person's account."

God has decided that all those who choose to humbly put their faith in Jesus for their salvation, will be credited or counted as righteous. Although we didn't deserve for Him to do it, Jesus took upon Himself the punishment of our sins, to provide us forgiveness. Paul describes it like this in his second letter to the Christians in Corinth: *"He made Him who knew no sin to be sin on our behalf, so that we might become the righteousness of God in Him"* (2 Cor. 5:21). Jesus Christ who lived perfectly while on this earth actually paid the price for the sins of the entire world in order to make it possible for sinners to become righteous! God determined that righteousness comes through obedient faith and not through works of the Law or works of the flesh. Look at the concept in these verses.

- Abraham **served** God and it was credited to him as righteousness (Rom. 4:3).

- But to the one who does not work, but **believes** in Him who justifies the ungodly, his faith is credited as righteousness (Rom. 4:5).

- Just as David also speaks of the **blessing** on the man to whom God credits righteousness apart from works (Rom. 4:6).

Paul points out in these passages that Abraham served and it was credited to him as righteousness. He believed and trusted God and he did not waver. Abraham grew in faith, gave glory to God, and he was fully assured that God would do exactly what he had promised to do (Rom. 4:20-21). Faith that trusts God enough to follow and obey is what God desires from all people. The one who believes in the Lord and believes the Lord is the one who justifies the ungodly, his faith is counted as righteousness. God by His grace provides the means to be made right with Him (righteous), and He reckons us as righteous when we put our faith and trust in Him. Through faith, anyone can be counted as righteous before a holy and just God.

What an amazing thought it is that even though we all are sinners, we all can be made righteous and receive forgiveness from our sins. In Romans 4:6-8, Paul refers to what David says in Psalm 32 regarding the blessing of having sins forgiven: *"How blessed is he whose transgression is forgiven, whose sin is covered! How blessed is the man to whom the LORD does not impute iniquity, and in whose spirit there is no deceit"* (Ps. 32:1-2).

Where Does Righteousness Come From?

David had his share of sin and evidently carried the guilt of sin with him for a time. But he would also come to know the great joy and relief when his sins had been covered. Because of David's faith, God blessed Him by not holding his sin against him and forgiving him.

The gift of standing before God justified and not guilty of sin should motivate every disciple of Jesus to follow Abraham's lead and not waver in belief and trust in God. As we continue to grow strong in faith, we give glory to God being fully assured that what God has promised He will carry out. What a blessing to know that by God's grace, He has found us not guilty of any of our sin because of the redeeming blood of Jesus Christ and His sacrifice offered at the cross!

There is a great day coming when Jesus returns, and when He does there will be no greater blessing than to stand justified before God. It's a day that every blood-bought believer in Jesus Christ can look forward to with great hope and great assurance!

Excel Still More Bible Workshop

ACTIVITY

1. How did Abraham attain righteousness?

2. How does David describe the righteousness which is imputed to man?

3. How is Abraham the father of the uncircumcised who possess faith?

4. In what ways did Abraham demonstrate his faith?

5. In what ways do you demonstrate your faith?

6. What are some things we could foolishly trust in to be justified?

Describe the blessing of a righteous man whose sin the Lord will not take into account:

Building
YOUR POTENTIAL CHOICES

ROMANS 5

GARRETT BERNETHY

"So then as through one transgression there resulted condemnation to all men, even so through one act of righteousness there resulted justification of life to all men. For as through the one man's disobedience the many were made sinners, even so through the obedience of the One the many will be made righteous."
- Romans 5:18-19 -

INTRODUCTION

Romans 5 considers two potential choices with two potential outcomes: spiritual life and spiritual death. Each of these two potential outcomes derives from one of two decisions. The first decision is to be baptized into Christ (Rom. 6:3), allowing you to be reconciled to God (5:10) and justified by His blood (5:9), and second decision would be to live a life of sin outside of Christ, which results in condemnation (5:16) and ends with the reign of death (5:21). Adam, the man through whom sin entered the world, sprouted forth the consequence of spiritual death (5:12), and Christ, the Man through whom one can be saved from the wrath of God (5:9) through the death of His Son (5:10) allowing one to have spiritual life. Paul's point is driven toward those who have already obeyed the Gospel message (Rom. 1:16-17) to help them understand their *justification by faith*, the results of being *reconciled to God*, and what God did to *free them from the result of sin*.

FOCUS

Paul's focus here, as Denny has pointed out in the Learning section of chapter 5, is directed at those who have already become Christians. In other words, one who has been baptized *"into Christ"* (Rom. 6:3) an important variable to this conversation, as only those *"in Christ"* can receive *"every spiritual blessing in the heavenly places"* (Eph. 1:3), which initiates forgiveness (Acts 2:38), frees you from wrath (Rom. 5:9) and gives freedom from sin (Rom. 5:16; 6:20, 23; 8:2; cf. 1 Tim. 5:22), eternal life (John 10:27-28; Rom. 5:21; 1 John 2:25; 5:11), and much much more.

Eternal life is a guarantee; we read in 1 John 5:13 that *"you may know you have eternal life,"* no doubt a favorite passage of many. But is it truly the case that we know? The answer lies within you. Just as Paul was talking to those already *in Christ,* the apostle John was equally talking to those *"in Christ;"* therefore, this was a statement made to those *"in Christ."* This means the **potential** is there for you to have eternal life rather than eternal death. The potential is found in your ability to be ***faithfully obedient*** to the will of God. It's your choice. The word *potential* in English means "an existing in possibility: capable of development into actuality."[1] With this definition, we can see that we are dealing with **what you are capable of** in your walk with or away from the Lord, which leads to what you can receive because of the choices of your life. In chapter 5:17, Paul writes, *"Those who receive the abundance of grace and the gift of righteousness will reign in life."* The word *receive* means the act or action or an instance of receiving.[2] In Greek, the word λαμβάνω (*lambano*) is the action of "getting a hold of something by laying hands on or grasping something., directly or indirectly, by grasping it or taking it in hand."[3]

> Potential is about what you can be and choice is what you decide to do. When your potential and decisions are in line with God's will, great blessings will happen.

In this instance, we are talking about eternal life. Is it possible to say that you have eternal life awaiting you at the end of this life? Again, it has to do with a few things, mainly what you will do with the potential you have. I remember being at football or basketball camps I was a part of as a player or even those that my sons have been a part of as players, and the one thing I have heard and many other parents or coaches have heard about their children or other players is, "They have potential." Potential is what we are looking for, isn't it? Whether in business, a team, or Christianity, the potential of a person is key because it means he or she is capable of being something great!

---

1. "Potential." Merriam-Webster.com Dictionary, *Merriam-Webster*, https://www.merriam-webster.com/dictionary/potential. Accessed 13 Jan. 2025.
2. "Reception." Merriam-Webster.com Dictionary.
3. Arndt, William, Frederick W. Danker, et al., *A Greek-English Lexicon of the New Testament and Other Early Christian Literature*. Chicago: University of Chicago Press, 2000, 583.

Your Potential Choices

Each of us has spiritual potential—did you know that? If you didn't, take a deep breath of realization and let it sink in. You have spiritual potential—to lead, teach, preach, evangelize, and live a life of obedience to God. You can do it! Every one of us can do it! What matters is that every one of us knows it. That we can be what God desires us to be, faithfully obedient (Rom. 1:5; 16:26).

When we live a life of obedience to God, it means that we are living up to our *potential*! In other words, we are living up to what we are capable of, *"walking in the light as He is in the light"* (1 John 1:7), something God has deemed the right way for His children. When we walk in this light and continue to abide or remain in His lighted path, the apostle John states that you can know where you are going and what you will receive: **eternal life**. Unfortunately, I have found that there are many who are just not comfortable with the idea that they can know they have a guarantee to be at home with God. However, that is what Scripture teaches, and we should not be apologetic for that, nor feel bad or uncomfortable with what it says.

Remember, eternal life is not for everyone, even though it is for everyone. I know it's a weird statement that may not make sense. How can something be for everyone and NOT for everyone at the same time? That's where potential comes in, which is what our study in this chapter is about. Our **potential** is to **receive** what God has in store for those who are faithful.

Focus Statement: Potential is about what you can be and choice is what you decide to do. When your potential and decisions are in line with God's will, great blessings will happen.

STUDY KEYS

Note: Take some time as you study through chapter 2 to mark each of these words and phrases individually with different color pens, markers, colored pencils, or highlighters of your choice. If possible, make notes in your margins to reflect the meanings of these words or phrases that may help you understand the overall context to a better degree.

WORDS OR PHRASES OF IMPORTANCE

- **God** (θεός)—vv. 1, 2, 5, 8, 9, 10, 11, 15
- **Faith** (πίστις)—vv. 1, 2
- **Grace** (χάρις)—vv. 2, 15, 17, 20, 21
- **Righteousness/Justified** (δίκη)—vv. 1, 7, 9, 17, 18, 19, 21
- **Law** (νόμος)—vv. 13, 20
- **Christ** (Χριστός)—vv. 1, 6, 8, 11, 15, 17, 21
- **Life** (ζωή)—vv. 10, 17, 18, 21
- **Death** (θάνατος)—vv. 10, 12, 14, 17, 21

Excel Still More Bible Workshop

PAUL'S LISTS

Four Results of Becoming and Living the Christian Life...5:1-4

1. **Peace** with *God*—This is a major result of the reconciliation process that Jesus provides the opportunity for—the ability to no longer be *enemies* of God but rather a friend. Note: This peace is not directed towards man but God.
2. Introduction by *faith* into His **grace**—The word *introduction* (προσαγωγή *prosagoge*)means to *bring into someone's presence*.[4] In secular literature, it was sometimes used for admission with an audience to a great king or even an introduction such as, "I would like to introduce you to...." The introduction to grace was by faith, ["let me introduce you to grace"] which makes it possible to obtain grace otherwise not possible outside of a faith in Christ.
3. *Exalt* in **hope** of the *glory* of God—The word *exult* (καυχάομαι *kauchaomai*), which was translated as *boast* earlier (2:17, 23; 3:27; 4:2) is not geared toward self-pride and the puffing up of one's self, but rather a boasting in what God has done (cf. 1 Cor. 1:31), which leads us to our reason for our exultation—*hope*. Hope saves (Rom. 8:24) and is the one thing that all of mankind is searching for. The possibilities for the future where things are better than our current situation. It is the motivating movement within a man's heart and, as the Hebrew writer proclaimed, *"an anchor of the soul"* (Heb. 6:18-19).
4. *Exult* in our **tribulation**—Many versions translate this *rejoice* (ASV) or *glory* (NKJV). However, we are still dealing with the same word καυχάομαι. Just as we can *boast* about the things that God has done, we can also *boast* about our tribulations (θλῖψις *thilipsis*). The ESV translates this *suffering*. It is the trouble that inflicts distress.[5] Barclay gives a literal definition of "pressure," discussing all the things that press in upon the Christian in life: the pressure of want, need, sorrow, persecution, unpopularity, and loneliness.[6]
    A.   See Denny's Sermon Seed Results of Justification on Romans 5:1-4.

Three Reasons Why We Exult in Tribulation...5:3-4

1. It brings about **perseverance**—The first reason one may exult. Sometimes, the more one goes through, the stronger one gets. James writes that the *"testing of faith produces endurance"* (James 1:3) could it be the same here? That the more pressure you feel from every side, the stronger you get? The word ὑπομονή (*hypomone*) also translated as *endurance* (ESV) or *steadfastness* (ASV) has to do with the idea of overcoming. Therefore, the more tribulations one goes through, the stronger you are to overcome future obstacles and struggles.
2. It brings about **proven character**—A result of one's *perseverance* as they have met their trials head on and—with God's help—have overcome. Now they are "battle-tested" (Roper) faith

---

[4]. Roper, David. "Chapter 5, Peace with God Through Jesus Christ, Romans 5:1-11." *Truth for Today Commentary, Romans 1–7, A Doctrinal Study*. Searcy: Resource Publications, 2013, 321.
[5]. Arndt, Danker, et al. 457.
[6]. Barclay, William. "Romans 5:1-5, At Home with God." *The Daily Bible Study, The Letter to The Romans*, Philiadelphia: The Westminster Press, 1957, 72.

veterans who have faced adversity and pressure from every direction and understand their ability to stand in the face of anything that comes their way. It is the showing of establishment within the heart of a person now displaying the character of a child of God.

3. It brings about **hope**—A result of proven character that shows your ability to stand the test of life's tribulations and now grow in spiritual maturity. Walking with God through our trials gives us a stronger understanding of God's reliability and allows us to set out hope fully in Him. When we do this, our ability to hope in God and His promises will reach new heights every day.

What You Used to Be Outside of Christ...5:6-10

1. **Helpless**—The KJV translates the word ἀσθενής (*asthenes*) as *without strength*. The word gives off the idea of a feeble man, one who has the disease of sin, causing his life to wither away from God and His healing power for the soul. BDAG defines the word in this way: pertaining to suffering from a debilitating illness, *sick,* ill.[7] You may have heard the term, "You can lead a horse to water, but you can't make him drink." The same concept exists here: You cannot help someone who refuses to help himself.
2. **Ungodly**—This is a spiritual condition of one without God outside of Christ, one who lives in the darkness (1 John 1:5-6; cf. Col. 1:13). Denny states it is one saying to God, "I don't want to be like you, I want to be the exact opposite." It is a refusal to worship and a direct attack on the character of God. The ungodly have a dark walk full of lust and pride, deserving of spiritual death.
3. **Sinners**—Paul defines this as being *"separated from Christ,"* which results from sinful lifestyles, bad decisions, and the absence of the blood of Christ (the soul-cleansing agent), failing to be what God intends for us to be. It is the state of a person's soul that has not been brought near to Christ. A sinner is of the world, resulting in him being seen as an enemy of God.
4. **Enemies**—An enemy is defined as being subjected to hostility, hated,[8]—one from an opposing camp, an adversary. C.S. Lewis wrote, "We are not merely imperfect creatures who must be improved; we are... rebels who must lay down our arms."[9] Enemies take part in everything contrary to the opposing force, completely against all they stand for and all they strive to accomplish. In this case, enemies of God are against all the work of the kingdom of God, as they walk in darkness.
   A. See Denny's Sermon Seed: What You Were, What You Are (pg. 41).

What You Are Now in Christ...5:8-10

1. God *"demonstrate"*s His own **love** toward us: The phrase *"His own love"* is unique to God. This love was demonstrated in the death of Jesus, who is His own Son. However, there is

---

7. Arndt, Danker, et al. 142.
8. Arndt, Danker, et al. 419.
9. Lewis, C. S. *The Problem of Pain.* Oxford: N.p., 1940; reprint, New York: MacMillan Publishing Co., 1962, 91. Lewis was an Oxford University agnostic who became a believer in God; Roper 332.

more to it than that. The Father and Son are one as They are part of the Godhead, so as Jesus gave His life on the cross, so did God in the sense that They are one and not separate.[10] This demonstration of love is and was not something that happened one time and only one time, but rather one time for all time (Heb. 10:14). Therefore, this is a continued action of showing love to all the world (John 3:16) daily as He offers His love to all of man. **You are loved in Christ**.

2. Been **justified** by His blood: The word *justification* carries with it a great meaning. The word δικαιόω (*dikaioo*) means to take up a legal cause, *show justice, do justice, or take up a cause*.[11] This is the legal action of doing justice against the sin in our lives. In other words, Jesus took on our cause as we were once enemies of God so He could allow us freedom from judgment. When Jesus died, He invested in those who would accept Him as the Son of God and Savior of the world. The blood investment, if you will, was shed so that it might **wash** (Acts 22:16), **cleanse** (1 John 1:7; cf. Heb. 9:22), **clothe** (Gal. 3:27), **purify** (1 Pet. 1:22), **sanctify** (1 Cor. 6:11; cf. Heb. 10:10), **redeem** (1 Pet. 1:18-19), and **free us from the wrath of God** (Rom. 5:9-10). There truly is power in the blood which, when used, will make you "just-if-Ied never sinned," as Dan Winkler likes to put it.

3. **Saved** from the *wrath* of God: The wrath we receive is our due from the unforgiven sin in our lives. The wrath of God is saved for those who are against the gospel, which Paul defines as *"helpless," "ungodly," "sinners,"* and *"enemies,"* as we have previously described. As we defined in our first Building lesson, the wrath of God is equivalent to the anger of God against all unrighteous acts within a person's life. It invokes the righteous punishment of God given to the ungodly. However, here Paul is describing our ability to be freed from such a punishment. *"In Christ,"* one is brought out of the kingdom of darkness (Col. 1:13) and into His marvelous light (1 Pet. 2:9), allowing us to be seen differently. This, of course, happens when the blood of Christ washes us through baptism (Rom. 6:1-12), which is the only way that a person can *touch* the blood of Christ (Gal. 3:27). Through our obedience to the will of the Father and the *power* of His Gospel (Rom. 1:1, 16), the blood of Christ will save us from the wrath of God and allow us to *receive* the blessings of God through both forgiveness and reconciliation.

4. Having been **reconciled**, we shall be saved by His life. Roper presents two different possibilities of what this means. First, this could refer to the resurrection of Jesus as He was raised from the dead after making an acceptable sacrifice, which allows us to be saved. We can reference chapter 4:25, which emphasizes that Christ was *"raised because of our justification."* A second meaning is that we are saved through the *"sharing of His life"* (Goodspeed). If we note chapter 6:8, *"If we have died with Christ....we shall also live with Him"* (cf. John 14:19). Paul would also say in Galatians 2:20, *"It is no longer I who live, but Christ lives in me."*[12] However, we shouldn't overlook what some have called the commentary verse for Romans 5:10—Hebrews 7:25—which states, *"Therefore He is able also to save forever those who draw near to God through Him since He always lives to make intercession for them."* Truly, our lives could not be saved unless He raised us from the dead, so in this sense, we are saved because He rose from the grave, which seems the likely meaning here. After all, Paul is about to begin speaking about the **spiritual life** we have *"in Christ,"* as He and Adam are compared in terms of what they brought into the world.

---

10. Roper 330-331.
11. Arndt, Danker, et al. 249.
12. Roper 333-334.

Your Potential Choices

The Comparison of Adam and Christ

Adam the man: Upon going back to the book of Genesis, we look back at the first man who ever lived. The molded creation of God from the dust of the ground (cf. Gen. 3:19) became a living human creation which God took great pride in and loved dearly as he was made in His image. However, the deception of the serpent led man to disobey the direct law of God and eat from the Tree of the Knowledge of Good and Evil (Gen. 2:17), which is what created a **divided relationship** between God and man. Thus, sin entered into the newly created world. This introduction of disobedience is the basic function of the ungodly sinner who walks in sin because he has not followed the commands of God. This brought about *spiritual death* for man as he walked in the same way as those before him. However, the sin of Adam is not inherited by those who come after him as some teach, but rather *"because all sinned"* and therefore fall short themselves (Rom. 3:23), producing the same results as those before them: spiritual death away from God. (See Denny's special notes on chapters 5:12-21 in the Learning section). Here, Paul is focusing on what Adam brought into the world beginning in verse 14, which says, *"Nevertheless death reigned from Adam until Moses, even over **those who had not sinned in the likeness of the offense of Adam**, who is a type of Him who was to come"* (emp. added). Here, Paul says, *"Again, who is a type of Him who was to come."* Paul here compares and contrasts Adam's "gift" to the world versus Jesus' "gift." The comparison leads us to look at their place or position. Adam is the physical head of the human family, whereas Christ is the head of the spiritual family (i.e., the church [Col. 1:18]). Both had a great impact upon mankind: Adam's sin in the garden brought **spiritual death** and Jesus' death on the cross brings **spiritual life**. They contrast in this way, "Adam got us into this mess, and Jesus came to get us out" (a quote from Eugene Peterson). We can also note the following texts: 1 Corinthians 15:21-22, 45, 47, 49. In each case, Adam is found on the negative side of the conversation in his impact on the world because sin entered through his disobedience.

Jesus the Man: The gift of Jesus reversed the effect of Adam's sin on the world, a powerful process, action, and result all from the event on the cross and resurrection from the grave. Paul writes that this was planned before the *"foundation of the world"* (Eph. 1:4), which is a great insight into the wisdom of God. Unlike Adam, Jesus is always offered on the positive side of the comparison and contrast between the two. While books upon books could be written on the majesty of Christ, there is a significant detail that we must not forget. Sin is the result of a lack of obedience to the will of God. While this is the case, it doesn't mean that everyone who sins is an inherently bad person whose evil resonates within every detail of his life. That simply isn't the case. There are a lot of good people in the world who are stained with sin. The reality is that Adam himself, along with Eve, of course, did not mean for all of this to happen. If there were ever a mistake that had lasting consequences, it would be this one. I do not believe that we can prove or take from the story that it was Adam's destiny or plan to bring about spiritual death into the world. He made a mistake like so many of us do today. That is why Jesus came to the world, to *"save man from their sin."* Why? Because God loves us, and He knows that just one sin is enough for an eternity of separation. That is not something He ever wanted to happen. Therefore, Jesus came to live and die as a man so that we might have the opportunity to choose something other than eternal death, and that is life. Therefore, Paul says in verses 15-18:

But the free gift is not like the transgression. For if by the transgression of the one the many died, much more did the grace of God and the gift by the grace of the one Man, Jesus Christ, abound to the many. The gift is not like that which came through the one who sinned, for on the one hand, the judgment arose from one transgression resulting in condemnation, but on the other hand, the free gift arose from many transgressions resulting in justification. For if by the transgression of the One, death reigned through the One, much more those who receive the abundance of grace and of the gift of righteousness will reign in life through the One, Jesus Christ. So then as through one transgression there resulted in condemnation to all men, even so through one act of righteousness there resulted in justification of life to all men.

As Jesus rose from the grave, several things happened. First, the Law of Moses was done away (Eph. 2:15; Heb. 8:13; 9:15-18), and a new covenant was made, which Paul says is the *"Gospel"* (Rom. 1:1, 16). Second, we gained a *permanent* High Priest and offering (Heb. 10:10-18). Third, Christ entered a *perfect tabernacle* (Heb. 9:11). Fourth, His blood allowed Him to be the *Mediator* of the New Covenant (Heb. 9:15), which allowed Him to *"bear the sins of many"* in order to bring salvation to those who *"eagerly await Him."* Jesus brought about the gracious gift of God, which is reconciliation and freedom, through the Gospel of God. As the Head of the church, which is His body (Col. 1:18), Jesus offers us spiritual life through His sacrifice as we reenact His **death** (Rom. 6:3), **burial** (Rom. 6:4), and **resurrection** (Rom. 6:5) that we might be *"raised in newness of life"* clothed in Him (Gal. 3:27). We have a clear and clean conscience (1 Pet. 3:21) and are placed within His wonderful kingdom of light (Acts 2:47; Col. 1:13; 1 John 1:7). While Adam brought the introduction of transgression, Jesus brings transformation.

STUDY

Bernard Shaw played the "What If" game shortly before he died. "Mr. Shaw," asked a reporter, "if you could live your life over and be anybody you've known or any person from history, who would you be?" Shaw replied, "I would choose to be the man George Bernard Shaw could have been but never was."[13]

Within our **Focus Statement,** we stated that potential is about what you can be; the choice is what you decide to do, when both are pointed in God's direction, great blessings can happen. As the apostle Paul makes his way through the thought of chapter 5, he is leading us to the options that we have spiritually speaking. Then he reminds us of three things we now have in Christ, so that we do not fail to live up to our spiritual potential in the Lord.

As Paul writes to those *"in Christ,"* the need to remember is of great importance. Let's face it: when we get our minds on other things, we tend to forget or take for granted what we have. Never let it be said that we have done this from a spiritual standpoint. Know what you have. Remember

---

13. Qubein, Nitto R. "Potential." *Sermon Illustrations*, www.sermonillustrations.com/a-z/p/potential.htm. Accessed 15 Jan. 2025.

Your Potential Choices

what Christ has done. Understand the results of your obedience. This is crucial from an eternal perspective.

Let's think about the key verses we began with at the beginning of this study. Romans 5:18-19 says, *"So then as through one transgression there resulted condemnation to all men, even so through one act of righteousness there resulted justification of life to all men. For as through the one man's disobedience the many were made sinners, even so through the obedience of the One the many will be made righteous."*

From our text, let's note the word *result*. In English, the word *result* is defined as a consequence or conclusion. Here, Paul states that the result of one's **transgression** is **condemnation**. In other words, this is what you get if you live a life where transgression/sin (παράπτωμα, *parastomal*) rules over your life. A walk in the darkness, if you will. This, from God's perspective, is spiritually failing to live up to your potential. You see, all men can obey God. All can live for God. No one is exempt from that opportunity; it is simply whether one chooses to do so.

On the other hand, an act of righteousness results in justification. Again, this results from what you get when you live a certain way. If you live for God, you get the blessings of God. In other words, when you are seen as righteous *"in Christ"* in the eyes of God, you can receive eternal life.

Contextually here, however, we are not discussing you and me, but instead Adam and Christ. Through Adams's transgression, condemnation arose, and then through the righteous actions of Jesus, justification came. Therefore, the concept of the sinner and being made righteous are major topics that the "man of potential" will receive due to his decisions. Therefore, man potentially has the opportunity to reign in life if he makes Christ the Lord of his life. Equally so potentially, man can reign in death if he does not. A clear choice one can make. What is yours?

It is important in our study to note that Paul is not driving away people by the things that he is saying. Instead, he is leading the Christians to understand what they have so that they will not forget the potential they have to go down either path—the path of righteousness or the path of disobedience.

No matter which choice one makes, it is genuinely one's choice. I am so thankful, and I know you are too, that we have not inherited the sin of Adam, nor our parents, or any other living being. Unfortunately, some teach that very thing in the doctrine of Calvinism. On the other hand, some teach "universalism," which says that all people will be saved, contradicting the Bible's plan of salvation and doctrinal teaching. Both fail to see the actual teachings of God, which show by both example and doctrine that all people can choose faithfulness or a lack thereof.

Therefore, **potential**, **choice**, and **reception** are certainly three significant points to be examined in one's life:
1. Your *potential* is your capability of spiritual growth, which can be impacted by what you know you now have *in Christ,* such as **peace, grace, hope,** and **tribulation,** which allows you to **persevere, prove your character**, and **grow in your hope**. Your potential is in your capability to live a certain way, be molded by a certain one, and walk a particular walk.

Remember, the potential is about what **you can** be, and God knows **you can** be faithful. **You can** be His child. **You can** be saved. **You can** teach others. **You can** be the spiritual leader in your family and in the church. These are things **you are capable of if you will let yourself grow**, and growth comes from knowing what you now have *"in Christ Jesus"*: justification! Your spiritual potential is about who you can be *"in Him."*

2. Your *choice* is based on knowing that you used to be **helpless**, **ungodly**, **a sinner**, and an **enemy** of God, but now, because you understand the Gospel message and its requirement of faithful obedience and have obeyed the Gospel, you are **loved**, **justified**, **saved**, and **reconciled** to God. These things cultivate growth in your spiritual life and should move you to reach your spiritual goal in being a child of His. The choice is based on knowledge; the more you know, the better you can choose. If all blessings and justification are found *"in Him,"* your choice of Him is an educated one.

3. Your **reception** of grace and the gift of righteousness, which will reign in life, results from a righteous decision. It is the fulfillment of your potential and the way that you— unlike Mr. Shaw in our opening illustration—will not have to or want to say, "I wish I would have been who I never was," but rather, "What I was is who I wanted to be." This is the outcome of no regrets, a result of the blessed and a finish line full of honor. It is a result of an obedient faith, one that makes you forever a child of God. Again, that is what you are striving to live up to be: **a child of God**, nothing more and nothing less—just His.

CHRISTIANS NEED TO UNDERSTAND

First, Their Justification Through Faith

Chapter 5:1 says, *"Therefore, having been justified by faith, we have peace with God through our Lord Jesus Christ."* Here, Paul is not saying that a person is "saved by faith alone" but rather is saved by the results of what his faith has led him to do. This faith he is discussing is a heart faith that leads one to obey from the heart itself. This is a God-approved faith.

Within Scripture, faith is used in a few different ways:
- **Subjectively**: concerning the act of believing (Mark 16:16)
- **Objectively**: concerning that which is believed (Phil. 1:27; Jude 3)
- **Comprehensively**: concerning a faith that obeys (Acts 18:8, 1 Cor. 1:14; cf. John 3:16, 36)[14]

These have to do with understanding faith itself and how it is used, whether translated as belief or faith. On the other hand, it must be understood that faith is essential to salvation (John 3:16-18; Acts 16:30-34; Rom. 5:1). It has the ability to save people as evidenced by Abraham, who expressed and lived within the parameters of an obedient faith (Rom. 4:1-4; Heb. 1:8).

It is important to note that justification results from faith, not the other way around, and not from the works of the Law, as mentioned in chapter 3. It is the result of obedience to the will of the Father in

---

14. Winkler, Dan. "Chapter 4, Just-If-Ied Never Sinned and at Peace with God, Romans 5:1-21." *Life-Changing Studies with an Open Bible, Just-If-Ied Never Sinned, A Study of Romans*, Madison: Winkler Publications, 2005, 32.

following the Gospel, allowing you to be washed by the blood of Christ and therefore justified by His blood (Rom. 5:9). Because of our justification, we can be *"reconciled"* (Rom. 5:10) or *"brought near"* (Eph. 2:13) to God, thus establishing the spiritual family relationship that man once had with God in the early days of Adam, where man and God walked together (cf. Rev. 21:3, 7).

Faith is subjective in the fact that we must live faithfully to the Lord (cf. Heb. 11:1, 6) day by day as we walk in the light. Walking in the light is a continuous action of choosing to have Him in our lives through each moment of every day.

Faith is objective. As we look back at our lives and our current state, we can speak truly to what and who we believe in as we *"strive for faith"* (Phil. 1:27)—faith in the Gospel and faith in the Lord. This is not only a daily walk but also a daily decision to believe, to confirm, to contend for. It is not only a thought but an investment of your life, a conviction deep within your heart's roots.

Faith is comprehensive in the fact that it drives you to do; it drives you to obey. This was the case for jailer and his family (Acts 16:22-34), Crispus in Acts 18, and many more as the church was taken throughout the known world. James states that faith without works is dead (James 2:17). Anybody can believe in something, but to act on that belief is faith. That is why I believe that Hebrews 11:2 is so essential to this part of the conversation, *"For by it the men of old gained approval,"* meaning they did things according to verse 1 which they were in the dark about, not knowing the outcome. This can be seen in Moses beginning his journey to release Israel, Abraham living in the land of promise before it was the Promised Land, or even the apostles' journey to take the Gospel into the world. Uncertainty was always at their doorstep, but their faith continued to push them forward.

Second, Their Reconciliation to God

Chapter 5:10 says, *"For if while we were enemies we were reconciled to God through the death of His Son, much more, having been reconciled, we shall be saved by His life."* Of interest, this is the first time that the word *reconcile* (καταλλάσσω *katallasso*) is introduced in the letter to the Romans. First, Paul said that we were *justified* in Christ; now, he says we are *reconciled*. According to Roper, these words cannot be separated as they both refer to becoming a child of God. However, both give us added insights into what the Lord has done for us.

The word καταλλάσσω denotes the exchange of hostility for a friendly relationship.[15] It has been said that a good simple definition of this is simply, "to be friends again." This is where Paul gives a good definition within the Ephesians letter, when he wrote, *"Remember that you were at that time separate from Christ, excluded from the commonwealth of Israel, and strangers to the covenants of promise, having no hope and without God in the world. But now in Christ Jesus you who formerly were far off have been brought near by the blood of Christ"* (Eph. 2:12-13).

---

15. Arndt, Danker, et al. 521.

The context here refers to the Gentile brethren and the Jewish brethren all being brought together. However, the meaning is the same. Those outside of Christ have now been brought inside of Christ, as they now have the blood of Christ.

Those reconciled are now a part of the family of God. It was never God's intention nor goal to separate man from Himself, but rather, man did that through the actions of the man Adam. Therefore, God carried out His desire through Jesus to bring man back to Himself (2 Cor. 5:20).

Paul would write in his inspired second letter to the Corinthians (2 Cor. 5:18-21) and say:

> *Now all these things are from God, who reconciled us to Himself through Christ and gave us the ministry of reconciliation, namely, that God was in Christ reconciling the world to Himself, not counting their trespasses against them, and He has committed to us the word of reconciliation. Therefore, we are ambassadors for Christ, as though God were making an appeal through us; we beg you on behalf of Christ, be reconciled to God. He made Him who knew no sin to be sin on our behalf, so that we might become the righteousness of God in Him.*

Our obedience to the Gospel is what allows us to be added into the body (Acts 2:38, 41, 47) in one body through the cross (Eph. 2:16), which is the church (Eph. 1:22, 23). When you are added to the family, Paul says you become **sons of God** (Rom. 8:14, 19) receiving a spirit of **adoption** (vv. 15, 23), **children of God** (vv. 16, 21), **heirs of God** (v. 17), and **fellow heirs with Christ** (v. 17). What does this mean? God is your Father; we are all His children, heirs **with** Christ.

Just like the father who waited for his son to come home after the son squandered all he had, so does God. When the son came back, the father loved, accepted, celebrated, forgave, clothed, fed, and adored him because his son was now home. They could now be a family again. This is the will of the Father for you to come home as a part of the family!

Third, Their Freedom from the Result of Sin

We all love the idea of freedom! In fact, if you are a movie buff, you probably hear the words of Mel Gibson in the movie *Braveheart* every time it's mentioned. To be freed from something is to not be bound to it anymore. In other words, it has no grip on you and no strength to hold you back—the very thing that sin is able to do—hold you back from a life with God.

Sin is a stain (2 Pet. 2:13) upon the soul. It is the blemish that makes you unpleasant to the eye of God and what makes it impossible for the relationship to stand (1 John 1:5). The unfortunate situation for Adam was that he decided to walk in the mess of sin, and the blessing of Christ is that He established a way for you to get out of it. There, Paul says that you were *washed* (1 Cor. 6:11) and therefore clean so that you might be presented without spot or blemish (Eph. 5:27).

Your Potential Choices

With no sin to hold you back, you may step into the realm of righteousness as a part of the family of God. That is why Paul writes, *"The gift is not like that which came through the one who sinned; for on the one hand the judgment arose from one transgression resulting in condemnation, but on the other hand the **free gift arose from many transgressions resulting in justification**"* (Rom. 5:16, emp. added)

Later in his letter to Timothy, he tells Timothy to *"keep yourself free from sin"* (1 Tim. 5:22), which expresses his current state of freedom. Within this freed state, you are blessed. However, if we are not careful, it is something that we may lose. You see, the freedom we have is a result of grace, something we can gain and something we can lose (Gal. 5:4). It has been said the most dangerous time within a person's life is when he has the ability to do as he chooses.

What a person must remember is what he gains from being in Christ and His purpose for him. The life of a disciple is not one of self-service but rather the serving of self to others. This was shown in all of its beauty when Jesus washed the feet of the disciples (John 13:5). While our freedom may not cost us anything financially (in most cases), our spiritual freedom certainly did cost something in order for us to have it—paid by the blood of Jesus.

All these things play into our **spiritual potential** as we strive to receive the blessings of God. Remember, the potential is about what you can be; the choice is what you decide to do; when both are pointed in God's direction, great blessings can happen.

ACTIVITY

This activity can be done as a group or individually. Each person will need a copy of the worksheet, something to write with, and his/her Bible.

The goal of this activity is on a more personal level as we think about our spiritual development and the potential we have spiritually within our lives.

Know Our Three Points of Examination:
1. **Potential**—What you are capable of.
2. **Choice**—What you decide to do.
3. **Reception**—What you receive in the end.

Each person will need to answer the questions given on the worksheet. Once they are done, the class or group leader will begin asking people to share their answers as you go down through the questions on the page. After each of the answers to the question, add in some discussion around some possibilities for the answer and things that could help that person and others grow as you begin to ***think together***.

Excel Still More Bible Workshop

Remember, while this activity is for people to think about themselves and give their answers, it is equally an activity that can help others who may be going through or dealing with the same things. We oftentimes go through similar situations at different times of our lives, but unfortunately, we are not very good at discussing them.

Through the discussion, we can offer practical advice or helpful thoughts to help each other grow spiritually—to be encouraged to move forward and reach his/her spiritual potential. When we grow stronger individually, the group naturally becomes stronger for it.

While working through each question, be sure to implement what we have learned from Paul's Lists, Reasons, and Results to help you answer your questions:

Four Ways a Christian Life Is Impacted	Three Reasons Why We Exult in Tribulations	What We Were Outside of Christ	What We Are now in Christ
Peace	Perseverance	Helpless	Loved
Grace	Proven Character	Ungodly	Justified
Hope	Hope	Sinners	Saved
Tribulation		Enemies	Reconciled

You will also need to have in mind and look back on our Study Keys to help you think about the different aspects of Paul's discussion and how they might pertain to your own life.

WORKSHEET

1. List three things you are thankful for from a spiritual standpoint.

2. Why are you thankful for them?

3. List three of the greatest struggles in your life. (Personal, sinful, emotional, etc...)

Your Potential Choices

4. For each listed above, why are they a struggle for you, and what do you believe continues to connect you with them?

5. Using your Study Keys, pick three things you believe apply to you based on how you feel spiritually now, based on your previous answers.

6. According to Romans 5, what are some ways that you believe you can begin overcoming these struggles based on what you know you have in Christ?

7. What do you believe your spiritual potential is?

8. Do you believe truthfully that your choices reflect what you're capable of?

9. Will what you receive be a product of Adam or Christ from an eternal perspective based on your answers above?

10. What do you believe you need to work on the most? Perseverance, personal character, or hope? Why?

Building

SIN, DEATH LIFE

ROMANS 6

GARRETT BERNETHY

"Now if we have died with Christ, we believe that we shall also live with Him, knowing that Christ, having been raised from the dead, is never to die again; death no longer is master over Him. For the death that He died, He died to sin once for all; but the life that He lives, He lives to God. Even so consider yourselves to be dead to sin, but alive to God in Christ Jesus."
- Romans 6:8-11 -

INTRODUCTION

After Adam's sin, the man had a significant problem due to the great divide of sin that now existed in his relationship to God. Because of man's sin, God could no longer have the connection with him that He once did. When we think about Adam and Eve's sin, we often only see that Adam and Eve were cast from the garden and punished (Gen. 3:24). But have we ever thought about things from God's perspective? You see, ever since that moment, the plan created before the world began (Eph. 1:4) was put into play. It was a plan of grace that would allow mankind to live under something that would not condemn them but rather save them. In chapter 6, three words represent significant realities for both those who strive to obey the Lord and for those who do not: sin, death, and life. In this lesson we will be looking at both the positive and negative sides of these three words: *sin*, *death*, and *life*.

Excel Still More Bible Workshop

FOCUS

The focus of Paul's letter is still on basically two things. His first focus is the opportunity that one has to gain *"eternal life"* from a spiritual standpoint by obeying the *"Gospel of God"* (1:1) to be *"raised in newness of life"* (6:4) and *"freed from sin"* (6:7). Second, he focuses on the choice to live a life of sin, resulting in spiritual death (6:23) which lasts for all of eternity. Each person must make a decision about how he or she will live here on this earth and that decision will have eternal consequences. Is it possible for a person to reach one and not the other? Absolutely! It is a guarantee that you will obtain one of these outcomes depending on how you live your life, your connection to God, and your spiritual state.

We must remember that in Romans 6, Paul is directly talking to those who have already become Christians (a name used three times in the text [Acts 11:26; 26:28; 1 Pet. 4:16]), now known as *"saints"* (1:7) as they are *"beloved of God."* However, these terms do not define them from a physical standpoint as your own name might. Instead, the terms *Christian* (originally a derogatory term for those who followed Christ), *saint,* or even *disciple* are descriptive terms that define the Lord's spiritual understanding of you and how He sees your soul. This is an important fact. Many claim to be a follower of God, yet their lives do not reflect that claim. What you are and how God sees you must line up with Scripture! If they do not, the results will be catastrophic.

One of the main topics in the chapter is baptism. In the book of Acts, we find that upon obeying the Gospel and being *"baptized for the forgiveness of sins"* (Acts 2:38), many were *"added"* (Acts 2:47) to the body of Christ (Gal. 3:27). According to the apostle Paul, this very act of baptism *"washed away...sins, calling on the name of the Lord"* (Acts 22:16). According to the New Testament, this was and still is an essential piece of the Gospel message that must not be overlooked! If overlooked, eternal failure is certain. As Denny stated in his notes in chapter 6:4, the only way one may be united with Christ and placed within His body is through the act of baptism! There is NO OTHER WAY!

The reason one must be baptized is very simple: sin! From the beginning, sin is the one thing that separated man from God. Why? Because sin represents the results of disobedience within a person's heart that pushes him to commit acts of unrighteousness in his life. We read in 1 John 3:4, *"Everyone who practices sin also practices lawlessness; sin is lawlessness."* Mark writes in Mark 3:29 that sin has eternal consequences. Paul states here in chapter 6:23 that *"the wages of sin are death,"* and John says in his epistle that *"sin is unrighteousness"* (1 John 5:17). The Bible makes clear God's stance on sin, and there is no mistaking the outcome of such an act.

However, while not every sin that has ever been committed was done with evil intentions, sin is sin, even if done in ignorance. Remember, Moses said that the Law would remain there as a *"witness against you"* (Deut. 31:24-27), which means it simply lies and waits for the opportunity to condemn. That is what the law does—it condemns. So when God's laws are broken, sin is the outcome of the action, and separation is the consequence. The problem is, and always has been, that the *Law* could do nothing else. It simply has no way to save but only to condemn and judge. However, *"in Christ,"* God has caused grace to come to you who believe and are baptized (Mark

Sin, Death, Life

16:16), which brings salvation. Therefore, where sin is in your life, God has caused grace to enter in and dismiss sin in Christ.

Notice the term *in Christ*. That is where grace is found. The only place the grace of God can be accessed is through the blood of Jesus. While the law requires perfection, grace requires obedience to a pattern, which is why God can forgive one's sins under the grace found in Christ (6:14). Thus, the one who is baptized has received the grace of God and is therefore *"freed from sin"* (6:7, 18, 22). At the close of the chapter, Paul says, *"For the wages of sin is death, but the free gift of God is eternal life in Christ Jesus our Lord"* (6:23). That statement connects us back to the end of chapter 5, where Paul states, *"The Law came in so that the transgression would increase; but where sin increased, grace abounded all the more, so that, as sin reigned in death, even so grace would reign through righteousness to eternal life **through Jesus Christ our Lord**"* (5:20-21, emp. added).

> The words sin, death, and life represent the path once must take to become a child of God and access grace, which can only be found in Christ Jesus.

This simply means, as Paul states, *"If we have died with Christ, we believe that we shall live with Him"* (6:8). But how can one die and then live? If we think about our previous studies, we must remember that **spiritual death and life** are our matters of discussion, the eternal state of the soul. Where **sin** has accrued, **death** must occur so that **life** may be found. **Sin** is something we have done through acts of disobedience. **Death** is the wages of sin. God gives **life** to those who spiritually die to the person they once were, as they have now become children of God (Rom. 6:3, 4, 5), being *"raised in newness of life"* (6:4).

Focus Statement: The words *sin, death,* and *life* represent the path one must take to become a child of God to access grace, which can only be found in Christ Jesus.

STUDY KEYS

Note: Take some time as you study through chapter 6 to mark each of these words and phrases individually with different color pens, markers, colored pencils, or highlighters of your choice. If possible, make notes in your margins to reflect the meanings of these words or phrases that may help you better understand the overall context.

WORDS OR PHRASES OF IMPORTANCE

- **God** (θεός)—vv. 10, 11, 13, 17, 22, 23
- **Christ** (Χριστός)—vv. 3, 4, 8, 9, 11, 23
- **Grace** (χάρις)—vv. 1, 14, 15
- **Death** (θάνατον)—vv. 3, 4, 5, 9, 10, 16, 21, 23

- **Life** (ζωή)—vv. 4, 10, 22, 23
- **Sin** (ἁμαρτία)—vv. 1, 2, 6, 7, 10, 11, 12, 13, 14, 15, 16, 17, 18, 20, 22, 23
- **Righteousness** (δικαιοσύνης)—vv. 13, 16, 18, 19, 20

PAUL'S STATEMENTS, QUESTIONS, AND POINTS

Three Questions

1. **Are we to continue in sin so that grace may increase?** Two words of importance exist in this question—the words *sin* and *grace*. The word *sin* (ἁμαρτία, *hamartia*) is discussing an offense, a departure from either human or divine standards of uprightness.[1] The second word *grace* (χάρις, *charis*), according to Vine, *causes a favorable regard* which has to do with God's redemptive mercy.[2] Each of these represents a positive and negative within a person's life. Sin is the negative, a result of lawlessness, which leads to eternal death. Grace is the positive, which results from being washed by the blood of Jesus, transferring you to the kingdom of light (Col. 1:13). While one may exist to dismiss the other (grace over sin), God did not model His Gospel for people to do more wrong so that He could make them more right. Rather, the model and pattern of the Gospel are for the purpose of releasing one from sin, no matter how much they may have. Where sin has increased, so will the grace of God, meaning there is nothing grace cannot cover for one *"walking in the light"* (1 John 1:7). However, we cannot overlook another word of importance here—the word *continue* (ἐπιμένω, *epimeno*)—which suggests, as Dan Winkler puts it, a "continuing to continue" in sin after conversion.[3] According to the major theme of the Bible, faithful obedience to the will of God is a required command, which means that to walk in His path, one must obey His will, not having a lifestyle of disobedience and "dark walking," as this is contrary to who God is and who His children are supposed to be. One cannot continue to live a life of sin and expect to be given the grace of God (cf. Gal. 5:4). Grace is given to those who have been *"baptized into Christ"* and live a transformed life.

2. **How shall we who die to sin still live in it?** When one has *"died to sin,"* they are at that time *"justified by grace,"* which has come through a person's faith. It is this that separates us from our past sins. When one is dead to something, they are no longer bound to its consequence. Remember that when people are baptized, they have died to their old self, leaving that person behind, and now they are committed to the Lord as they have repented from all their old ways. The word *repent* has been defined by several as "to change the way one thinks" regarding who they are, how they do things, and the things they do (Note: BDAG, change one's mind).[4] Can a person go on living the same life he did before conversion? Paul says, No! There must be a conforming to the will of God and a transformation by *"the renewal of your mind so that you*

---

1. Arndt, William, Frederick W. Danker, et al. *A Greek-English Lexicon of the New Testament and Other Early Christian Literature*. Chicago: University of Chicago Press, 2000, 50.
2. Vine, W E. "Grace." *Vine's Concise Dictionary of the Bible*. Nashville: Thomas Nelson, 2005, 162.
3. Winkler, Dan. "Just-If-Ied Never Sinned and Determined to Stay That Way." *Life-Changing Studies with an Open Bible, Just-If-Ied Never Sinned, A Study of Romans*. Madison: Winkler Publications, 2005, 37.
4. Arndt, Danker, et al. 640.

Sin, Death, Life

may prove what the will of God is, that which is good, acceptable, and perfect" (Rom. 12:2). One must think of it from this perspective. When Jesus called His twelve, He said, *"Follow Me, and I will make you fishers of men"* (Matt. 4:19). Jesus was their rabbi (cf. Matt. 26:25), and they were His disciples (cf. Matt. 8:23). A disciple's entire goal is to become like the rabbi (teacher) to be and become like Him. If we are called to be disciples of Christ (cf. Matt. 28:18-20), then are we not to do the same? Jesus did not live a life of sin but a life of righteousness. While Paul is NOT saying that the Christian cannot sin or won't sin, a sinful lifestyle is both contrary and inconsistent with one's new status of *"being dead to sin."* One cannot live a life of sin purposefully and expect to be rewarded with His righteous sanctification in the end.

3. **Do you not know that all of us who have been baptized into Christ Jesus have been baptized into His death?** It is important to note that Paul and those he is writing to, including who Barclay has called "the objector," are all on the same playing field. All needed Jesus. All needed to have their sins washed away (Acts 22:16). Therefore, Paul used the word *us*, including both him and those *"who have been baptized into Christ."* What a noteworthy statement that shows this was a **universally understood act of obedience to the Gospel message!** F.F. Bruce wrote, "From this and other references to baptism in Paul's writings, it is plain that he did not regard baptism as an 'optional extra' in the Christian life."[5] Before both Paul and those in Rome were baptized, they were "outside of Christ" as they had NOT been *"baptized into Christ."* Baptism "ushered the candidate into the death of Jesus and into the benefits of His death."[6] One cannot pass from one life into another physically or spiritually unless one dies first. To be baptized into the death of Jesus allows you to gain a personal relationship with Him as you are in Him, and He is in you. William Barclay illustrated it in this way, "We cannot live our physical life unless we are in the air, and the air is in us. It is so with Christ. Unless we are in Christ, and Christ is in us, we cannot live the life of God."[7] Therefore, to be baptized *"into Christ"* and *"into His death"* is to join Jesus in the grave. He died because of our state of being *"dead in sin"* (Eph. 2:1, 12) so that we could die *"old self was crucified with Him"* (6:6). Therefore, as Denny states, "It is clear that Paul wants our physical act of immersion (burial) to establish a spiritual link to the death, burial, and resurrection of Christ" (See Denny's notes on Romans 6:5). Therefore everything we have done and who we have been outside is buried and dead in the grave.

Statements About Death

- **Baptized into His death** (6:3): As stated previously, when a person is baptized into the death of Christ you have died to sin because you have died with Christ, thus participating in Jesus' death and its results.
- **Buried with Him in baptism through death** (6:4): A declaration of the union one has with Christ's death, in the momentary burial of your body in the watery grave. We must remember

---

5. Roper, David L. "Having Died, We Live, Romans 6." *Truth for Today Commentary, Romans 1–7, A Doctrinal Study*. Searcy: Resource Publications, 201, 377.
6. Jackson, Wayne. "Romans Chapter 6:3-11, Baptism: The Point of Transition." *A New Testament Commentary, Third Addition*. Jackson: Christian Courier Publications, 2012, 297.
7. Barclay, William. "Dying to Live, Romans 6:1-11." *The Daily Study Bible, The Letter to the Romans*. Philadelphia: The Westminster Press, 1957, 86.

that baptism is an act of memorial and reenactment of what Jesus has done on our behalf, thus, when we are completely immersed under water (i.e., buried, cf. Col. 2:12), sin ceases ALL contact with us as we are united with Him and dedicated to God. William Sanday wrote, "Baptism is a double function. (1) It brings the Christian into personal contact with Christ, so close that it may be fitly described as union with Him. (2) It expresses symbolically a series of acts corresponding to the redeeming acts of Christ. Immersion = Death. Submersion = Burial (the ratification of death). Emergence = Resurrection. All of these the Christian must undergo in a moral and spiritual sense."[8]

- **United with Him in the likeness of His death** (6:5): The term *united* (σύμφυτος, *symphytos*) carries with it the idea of growing together, or more literally defined as *identified with* (BDAG) or closely *united* to:—planted together.[9] The KJV uses the term *planted together* to which Roper suggests the idea of Paul comparing the concept of *being immersed in* water to the planting of a seed in the earth. The seed must die in order for new life to come forth (cf. John 12:24; 1 Cor. 15:36).[10]

- **He who has died is freed from sin** (6:7): The term *"freed from sin"* is used both here and in verses 18 and 21. The term *freed* (δικαιόω, *dikaioo*) is also translated as *justify* or *justified* as one has NOT been found guilty in a court of law. The death that we have died in the *"watery grave"* of baptism has thus *"set us free"* from sin. In fact, rabbis taught that death cancels out obligations. Where there is death, there is no more obligation as those who were slaves of sin have been set free from their master. Sin no longer has reign over you.

- **If we have died with Christ** (6:8): The term *if* is a marker of a condition, existing in fact,[11] referencing the reenactment of the baptism burial, dying with Christ to sin. Therefore, "if" you have done this, Paul states that *"we believe that we shall also live with Him."* Thus, we establish the fact that one must die a spiritual death in order that he may have spiritual life in Christ.

- **Raised from the dead, never to die again** (6:9): When Lazarus was raised from the dead by Jesus (John 11:1-46), he went on to live his life, only to die again a physical death. Others would experience this, too. However, when Jesus rose from the grave (Matt. 28:6; Mark 16:6; Luke 24:6; John 19:1-9), He rose to never die again (cf. Rev. 1:18) as *"death no longer is master over Him."* Jesus is alive and will forever be (cf. 1 Cor. 15:1-19; cf. Heb. 7:17, 24; 13:8; 1 Pet. 4:11; Rev. 11:15). When Jesus came to earth, He *"came in the likeness of men"* (Phil. 2:7), John states that He became flesh (John 1:14) like you and me, which means that His body was governed by the laws of life. Paul says, *"Being found in appearance as a man, He humbled Himself by becoming obedient to the point of death, even death on a cross"* (Phil. 2:8). The purpose of this was so that He could be a mediator of a New Covenant (Heb. 10:15). While Jesus had to die, equally He had to be raised, and He was! Therefore, death is over for Jesus, who rose from the grave, and for the Christian who will rise with Him.

---

8. Lipscomb, David. "The Reign of Grace Affords no Encouragement to Sin, Romans 6:1-14." *A Commentary of the New Testament Epistles, Romans*, Nashville: Gospel Advocate Co., 1967, 116.
9. Strong, James, *A Concise Dictionary of the Words in the Greek Testament and the Hebrew Bible*. Bellingham: Logos Bible Software, 2009, 68.
10. Roper 381.
11. Arndt, Danker, et al. 277.

Sin, Death, Life

- **Death no longer has master over Him** (6:9): The power of death to touch Him is no more. While He did die, the power of death could not hold Him! Rev. 1:17-18 says, *"Do not be afraid; I am the first and the last, and the living One; and **I was dead, and behold, I am alive forevermore, and I have the keys of death and of Hades**"* (emp. added). Where death was once master, now **He** is!
- **The death that He died** (6:10): The death of Jesus was an intentional, on-purpose death because it was a part of the eternal plan of redemption (Eph. 1:3-14). So the death that He died, according to Hebrews, was for the purpose of offering (Heb. 10:10) in order that it may take away sins. His death was the ONE and ONLY sacrifice that was needed on behalf of mankind. It is worthy to note the words of John the Immerser who said, *"Behold, the Lamb of God who takes away the sin of the world"* (John 1:29).
- **He died to sin once and for all** (6:10). Again, we note Hebrews 10:10, *"By this will we have been sanctified through the offering of the body of Jesus Christ once and for all."* It was His act on the cross that dealt with sin. His death was so powerful and meaningful that it only took one time for Him to do it, unlike the daily sacrifices offered under the Old Covenant (Heb. 10:11). The blood of bulls and goats was of no comparison to His ultimate act of selflessness. While other sacrifices would be made on behalf of one or some, His was for all of mankind for all time (Heb. 9:24-28)!
- **Dead to sin** (6:11): As Paul writes, he is discussing two important truths. First, you in Christ are **dead to sin,** meaning, as we have discussed, it no longer is master over us as it is no longer master over Jesus. Secondly, you are *"alive to God in Christ Jesus."* God is our NEW Master, as Jesus has made it so, creating the opportunity for the believer and God to be unified through His and your resurrection from the grave. Christ is with us and we are in Him.
- **Alive from the dead** (6:13): Wayne Jackson writes, "Following his conversion, the child of God is to refrain from letting sin 'reign' in his body, yielding to the carnal desires thereof. His bodily members are not to be used as instruments of unrighteousness. Instead, he is to present his body as 'alive' in contrast to his former 'dead' state (i.e., separated from God) using his body to the glory of God."[12] Paul is referring to a spiritual state of life as a result of being *"raised in newness of life"* (6:4).
- **Sin resulting in death** (6:16): Within its context, Paul discusses the servant-master relationship, whether one is a servant of obedience to God or to sin. Obedience to God is righteousness, which leads to eternal life. On the other hand, obedience to sin leads to death—eternal separation from God. Remember, Jesus said, *"Everyone who commits sin is a slave of sin"* (John 8:34). Truly, no one can serve two masters (Matt. 6:24), therefore the option to choose the path is given to everyone. And everyone must make the choice of whom they will serve (cf. Josh. 24:15).
- **The outcome of those things is death** (6:21): We have all experienced that sometimes "Sin looks good!" However, while it may present itself as attractive, it certainly is not. There is nothing good about sin. While it may seem or feel good in the moment, it is nothing but regretful in the end. Therefore, Paul says, what benefit is there from continuing in such acts? If we are living a sinful lifestyle on purpose, the grace of God will not bless us, so why do it? While sin may promise freedom, it most certainly brings about slavery, a prominent teaching in this chapter. Sin brings death because that is the only reward it can offer.

---

12. Jackson 280.

- **The wages of sin is death** (6:23): The only earned reward that sin can give is death, and it has always been that way. So why would we expect anything else? Within the verse however, Paul contrasts this idea with the *"free gift of God,"* which is eternal life **in Christ Jesus our Lord**. Again, the same principle can be applied. While sin has always brought about death, obedience to the will of the Father has always brought about life (6:16). This is the constant. Sin = Death; Obedience = Life. Note the phrase found in verse 17, *"You became obedient from the heart to that form of teaching to which you were committed and having been freed from sin, you became slaves of righteousness."*

The Christian's Conviction

- **DO NOT let sin reign** (6:12): Paul's focus here is on one who one will serve, which we have stated plainly is sin. However, Paul's words are directed toward the evil desires of the flesh, that which tempts and leads to the corruption of the heart. While our bodies do have natural desires as they have been designed, we are still expected to use our bodies to accomplish good things that align with His purpose. However, Satan has used this throughout time (cf. 1 John 2:16) to lure us away from the righteous ways of God to entice us to be instruments of his—we seek to please ourselves as lust sets its grip upon the heart. When this happens, we find great urges that seek to satisfy our own desires, sometimes in perverted ways that are not pleasing to God in the slightest (cf. James 1:14). As Paul knows this about the flesh, he says *"do not let sin reign...."* As Denny states in his notes on chapter 6:12-13, the idea of sinless perfection is not what is being required here but rather not letting sin control us so that we are instruments of unrighteousness. When sin reigns in your mortal body, lust becomes the god of your life, and you will only live to please that lust. Don't let it reign in you.
- **DO NOT go on presenting** (6:13): When one becomes a child of God, his life is supposed to change. Certainly, this may not happen overnight, but a new direction is required. There is no benefit that one may find in a continuation of feeding the desires of the flesh and promoting old sinful lifestyles and behavior in the new life. Therefore, do not go on presenting yourself as an instrument of unrighteousness. That is not who you are anymore. As Denny writes, we must respond to God's gift of grace and salvation by offering ourselves as **instruments** to God, ready to devote the members of our bodies to Him for His use.
- **Sin SHALL NOT be master over you** (6:14): The phrase *shall not* does not mean that you will not sin in your life, but rather, it refers to the mindset that you are determined NOT to sin in your life nor allow it to reign over you. Remember, victory is found in Jesus, not in sinful behaviors and lust. Therefore, we can have freedom from sin when we follow Jesus. This is important as Paul is now thinking about both **grace** and **sanctification**, two things that allow for the sin in our lives to be dismissed as a result of our obedience to the will of the Father. Grace is a result of our faith, which acts in conviction based on what we know to be true. When we act on our faith to obey, grace is the result of our obedience to the Gospel. Sanctification, on the other hand, happens when we dedicate ourselves to righteousness (right behavior). This is what allows us to be "set apart" as we have devoted our lives to Him. It is the result of our acceptance of His rule over our lives to *"cleanse ourselves from all defilement"* (2 Cor. 7:1) and pursue righteousness and peace with both man and God.

Sin, Death, Life

Therefore...

It is good to mark the word *therefore* as it acts as a bridge between what has been said and what will be said. Note the following verses and the context around them.
- 6:4—"***Therefore*** *we have been buried with Him through baptism into death, so that as Christ was raised from the dead through the glory of the Father, so we too might walk in newness of life.*"
- 6:12 —"***Therefore*** *do not let sin reign in your mortal body so that you obey its lusts...*"
- 6:21—"***Therefore*** *what benefit were you then deriving from the things of which you are now ashamed? For the outcome of those things is death.*"

Death, Burial, and Resurrection

While marking in your Bible, make sure to highlight the main point of each verse. Here, Paul uses these three verses to both illustrate and define exactly what one does in the act of being baptized. Death = dying with Jesus to our old self of sin. Burial = to be completely immersed in water, not as a washing of the dirt off the flesh but as an appeal to God for a good conscience (1 Pet. 3:21), i.e. you are buried with Christ in the grave. Resurrection = being raised in *"newness of life"* with and in Christ as you have now been *"clothed in Christ"* (Gal. 3:27).

- 6:3—"*Or do you not know that all of us who have been baptized into Christ Jesus have been baptized into His* ***death****?*"
- 6:4—"*Therefore we have been* ***buried*** *with Him through baptism into death, so that as Christ was raised from the dead through the glory of the Father, so we too might walk in newness of life.*"
- 6:5—"*For if we have become united with Him in the likeness of His death, certainly we shall also be in the likeness of His* ***resurrection****.*"

Result in Sanctification

A phrase found twice in chapter 6 (vv. 19, 22) is referenced by William Barclay as "the road to holiness."[13] Denny writes that sanctification represents the goal of one saved: to be like Christ (see 6:19 note in the Learning section). The word ἁγιασμός (*hagiasmos*) is the personal dedication to the interests of the deity, holiness, consecration, and sanctification.[14] In verse 19, Paul is discussing one's dedication. In Christ, we should be dedicated to presenting our bodies as slaves to righteousness, just like we did when we were slaves to impurity. It seems that when we give into the lusts of life, it begins to feed a gross desire for more. It consumes our minds and our hearts, therefore creating a situation where we truly are slaves to whatever our desire of choice might be. Paul says that our works of righteousness, in the same way, must consume us as every desire of our lives can revolve around the good works of the Lord. Thus, our bodies represent and are dedicated to doing those works of righteousness because our hearts and minds revolve around the blessings we have in Christ. Therefore, just as you were slaves to the sinful way of life, allow yourself to be slaves to the righteousness of God. The same dedication. The same involvement. The same level of

---
13. Barclay 93.
14. Arndt, Danker, et al. 10.

thinking. The same level of being consumed. The same level of desire. Only now you are in your entirety directed to the Lord and not the sinful behavior of your past. According to verse 22, as a result of our freedom from sin, we become enslaved to God; therefore, we take hold of the benefits or advantages that we have in Him, which results in sanctification and eternal life. Dedication leads to production, which represents the fruits of one's labor or obedience. In this case, both begin with obedience, which leads to labor. We labor not because we should or could "work our way to Heaven," but because our faith drives us to do for the Lord as He has done for us. This is the result of Him being the ruler of our life.

At What Point Is One Saved?
Romans 6:17-18 says, *"But thanks be to God that though you were slaves of sin,* ***you became obedient from the heart*** *to that form of teaching to which you were committed, and having been freed from sin, you became slaves of righteousness"* (emp. added).

True obedience can only come from the heart.

STUDY

Romans 6 serves as a staple in our New Testament with its plain teaching on the importance of baptism. With so many in our world today fighting against the idea that one needs to be baptized to have forgiveness of sins and be added to the body of Christ, it is no wonder that God made sure that we had access to this letter that Paul wrote to the church of Christ in Rome.

The reality is that many teach against baptism, which is so unfortunate. Their belief in the Gospel message is that baptism is not essential to become a child of God. For instance, we find in the claims of the Baptist church as well as the Mennonite church these statements:[15]

- **Baptist:** "Baptism may not be essential to salvation, but it is essential to obedience."[16]
- **Baptist:** "There is not one passage in the Bible that teaches that baptism is necessary for salvation."[17]
- **Baptist:** "It is, however, a witness and a testimony to the covenant since it is naturally and properly the first Christian act of the believer after the exercise of saving faith."[18]
- **Baptist:** "We believe the Bible teaches baptism does not save anyone. We are convinced God's Word teaches no form of baptism saves or has any part of salvation." [19]
- **Mennonite:** "Although baptism is a most meaningful symbol and the rite for admission to the church, and although it is based upon solemn vows, yet it is not an end in itself, nor is salvation dependent upon it." [20]

---

15. The following list was put together by H. Wesley Simmons, World Video Bible Course Notes, Romans, 118. Each of the statements is cited below.
16. Hiscox, Edward T. *The Hiscox Guide for Baptist Churches.* Valley Forge: The Judson Press, 1964, 87.
17. Odle, Joe T. *Church Members Handbook.* Nashville: Broadman Press, 18.
18. Hiscox 83.
19. Alvarez, Richard U. In a Letter to Don Crum, From *Jerry Falwell and The Old Time Gospel Hour.* Feb. 4, 1981.
20. Mennonite General Conference, Aug. 26, 1955..

Sin, Death, Life

While these are a very small portion of the belief systems that are out there, baptism, in many ways, has become nothing more than a great big show where everyone gets a t-shirt. You've seen them before, haven't you? A big "church" that has thousands of people, the swimming pools on stage, everybody wearing a shirt that says "I was baptized" or some form of that. People being dunked, the perfect pictures being taken, people hugging and dancing as they are joyous, thinking they have been saved! How sad that it has been made into a show over what it was intended to be: a memorial reenactment that places you in Christ.

On the other hand, baptism has been completely neglected by other groups who believe simply praying Jesus into their heart makes them saved. Again, you can almost see with your mind's eye a group of people trying to find Jesus sitting at a revival of some kind and being told, "If you will just say this prayer, you will be saved!" There are several problems with their way of thinking. First, many different prayers are out there, so how do I know which one is right? Second, none of them are in the Bible, which causes a major problem because that means that the prayer did not come from God. Third, there is no way to contact the blood of Christ by way of prayer, which is the soul-cleansing agent that will wash one clean (cf. Acts 22:16; 1 John 1:7). Fourth, there is a great lack of consistency within the teaching. Fifth, there is no way to be buried when you pray. Well, I guess you could be, but not in a spiritual way!

Everything that we do from a spiritual and Biblical standpoint MUST BE AUTHORIZED by Scripture. If it is not, then it is not worth doing because it simply isn't right. We also need to remember that baptism itself is not everything. Can a person be baptized for the remission of his sins and still not make it to Heaven? Yes. How? Either he believed that being baptized was the only thing he needed to do and nothing else and he went on living his life in the same manner as before baptism, or he fell away, meaning he had *"fallen from grace"* (Gal. 5:4). Some believe that is not possible, but Paul tells us it is very possible.

Salvation is something that is **completed** with baptism, not started. Neither is baptism just a sign after salvation, like some of the life churches and other denominational groups would lead you to believe with their baptism days, which are really just religious pep rallies. If sincere belief and repentance are not and were not a part of your baptism, then all you have done is simply get wet.

Remember, Peter said, *"Repent and be baptized for the forgiveness of your sins"* (Acts 2:38). **Repentance** is just as necessary as baptism. **Belief** is just as necessary as repentance. **Baptism** is just as necessary as both. You cannot have one without the others, and more is needed. The Bible shows that true baptism is always shown and preceded by actions such as **hearing** the Gospel, **believing** Jesus is the risen Lord, **repenting** of your sins, and **confessing** your faith in Christ as the Son of the living God. (Note: Acts 8:12-13; 16:14, 31, 34; 18:8; Rom. 10:9-10; Col. 2:12)

This also brings up the false teaching of infant baptism being a true form of baptism. Babies and small children **are not capable** of understanding the Gospel; they have no sin in their lives and do not have an actual ability to follow or believe. This is why we do not have one single account of a baby or child being baptized in the New Testament. Here are some points used by those who believe, teach, and practice infant baptism.

- They look to passages that say households were being saved or baptized.
- They say, "These households must have included infants and small children."
- They bring it together like this: "Since these households must have included infants, then infants must have been baptized too."

However, when you take a closer look at these household-conversion passages, you will find that the members of these households also did other things.

1. They feared God—Acts 10:2
2. They listened to the Gospel message—Acts 10:4; 16:32
3. They believed—Acts 16:34; 18:8
4. They rejoiced in their salvation—Acts 16:34

How can a baby or child do any of these? They cannot! The term *household* referred to only those capable of understanding and obeying the message received. If there were babies and small children in the household, they would later be converted as they grew and were able to understand and obey.

As we think about our Focus Statement at the beginning of our lesson, "*Sin, death,* and *life* represent the path one must take to become a child of God to access **grace,** which can only be found in Christ Jesus." We find this idea clearly stated within the chapter. Because the *"wages of sin is death,"* there must, of necessity, be a death to escape the outcome of God's wrath. When one dies from a spiritual standpoint, only then may he/she have life in an eternal sense! There is no other way!

It is important that we connect the meanings of the words *sin, death,* and *life* with what the Gospel teaches because we need to be right when it comes to how one can be saved. God is not good with partial obedience. Rather, He is looking for complete *"obedience from the heart"* (6:17). It seems that obedience is the key—something a baby cannot do, that prayer cannot accomplish, and that sprinkling cannot touch. Complete obedience is to follow the teachings and examples of the text. From the culture to historical tradition, to the Gospel teaching, to the first day of the church, one thing has been a constant: baptism.

So, let's look at each of these individually to begin to draw out some conclusions.

Sin

Radio personality Paul Harvey tells the story of how an Eskimo kills a wolf. The account is grisly, yet it offers fresh insight into the consuming, self-destructive nature of sin.

> First, the Eskimo coats his knife blade with animal blood and allows it to freeze. Then, he adds another layer of blood and another until the blade is completely concealed by frozen blood. Next, the hunter fixes his knife on the ground with the blade up. When a wolf follows his sensitive nose to the source of the scent and discovers the bait, he licks it, tasting the fresh, frozen blood. He begins to lick faster, more and more vigorously, lapping the blade until the keen edge is bare. Feverishly now, harder and harder, the wolf licks the blade in the arctic night.

Sin, Death, Life

So great becomes his craving for blood that the wolf does not notice the razor-sharp sting of the naked blade on his own tongue, nor does he recognize the instant at which his insatiable thirst is being satisfied by his own warm blood. His carnivorous appetite just craves more—until the dawn finds him dead in the snow!

It is a fearful thing that people can be "consumed by their own lusts." Only God's grace keeps us from the wolf's fate.[21]

While we may not be wolves, this too is what can happen when one is enticed by lust and pride (cf. 1 John 2:16). One sin usually leads to another and then another until you can **change** how you feel about the sin you are committing. Earlier in chapter 1, Paul referenced several sins being committed by the Gentile brethren and also by the Jewish brethren.

Romans 1:26-32,

> *For this reason God gave them over to degrading passions; for their women exchanged the natural function for that which is unnatural, and in the same way also the men abandoned the natural function of the woman and burned in their desire toward one another, men with men committing indecent acts and receiving in their own persons the due penalty of their error. And just as they did not see fit to acknowledge God any longer, God gave them over to a depraved mind, to do those things which are not proper, being filled with all unrighteousness, wickedness, greed, evil; full of envy, murder, strife, deceit, malice; they are gossips, slanderers, haters of God, insolent, arrogant, boastful, inventors of evil, disobedient to parents, without understanding, untrustworthy, unloving, unmerciful; and although they know the ordinance of God, that those who practice such things are worthy of death, they not only do the same, but also give hearty approval to those who practice them.*

Within this list, we can clearly see that there was no excuse for the actions of the people. They were sinning in several different ways, and there was no escaping that fact. Their ***ingratitude*** (1:21), ***idolatry*** (1:22-23), and ***immorality*** (1:24-32) were a product of their own selfish, lustful ways.

Dan Winkler writes further on Romans 1 and the Gentiles' transition into their shameful ways. He titles this section "The Evolution of Evil" and makes three observations. First, there was a *philosophical* breakdown (1:18-21), and they became futile in their thoughts. They refused to properly reason from the creation of God. Second, there was a *theological* breakdown (1:22-23) as they adopted an idolatrous belief system where they exchanged the truth about God for a lie and created gods to fit their own wishes. Third, there was an *ethical* breakdown (1:24-32) as they became immoral and approved of immorality in others[22]

---

21. Zwingelberg, Chris T. "Sin to Slavery." *Sermon Illustrations*, www.sermonillustrations.com/a-z/s/sin_slavery_to.htm. Accessed 21 Jan. 2025.
22. Winkler 16.

Is this different from the day in which we live? Absolutely not. It is the same. People of today are completely engulfed in this type of behavior. From homosexuality, transgenderism, political forms of racism, drugs, adultery, murder, you name it—we have it still to this day. Nothing has changed. The sin of lust and pride will forever haunt us until we turn our lives to the Lord to leave them behind.

However, we must remember that the sinful relationship is a servant-master one. Can it get its grip on you tightly? Yes! That is why the pornography industry is so successful. In 2023 alone, the global adult entertainment market was valued at US $287.8 billion! One study showed that in 2016, people watched **4.6 billion hours of pornography** on one of more than 42 million pornographic websites. That's **equivalent to 524,000 years spent watching porn in one year!**[23]

The question is, do we still have a problem with sin? Absolutely we do! And we see the ramifications of it every single day, from broken families to broken people because of lives they wish they had never lived. As we have stated before, while sin may be "rewarding" now, it is detrimental to your life. Nothing good comes from sin, so don't let it be a master over you!

As we have said before, the disobedience which led to sin is the reason for our separation from God in the first place. Since sin separates us from God, is it worth it? Since it sends us to Hell, is it worth the moment of pleasure? Don't be fooled by the deception of a feeling or how something looks. It is nothing more than a lie to lead you away from righteousness. This is why being able to discern the text is so important because it can help you identify sin and give you enough strength to overcome it! Satan is continually throwing arrows of temptation at us every day. Is your shield up? He is coming at you with every deception known to his mind. Is your sword up? He is trying to bash you in the head with trial after trial physically, spiritually, and psychologically. Is your helmet on? Let's be clear: this is a spiritual war that we are facing, and we need God's armor to face it, but we can't wear God's armor and be a part of the enemy's army at the same time.

Just as Joshua told Israel, we must choose whom we will serve (Josh. 24:15). Sin or God. The reason that Jesus came is so that He could save you from sin (Matt. 1:21; John 1:29; Acts 2:38; Rom. 6:23; Gal. 3:22; 1 John 1:7, 2:1; Rev. 1:5)!

Death

While we have spent some time looking at the concept of death here in chapter 6, there is no doubt more to be said about the great importance that it serves for the one who is seeking to be brought to salvation. Paul looks at the concept of death in three ways.

First, the death of Jesus. As Jesus hung on the cross at Golgotha, His mind was focused on what He had to do. He wasn't up there for Himself; it was for you and me. Paul writes in 6:20, *"For the death that He died, He died to sin once for all; but the life that He lives, He lives to God."* Peter later wrote, *"For Christ also died for sins once for all, the just for the unjust, so that He might bring us to God, having been put to death in the flesh, but made alive in the spirit"* (1 Pet.

---

23. Azcuna, Lyndon. "The Porn Pandemic." *LifePlan*, www.lifeplan.org/the-porn-pandemic/. Accessed 21 Jan. 2025.

3:18). The death of Jesus was necessary (Heb. 7:12; 9:16) as it was the only thing that could and would allow us to have an eternal **High Priest** (Heb. 7:23-28), a **New** Covenant (Heb. 8:6, 13), an eternal **sacrifice** (Heb. 10:10-14), the **continual cleansing of blood** (Heb. 10:19; cf. 1 John 1:7); **forgiveness** (Acts 2:38; Col. 1:14; cf. Heb. 10:18; 1 John 1:9), **justification** (Rom. 3:24; 5:9), **sanctification** (6:19, 22), **grace** (Eph. 1:7; 2:5, 8), and much more. Without the death of Christ, we would have nothing and would still be living under the Mosaic and/or moral system of law that could only condemn. The death of Jesus created a NEW REALITY for us, one that the angels long to look at (1 Pet. 1:12). How blessed we are that Jesus died on our behalf.

Second, our dying with Christ. To die with Christ is to live with Christ. They are inseparable. Spiritually speaking, this is the essence of our baptism—that we die and are buried with Him. When we do this, we are dying to everything that we once were. If you are addicted to alcohol, you are dying of that addiction. If you were living in adultery, you are dying to that way of living. If you are living a life of deceit, then you are to walk away from that life. Why? Because when you die to who you used to be, the "new you" is no longer associated with the deeds of the flesh and its lustful desires. When you die with Christ, you die with Christ. Therefore, you CANNOT be who you used to be before you repented. You cannot go on living the same life you lived because you will never reach your transformed state. To die with Christ is to change with Christ so that you may be His and a product of Him. Death is and has always been about the end of something. In this case, it is the end of your past life.

Third, our spiritual death. When Adam and Eve were cast out of the garden, death was considered while in the process of their committing sin (Gen. 3:3-4). However, this was not a physical death that the serpent was discussing it was spiritual. Unfortunately, Eve did not know that at the time, no doubt it was a result of his deception. Spiritual death is a result of a continued life of sin. It is a lifestyle and mindset that refuses to admit sin in any way as a part of your life (1 John 1:8, 10). It is lawlessness (1 John 3:4) and unrighteousness (1 John 5:17) that lead to spiritual eternal death, which has the outcome of an eternal separation from God (cf. Luke 16:19-31). Spiritual death is a representation of a soul that has not been saved and is therefore condemned by God to receive His wrath (Rom. 1:18). It is the lack of conforming to His will and an unwillingness to obey.

Within these three concepts, we can clearly see that the concept of death is a big one. In one sense, it places you with Christ; in another sense, it separates you from who you used to be. In yet another sense, it separates you from God. Clearly, death is an important subject that has a clear connection to every human being.

The reality is that we will all die. You will, of course, die at the end of your time here on earth from a physical standpoint, which simply means that you will leave this place to go to another. It is at that point that all spiritual things will matter more than anything to every single soul. The problem is that at that point, it will be too late! It is too late to serve, to be obedient, to love, to walk in the path of righteousness, and—the big one—to obey the Gospel. If you are spiritually dead at your physical death, it only leads to one place. Remember, our death here is not the end, as we should live forever. Where it lives is the key to knowing the two directions of life: toward God or away from God.

Don't let yourself come to that point! Physical death is coming for everyone. There is nothing we can do to escape that truth. It is how God designed life. Spiritual death is an eternal sentence! It is not worth pursuing. However, when we die with Christ, we receive nothing but blessings!

Life

I love 1 John 5:13, *"These things I have written to you who believe in the name of the Son of God, so that you may know that you have eternal life."* We have looked at this in our building studies in the past years, and I just don't believe we can look at this passage too much. How awesome it is that we can know that we have eternal life! It is assuring, convicting, comforting, cultivating, and something that will continue to strengthen you because you know what the end is.

However, in order to have eternal life, there are things I must do! For instance, I must conform to the *"words of sound teaching"* (1 Tim. 6:3; 2 Tim. 1:13). I must *"walk in a manner worthy of my calling"* (1 Thess. 2:12) so that I may *"walk in the Light as He is in the Light"* (1 John 1:7). I must **hear** the Word of the Lord and let it ring true in my ears down to my heart with an openness that allows me to comprehend and consider what is being taught. Bob Turner said in a sermon one time, "How often do we limit ourselves because of the way we see ourselves?" If we are unable to listen to the message, are we not limiting ourselves to what we could know and what we could be?

I must also **believe** (John 3:16; 8:34; Heb. 11:6) in the message that is given. Paul began the book by discussing the *"holy Scriptures"* (1:1), which proclaimed what was to come. The Scriptures were given to the prophet, who was universally accepted by the people of God, so what he wrote is what they believed. Are we able to do the same thing? Are we applying ourselves to take in all of Scripture and not just some of it? Are we thinking, meditating, researching, and praying about what we study in Scripture? If God wants us to know something, do you not think He will help us to understand? The problem some face is found in their unwillingness to be open to something outside of what they have always been told and taught. To let go of a tradition for some will be an ongoing battle as they would hold on to tradition rather than the text because change is not an option. Listen, there is no room for pride in the heavenly home. Jesus taught humility and kindness, not hardheartedness and pride. Therefore, when we study the Gospel itself, is it not important to take into account ALL that it teaches? To believe in the Gospel is more than just believing in Jesus, it is also believing in how to follow and obey it. Many believe in Jesus, but is that believing in the Gospel? Many believe in both faith and grace, but is that believing in the Gospel? To believe in His plan requires full attention to each detail, not just parts of it. If Jesus said it, I believe it. If Paul taught it, I believe it. If Peter proclaimed it, I believe it! It is that simple. What the Bible says I will do, and where it sends, I will go. True faith allows God to lead in all times of your life, including your journey of faith.

Repentance is also key to our obtaining eternal life. To repent is to change the way we think. It means I must change the way I think about sin, my actions, my addictions, my faults, my outbursts of anger, my insecurities, my anxieties, and my sinful tendencies. To be transformed is in the mind; it is a change of the inner man. People will only truly repent when they are convicted within their heart. Therefore, the people at Pentecost said, *"Brethren, what shall we do...?"* (Acts 2:37). Conviction causes immediate change because you know that you are not right. It causes

Sin, Death, Life

you to change direction in a drastic way. Sure, some things will take time. The reality is that after conversion, your life stays the same with all of its consequences. However, you are the different part of the equation now. To follow the Lord is to walk away from sin and all that leads to eternal death. It is to create a personal culture within your heart and mind that will not allow sin to rule in your heart any longer. It is changing your ways and making everything right—to right the wrongs, to be forgiven, to evaluate your time and energy, and to have an awareness of what you are feeding the soul. Once you were feeding your heart and mind all the things that the flesh desires; now you are only putting in the things that God desires for you. When you fill your life with God, your life begins to revolve around Him. This is true change.

Confession is only found in the heart of a true believer. Only one who truly believes in Jesus will confess Him as Lord. Peter's confession is a great example: *"You are the Christ, the Son of the living God"* (Matt. 16:16). His confession was rewarded with praise. Is yours? To confess to Jesus is to put Him above all else in life. He is Lord. The Son of God. The Savior of the world. Is this your belief? Rarely do people truly express what they do not believe. Certainly, there are many who will deceive another by making a false claim of their belief in Jesus, but it doesn't change the fact that God knows where the words are coming from. Our confession is a result of the faith we possess, which leads us to do, to act on, and to follow. The apostle Paul immediately followed, just like the apostles did as they were called. When Paul said, *"Do not let sin reign in your mortal bodies so that you obey its lust"* (6:12), does this not have to do with the one who reigns in your life? The servant-master relationship is one of importance, and if you do not see Jesus as King of Kings and Lord of Lords, the Son of the Living God, then a pure confession of the heart will never be possible for you. One can only reach eternal life when one confesses with sincerity and truth due to his true belief in Him (Rom. 10:9-10). To add to this, we must also remember the words of Jesus, *"Therefore everyone who confesses Me before men, I will also confess him before My Father who is in heaven"* (Matt. 10:32).

The next step is **baptism**. Let's look at a few passages:

> *"Go therefore and make disciples of all the nations, baptizing them in the name of the Father and the Son and the Holy Spirit"* (Matt. 28:19).

> *"He who has believed and has been baptized shall be saved; but he who has disbelieved shall be condemned."* (Mark 16:16).

> *"Peter said to them, 'Repent, and each of you be baptized in the name of Jesus Christ for the forgiveness of your sins; and you will receive the gift of the Holy Spirit.'"* (Acts 2:38).

> *"As they went along the road they came to some water; and the eunuch said, 'Look! Water! What prevents me from being baptized?' And Philip said, 'If you believe with all your heart, you may.' And he answered and said, 'I believe that Jesus Christ is the Son of God.' And he ordered the chariot to stop; and they both went down into the water, Philip as well as the eunuch, and he baptized him."* (Acts 8:36-38).

> *"Or do you not know that all of us who have been baptized into Christ Jesus have been*

baptized into His death? Therefore we have been buried with Him through baptism into death, so that as Christ was raised from the dead through the glory of the Father, so we too might walk in newness of life. For if we have become united with Him in the likeness of His death, certainly we shall also be in the likeness of His resurrection" (Rom. 6:3-5).

"For I delivered to you as of first importance what I also received, that Christ died for our sins according to the Scriptures, and that He was buried, and that He was raised on the third day according to the Scriptures" (1 Cor. 15:3-4).

"For all of you who were baptized into Christ have clothed yourselves with Christ" (Gal. 3:27).

"...Having been buried with Him in baptism, in which you were also raised up with Him through faith in the working of God, who raised Him from the dead." (Col. 2:12).

"...Who once were disobedient, when the patience of God kept waiting in the days of Noah, during the construction of the ark, in which a few, that is, eight persons, were brought safely through the water. Corresponding to that, baptism now saves you—not the removal of dirt from the flesh, but an appeal to God for a good conscience—through the resurrection of Jesus Christ" (1 Pet. 3:20-21).

John Moore wrote,

"Being born again and thereby becoming a child of God requires that one be born of water; that is to say, he or she must be baptized. According to Romans 6:17-18, to be free from sin and thereby become a servant of righteousness, one must be obedient *in baptism* to the form of doctrine that imitates the death, burial, and resurrection of Christ. In Romans 1:16, we learn that the Gospel is God's power to save. In Romans 6:17, we learn that a form of that Gospel can be obeyed. Since that is true, you and I must come to understand the gravity of the following statement:

and to give relief to you who are afflicted and to us as well when the Lord Jesus will be revealed from heaven with His mighty angels in flaming fire, dealing out retribution to those who do not know God and to those who do not obey the gospel of our Lord Jesus (2 Thess. 1:7-8)."[24]

He goes on to say, "The Gospel must be obeyed! A sinner cannot save himself or herself by *literally* being crucified, by *literally* being buried, and by *literally* being resurrected from the grave....we can do something similar to this. A sinner can be buried with Christ in baptism for the remission of sins (Acts 2:38) and then arrive to walk in a new life (Col. 2:12)."

Baptism being the final step to bring into you a NEW state, placed in the kingdom of God (Col. 1:13), placed into the body of Christ (Acts 2:47) and saved (1 Pet. 3:21). Therefore we cannot overlook the gravity of these two passages of importance of baptism.

---

24. Moore, John. "About Baptism." *Searching for Truth,* Maxwell: World Video Bible School, 2007, 92.

Sin, Death, Life

*"Therefore **we have been buried with Him through baptism into death**, so that as Christ was raised from the dead through the glory of the Father, so **we too might walk in newness of life**"* (Rom. 6:4, emp. added).

*"having been buried with Him in baptism, in which **you were also raised up with Him** through faith in the working of God, who raised Him from the dead"* (Col. 2:12, emp. added).

There is a clear connection between baptism and life. You cannot have one without the other, and because through His death we are clothed in His blood that washes us clean from all of our sin (Gal. 3:27; 1 John 1:7)! It is the only way to receive the grace of God!

ACTIVITY

Our activity for this section will require everyone to be placed in small groups of 2 to 3 people (max). Be sure that each person has a worksheet, something to write with, and his/her Bible.

The goal of this activity is to discuss salvation from the standpoint of baptism, as discussed in Romans 6. Within each of the groups, one person will play the role of one sharing the **plan of salvation** while the other/others will play the role of those who are being taught. In each discussion, it will be important for us to challenge each other about what we know based on this chapter and the New Testament Scriptures given on the importance of both **baptism** and **being obedient from the heart**.

This exercise will also serve as good practice for those who may not be comfortable in a personal study type of setting. The key here is to "stick to the text." If we believe in what Scripture teaches, it will give us all we need to know. When it comes to salvation, opinions are a hard sell, but the truth needs no salesman, only a voice and an opportunity.

Within each group, set a time limit depending on the amount of time you have in class, and allow each person to be in each role. If there are more than two in a group, the third person can be there to oversee and help the one teaching when needed. This can also be a good time for the observer to learn certain techniques of those experienced and possibly what not to do in certain situations.

Remember, this is a learning exercise that is designed to help everyone grow in their knowledge of how one must be saved.

Be sure to include in each study the importance of understanding sin, death, and life and how they connect to our topic at hand. Remember, *faithful obedience to the Gospel* is key. If we cannot be fully faithful, then nothing we do will matter.

Be sure to use something you have learned from each section of our study and try to apply it to your conversational study.

*"Therefore **we have been buried with Him through baptism into death**, so that as Christ was raised from the dead through the glory of the Father, so **we too might walk in newness of life**"* (Rom. 6:4, emp. added).

Instructions:
- Assign each group a certain belief that does not require baptism for salvation. Be sure that the group has an understanding or information in hand about what a certain group believes.
- Hand the assignments out randomly to each group.
- After the designated time limit is up, allow the group to rotate, we want each person to have a turn.
- Once completed, designate some time to go around the room and have each group tell what belief they were up against, what they learned, how they decided to defend, and best practices to teach and reach the lost soul.

It will be up to the instructor to possibly give out some handout information about each of the different religious beliefs that are used within this activity. If you are doing this by yourself, choose a different belief and try to fill out the answer key in order to defend the teaching.

Sin, Death, Life

WORKSHEET

Study Partner's Story: My name is _____, and I was raised in the _____ church. I believe that a person is saved through _____.

1. Do you believe that you are a "saved person"? _____

2. If so, how is it that you were saved? _____

3. Discuss the importance of the blood of Christ and what it does for the believer who answers the Gospel call.

4. Discuss the importance of understanding sin, death, and life and how each of these connects to the biblical discussion of baptism in Romans 6:3-5.

5. List the Scriptures that discuss baptism and talk about why they are important.

6. Note what types of "death" a person can achieve and how a life in Christ or away from Christ can affect the type of death one will endure.

7. According to Scripture, Romans 6:3 tells us that sinners who want to be saved must be _____ into the death of Jesus.

8. Within your belief how is one able to have their sins washed away? (Note your Scriptural references of how this can happen)

9. What does 1 Corinthians 12:13 teach us?

10. Explain at what point a person is saved according to Romans 6:17-18.

Building

225

Building

THE STRUGGLE IS REAL!

ROMANS 7

GARRETT BERNETHY

"For what I am doing, I do not understand; for I am not practicing what I would like to do, but I am doing the very thing I hate. But if I do the very thing I do not want to do, I agree with the Law, confessing that the Law is good. So now, no longer am I the one doing it, but sin which dwells in me. For I know that nothing good dwells in me, that is, in my flesh; for the willing is present in me, but the doing of the good is not. For the good that I want, I do not do, but I practice the very evil that I do not want. But if I am doing the very thing I do not want, I am no longer the one doing it, but sin which dwells in me. I find then the principle that evil is present in me, the one who wants to do good."
- Romans 7:15-21 -

INTRODUCTION

As stated in the title of this lesson, the "struggle with sin is real," and that is most definitely what we see from Paul in chapter 7. Thank God, however, that we are no longer in Christ bound to who we used to be or a law of another kind from the ancient past. Rather, we are now under the law of Christ (7:14-25; cf.1 Cor. 9:21) as we have been unified with Him through our death, burial, and resurrection! What Paul realizes more than ever with the continued struggles that he deals with is that there is no one who is exempt from the need for Jesus. He is truly the only answer to our ability to overcome sin. There is simply no other way!

Excel Still More Bible Workshop

FOCUS

As Paul now turns back to the Jews in his discussion of the Law, he greatly desires to make a certain point. In Christ, you have been released from all other laws, in this case, the Law of Moses, as it no longer stands anymore. Just as a husband might die, the Law died, and therefore, there is no connection to that Law or the husband any longer. Therefore, everything you once held as important, every practice that you once held, every command that you once obeyed according to that Law is no longer needed or beneficial to you in any way. Why? Because it is dead.

On the other hand, the Law itself could only make you aware of the sin that you have committed. Therefore when you lied, the Law made you aware of it. However, there was nothing you could do about the sin. Consequently, the only thing the Law could produce was death.

One of the many blessings in Christ is that in Him we have been freed from the Law, thus now allowing us to know about our sin and be saved from it! In knowing this, however, it can produce a great struggle. Like Paul, we are certainly a blessed people to be able to have the forgiveness of our sins as we have received the grace of God through our faithful obedience. But due to the enticing and powerful pull of sin, somehow, it becomes a great struggle for us to let it go. In Paul's case, he says, *"For the good that I want, I do not do, but I practice the very evil that I do not want. But if I am doing the very thing I do not want, I am no longer the one doing it, but sin which dwells in me"* (7:19-20).

> Doing good is a state of mind, the struggle is the journey, and when we find true strength in our Lord, there is nothing that we cannot overcome!

Sin truly is a real struggle, one that should not be looked over or passed off as insignificant or nothing. Within our study so far in the book, we have identified that sin—with all its lusts and desires—is nothing short of dangerous to a person's life from a spiritual standpoint. It is the silent killer of life that eats away at you, deceiving you and making you think that things are so good, when really they are anything but.

However, Paul reminds us at the close of the chapter, *"Wretched man that I am! Who will set me free from the body of this death? Thanks be to God through Jesus Christ our Lord! So then, on the one hand I myself with my mind am serving the law of God, but on the other, with my flesh the law of sin"* (7:24-25).

What we must realize is that **sin takes every opportunity** to take advantage of you! From one perspective, Paul says it produced *"coveting of every kind,"* which is something that *"produced death for him."* On the other hand, sin deceived him, per Denny's note in chapter 7:11, the deception is found in the joy sin promises and the lack of consequence you think it has. It is the enticing tool of Satan.

So, while sin takes its opportunity, so must we. Not to sin, of course, but to do good. While the struggle of sin is real for each one of us, that doesn't mean that we cannot take the opportunities

The Struggle Is Real!

we have in our lives to overcome sin. Struggle can be seen or looked at from two different lights. From one perspective, it can be seen as a negative that puts you down and keeps you down. From another, it is a challenge issued.

William M. Batten once wrote, "When I hear my friends say they hope their children don't have to experience the hardships they went through—I don't agree. Those hardships made us what we are. You can be disadvantaged in many ways, and one way may be not having had to struggle."[1]

Paul wrote, *"For our struggle is not against flesh and blood, but against the rulers, against the powers, against the world forces of this darkness, against the spiritual forces of wickedness in the heavenly places"* (Eph. 6:12).

Here he is saying that our struggles are against Satan and all those with him who are striving to make the struggle even more real from day to day (cf. Job 1–3). Satan has proven to go against mankind (cf. Gen. 3; 1 John 2:16) in a continual effort to take as many souls away from God as he possibly can. Yes, some of our struggles may indeed be brought on by ourselves, something Paul is very willing to take the blame for. However, that doesn't mean they may not be enhanced by the works and schemes of the devil (1 Pet. 5:8; cf. Eph. 6:13, 16).

Within this lesson, we will work to identify first how sin takes its opportunity with you, and second, how you can take your opportunity to overcome it.

Focus Statement: Doing good is a state of mind, the struggle is the journey, and when we find true strength in our Lord, there is nothing that we cannot overcome!

STUDY KEYS

Note: Take some time as you study through chapter 7 to mark each of these words and phrases individually with different color pens, markers, colored pencils, or highlighters of your choice. If possible, make notes in your margins to reflect the meanings of these words or phrases that may help you understand the overall context to a better degree.

WORDS OF IMPORTANCE

- **God** (θεός)—vv. 4, 22, 25
- **Christ** (Χριστός)—vv. 4, 25
- **Law** (νόμος)—vv. 1, 2, 3, 4, 5, 6, 7, 8, 9, 12, 14, 16, 22, 23, 25
- **Sin** (ἁμαρτία)—vv. 5, 7, 8, 9, 11, 13, 14, 17, 20, 23, 25

---

1. Batten, William M. *Sermon Illustrations*, www.sermonillustrations.com/a-z/s/struggle.htm. Accessed 22 Jan. 2025.

- **Death** (θάνατος)—vv. 5, 10, 13, 24
- **Spirit** (πνεῦμα)—v. 6
- **Brethren** (ἀδελφός)—vv. 1, 4
- **Grace/Thanks** (χάρις)—v. 25

PAUL'S STATEMENTS, QUESTIONS, AND POINTS

Paul's Marriage Discussion...7:1-6

Marriage is the oldest institution we know of as we begin reading about it in Genesis 2:24. That *"man shall leave his father and mother and be joined to his wife, and the two shall become one flesh."* In marriage faithfulness is the requirement for each party. It is a lifelong commitment and foundational within the family unit. It is a relationship that builds comfort and confidence for not only those who are married but the children they may have.

As Paul was shifting his thoughts now to the Jews, they would have understood the laws of marriage—a relationship of unity and not division—where the husband holds his wife up and loves her as himself (Eph. 5:25), and the wife is to be *"subject to her husband as to the Lord"* (Eph. 5:22).

Equally, they would have known—despite the Pharisees' constant badgering of Jesus while they broke their own laws—that nothing can separate the husband and wife with the exception of two things: adultery (Matt. 5:32; 19:9) or death (Rom. 7:2). Outside of those two reasons, there is nothing that may release a husband and wife from the marriage covenant that they made. Therefore, if a divorce occurs for any other reason than adultery, a man or woman may not re-marry as God has not released her from that covenant relationship with her husband. This teaching is consistent despite many efforts to justify re-marriage within our current culture. To add to this Paul would write to those in Corinth, *"A wife is bound as long as her husband lives; but if her husband is dead, she is free to be married to whom she wishes, only in the Lord"* (1 Cor. 7:39).

The question becomes—was this truly a teaching on marriage or was this an illustration? The answer is the latter; it is an illustration of what the Jews already knew. Within their culture and under the laws of Moses, marriage was to be held in its highest regard, and any adultery that took place could and would have a high degree of punishment, which can be seen in the story of the adulterous woman in John 7:53–8:11. While they brought the woman to be stoned, the Pharisees did not follow the law to its fullest because they wanted to trap Jesus. In that situation (true or not), both the man and woman under Jewish law should have been brought to be stoned, not just her.

Paul used this illustration because the Jews and Pharisees had a good understanding of the marriage laws, and Paul knew that since he was also one (Phil. 3:5). Jesus was a master of using illustrations that people understood in the fullest, in most cases using things that may have been around them. Here Paul does the same.

The Struggle Is Real!

While marriage is important, he used it to illustrate that a wife cannot be bound to her husband if he is dead, as those alive cannot be bound to those who are not. In the same way, one cannot be bound to a law that is also dead. From a physical standpoint, one who is alive literally cannot have a relationship in any way with those who are not. The only thing we can have regarding them are the memories of our lives. The Law, however, was done away with when Jesus rose from the dead (Heb. 8:13; 9:15-28). Therefore, any connection that the Jew had with the Law of Moses was gone. Why? Because it no longer exists.

Therefore, Paul writes, *"For the married woman is bound by law to her husband while he is living; but if her husband dies, she is released from the law concerning the husband. So then, if while her husband is living she is joined to another man, she shall be called an adulteress; but if her husband dies, she is free from the law, so that she is not an adulteress though she is joined to another man"* (Rom. 7:2-3).

Wayne Jackson wrote, "The Jewish Christians were made 'dead' (i.e., separated) to the Law of Moses by means of the death of Christ (Eph. 2:13-15; Col. 2:14) so that they might be joined to another. Therefore, the death of Christ terminated the Law of Moses. Phasing into a new stage of the imagery, there is the reference to Jesus, who was raised from the dead. By implication, Jewish converts were joined to Him through the gospel that 'fruit' (spiritual offering) might be brought forth to God (v. 4). Clearly, the death of Christ was the 'continental divide' between the two covenants systems."[2]

This teaching on the marriage relationship is used as an illustration. The truth remains the same for both. While one is alive and the two are joined, faithfulness is the ultimate requirement, whether it be the law or the husband. But when one dies, you are released in every way from them. (See Sermon Seeds on Romans 7:1-6 and note the illustration).

May It Never Be!

No doubt one of Paul's favorite phrases from the book is used in 3:4, 6, 31; 6:2, 15; 7:7, 13; 9:14; 11:1, 11. The phrase μὴ γένοιτο is the "strongest negation possible in Greek."[3] According to Roper, English words cannot express the depth of emotion in the phrase. While the NIV has *"Not at all,"* the NKJV has *"certainly not,"* and the KJV has *"God forbid."* Paul's denunciation of the ideas was the harshest disregard as the notions made or brought up were completely absurd. Paul's emphasis was on the fact that the Law itself was not sin and did not in and of itself produce sin. What it did do, on the other hand, was reveal sin.

What Shall We Say?

Another one of Paul's favorite phrases occurs in 3:5, 4:1, 6:1, 7:7, 8:31, 9:4, and 30. Another way to say this would be to say, "What conclusion should we reach?" (Roper). Paul continues to question their understanding and logic of the rhetorical and not-so-rhetorical questions given throughout the text.

---

2. Jackson, Wayne. "Romans Chapter 7:1-6; Dead to the Law, Alive to God." *A New Testament Commentary, Third Addition.* Jackson: Christian Courier, 2012, 281.
3. Roper, David L. "Romans Chapter 3:1-8, Answering Objections." *Truth for Today Commentary, A Doctrinal Study of Romans 1–7.* Searcy: Resource Publications, 2013, 199.

Taking Opportunity...7:8, 11

The word ἀφορμή (*aphormae*) discusses the opportunity or occasion for that which is described. In this case, he spoke of sin to further prove his point that the Law itself was not inherently bad nor was it sinful; after all, it was God who gave it to the people. So that very notion would again be absurd. However through the law, sin searched for the occasion to generate sin where there was none. In this case, for Paul to covet. Through its work, Paul said *"it produced in him coveting of every kind"* (7:8).

However, while the Law of God was holy, righteous, and good to accomplish its own purpose, the Law seemingly provided the opportunity that sin was looking for—to violate the Law, which became an instrument of death (Jackson). So here again, the Law was able to make you aware of your sin, but it could not save you from it. Sin, or rather the *"father of lies"* (John 8:44), knew this, and therefore through deception (7:11) exploited the good nature of the Law itself to condemn those who were trying to follow it.

Paul's Constant Struggle

I suppose it would be fair to say that we, like Paul, struggle in our spiritual walk. I just don't know how life would be without it, to be honest. Of course, there are things that get easier through time and knowledge, but there are still things that we all struggle with. Now, we aren't talking about the financial struggle or a struggle with our weight. We are talking about our struggle with sin.

Hopefully, like Paul, we first have a great desire to serve the Lord! To simply speak on behalf of myself, there is no greater thing in my world than to serve God with all my heart! I truly love His church and all who are in it. I love worship, preaching, teaching, and doing things outside of the walls of our building that help to promote the very teachings of the Bible to others, not only around me but the world itself. Whether your work or reach is lesser or greater, to serve God in any capacity is truly one of the great blessings in life. I can only imagine the pride and conviction of Peter while he took his stand with the eleven before thousands of people and proclaimed Jesus to them, calling them out for their sinful behaviors. What an event to see and or be a part of!

That is no doubt Paul's greatest love: the work of the Lord. The promotion of the kingdom and the constant writing and teaching of Scripture to hundreds of billions of people throughout time over the last 2,000 years. Yes, that's right, billions. His words, through his letters, which he was inspired to write, have touched so many souls throughout time! There is no doubt that Paul loved the Lord and His Word until the very end.

However, on the other hand, every person who has the great desire to serve the Lord with all of his heart, soul, and mind struggles. The struggles come in the form of sin. Maybe for you it is coveting like Paul? Maybe it is another struggle. No matter what you struggle with from a sin perspective, we must know that we are all in this together. Paul, a pillar of faith, struggled with sin. While I should not be and will not be joyous about that, I can be relieved and comforted because **first**, Paul, an apostle, a pillar, a leader of leaders in the Lord's church, struggled with sin and was open about it. If he was, maybe I should be too. **Second**, while Paul struggled with sin, he never gave in to living that type of lifestyle. Was it a struggle? Yes, but that is where it remained. This makes him human and not exempt from what we go through each day. If he can push through, so can we! **Third**, he wanted to overcome his sin problem and knew that with Jesus, he could do just that! So can we.

Wayne Jackson adds, "Paul, therefore, pledges to continue serving God with his mind and within the framework of divine restraint, though he understands that sin will always be a problem as long as he is in the flesh."[4]

STUDY

Now, let's remember our Focus Statement: Doing good is a **state of mind**; the **struggle is the journey**; when we **find true strength in our Lord**, there is nothing that we cannot overcome! Paul's mindset must be ours because the struggle is real!

First, let's think about our state of mind. I read one time that someone said, "Let the mind of the Master be the master of your mind." I love that statement, don't you? It is so true on many different levels, especially with all that we have discussed in this study. If you let sin rule over you, will it not be the master of your mind? If you let God rule over you, will He not be the Master of your mind? Of course they will be.

Can different things mold our minds? Absolutely. Culture, doctrine, and media can mold them, along with so many other things. However, within this, it cannot be overlooked that most of the things that may mold our minds have to do with what we feed them. With this fact in mind, we must be honest with ourselves. Sometimes, our mindsets are what they are because we make them that way by what we continue to feed them. For example, when you look up different things in your search engine on your computer, an algorithm looks up what you desire by searching hundreds of billions of website pages.[5] When you click inside your search bar, a number of things will pop up automatically due to the number of times you have searched them. For instance, if you were to get on my laptop and type in the letter *e*, the first thing that pops up is www.excelstillmore.net, which is labeled as the "top hit." Below that are Google suggestions, which are given in this order: "eBay, Elon Musk, ESPN, equal opportunity employment act." Why are those there? Well, it is because other people are putting those things into Google, and it knows that I may have some interest in those things when I type the letter *e* because of the popularity of those search inquiries.

Here is where we are going with this. What you put into the search engine is what it is going to try and search for you based on what you have placed into it in the past. Our minds work the same way. If we put bad things in our minds containing negativity, anger, hatred, bias, pornography, and/ or anything that may not be good for our minds, then the output will be the same. For a person

---

4. Jackson 282.
5. Marsden, Sam. "How Do Search Engines Work?" *Lumar*. 9 Feb. 2024, www.lumar.io/learn/seo/search-engines/how-do-search-engines-work/.

who is addicted to pornography, what is it that his mind continues to bring up? Pornography. If a person has developed a certain mindset about a particular political party based on who is in office and begins listening to every negative and hateful thing that is said about that certain party or individual, what will be the first thing that is brought into that person's mind when something political gets brought up? You see, our minds essentially work the same way as the search engine. When you put trash in the search engine, trash is what it looks for.

But the opposite is also just as true. If you are interested in hunting, guns, horses, golf, Bibles, coffee, computers, etc., and those are the things you are continuously looking up, that is what will be supplied to you first. When it comes to your state of mind, what you feed it is what it will become. Therefore, if you are filling your mind up with Scripture, positivity, spirituality, love, mercy, and kindness, that will be reflected in your state of mind.

For Paul, that is his state of mind. It is filled with God. His Word. The church. People in need. Those who need help. Following doctrine and so much more. How do we know this? We can simply read through each of his letters, including Romans. What is his focus? Unity! Unity with the brotherhood and unity with God. When we condemn the brethren for the things we do ourselves, it will never cultivate an atmosphere of love, will it? If we continue to go back to our own sinful ways, it will never better our relationship with God, will it? You see, that is what is on the mind of Paul. The Gospel. How it works. What it does. What it creates. How it blesses. Therefore, his message is about how the Gospel will change your life—not just physically but even more spiritually.

Paul understands what the Gospel has done for him, and he is extremely happy and blessed by the grace that he has received from the Lord. The problem is he cannot figure out why he is still struggling with the sin of coveting! There is no doubt that we can see the turmoil that he is in. He doesn't deny his personal responsibility for the sin he is committing, but at the same time, he struggles, by his own personal diagnosis, to figure out why it is continuing to be a problem for him since he is an apostle and a saint.

As Paul bared his soul and discussed his experience, which is very hard but nevertheless needed, he knew what the right thing was. After all, he was inspired and gifted with grace (spiritual gifts), but for some reason, he just couldn't seem to do what was right all the time. Therefore, he knew he was wrong, and that is the last thing he wanted to be.

Barclay writes,

> He felt himself to be a split personality. It was as if two men were inside one skin. He felt himself pulled in two directions. He knew himself to be a walking civil war. He was haunted by this feeling of frustration, this ability to see what was good and this inability to do it, this ability to recognize what was wrong and this inability to refrain from doing it. Paul's contemporaries well know this feeling, as, indeed, we know it ourselves. No one knew this problem better than the Jews. The Jews had solved it by saying that in every man, there were two natures, two tendencies, and two impulses. They called them the *Yetser Hatob* and the *Yetser Hara*. It was the Jewish conviction that God had made men like that and that all men had a good impulse and an evil

impulse inside them. There were rabbis who believed that the evil impulse was in the very embryo in the womb, that it was there before a man was born at all. It was a malevolent second personality. It was man's implacable enemy, and it was there waiting to ruin a man in the end.[6]

He would go on to list three things that might be called a demonstration of inadequacies:[7]

1. **The *Inadequacy of Human Knowledge*:** This says that if you know the right things and do the right thing, life will be easy. But knowledge itself does not make a man good. It is the same in every walk of life. We know how things should be played, such as golf, but in most cases, we are far from being able actually to play it, or we may know how to behave in a certain situation, but we are unable to behave within it. That is the difference between religion and morality. Morality is knowledge of what to do; religion is knowledge of Jesus Christ. Morality is knowledge of code; religion is knowledge of person. It is only when we know Christ that we are able to do what we know we ought to do.
2. **The *Inadequacy of Human Resolution*:** To resolve to do a thing is very far from doing it. There is in human nature an essential weakness of the will. The will comes up against the facts, the problems, the difficulties, the opposition, and the will fails. Once, Peter took a great resolution, *"Even if I have to die with You, I will not deny You."* The human will without Christ's strength is bound to crack.
3. **The *Limitations of Diagnosis*:** Paul knew quite clearly what was wrong, but he was quite unable to put it right. He was like a doctor who could accurately diagnose a disease but was quite powerless to prescribe a cure. Jesus is the one person who not only knows what is wrong but who can also fix it. It is not criticism He offers but help.

It seems clear that mindset of Paul, like many of ours, is conflicted but nevertheless focused. It is conflicted in the fact that while he knows what he knows, he still struggles with sin, but on the other hand, he is focused because he knows that with Jesus, it will all be cleared in the end. Therefore, Paul's mindset is concerned with his actions but humbled by the grace of God through Jesus. Therefore, he states, *"The free gift of God is eternal life in Christ Jesus our Lord"* (6:23). Consequently, he says, *"Thanks be to God through Christ our Lord."*

To do good is a state of mind, and Paul's mind is focused on Jesus!

Second, let's think about the struggle. An article I found entitled "5 Habitual Sins Men Especially Struggle With" listed these things in this order: (1) anger, (2) sexual immorality, (3) greed, (4) sloth, (5) pride.[8] While these may be true for some and not for others, it proves a point. The struggle is real—the struggle with sin, that is.

---

6. Barclay, William. "Romans 7:14-25, The Human Situation." *The Daily Study Bible, The Letter to the Romans*. Philadelphia: The Westminster Press, 1957, 100–101.
7. Barclay 102-103..
8. Brown, Aaron D'Anthony. "5 Habitual Sins Men Especially Struggle With." *Crosswalk.Com*, Crosswalk, 7 Oct. 2024, www.crosswalk.com/faith/men/habitual-sins-men-especially-struggle-with.html.

The apostle Paul in his ministry discussed the concept of a struggle from three different perspectives:

1. **Spiritual Struggle**: In Ephesians 6:12, he writes that our struggle is not against *"flesh and blood"* but against those in the *"heavenly places."* Within this passage, Paul is discussing the spiritual war that is going on in the battle of the soul. It would include temptation, deception, and delusions that he discusses in both Ephesians and Colossians regarding Satan and his minions who are continually coming after you. Therefore, from a spiritual standpoint, there will be a struggle against those who are spiritually against us in the spirit realm. Here, the word πάλη (*pale*) means literally to struggle against or to engage in a challenging contest, meaning each team is at odds with one another.
2. **Collective Ministry Struggle**: In Philippians 4:3, Paul writes of those who have *"labored"* or *"struggled"* alongside him in the work of ministry for the case of Christ. Here, the word συναθλέω (*synathleo*) discusses those who struggle along with someone. Here, Paul is referring to those called *"fellow workers whose names are in the Book of Life."* To struggle here is to fight for the cause, but together and not as individuals. It is a unified battle of spiritual competition. Truly, those who work for the Lord are both a team and a family.
3. **Spiritual Leadership Struggle**: In Colossians 2:1, Paul is ἀγών (*agon*) struggling on behalf of those in Laodicea, laboring (1:29), earnestly in his prayers (4:12) for them so *"that their hearts may be encouraged, having been knit together in love, and attaining to all the wealth that comes from the full assurance of understanding, resulting in a true knowledge of God's mystery, that is, Christ Himself, in whom have hidden all the treasures of wisdom and knowledge"* (Col. 2:2-3). Here, the idea is to fight for those who are in need of being fought for. Everyone, at some point in their lives, needs to be fought for when it comes to their spiritual well-being. Everyone needs someone to look out for them. Jesus would even discuss leaving the 99 to go and find the one (Matt. 18:12-13; Luke 15:4-7).

What do we gain from this? The struggle is real. From one perspective, we have Satan fighting a battle and waging war on your soul to try and take it away from God. This is the **struggle of spirituality**. Second, we have a collective battle where the church fights together against the schemes of the devil with the armor of God. We all know when we are truly together, walking with God, there is nothing that can overcome the kingdom of God. This is the **collective struggle** that we face together. Third, we have the personal struggle where people need someone to fight for them so that they can fight for themselves. This is the **personal struggle** that needs to be looked at in two ways. First on behalf of the one fighting for someone, and then on behalf of those who need to be fought for.

With each of these words used in these three texts, each of them is about the struggle of life. To struggle **against** (Eph. 6:12), to struggle **with** (Phil. 4:3), and to struggle **for** (Col. 2:1). While all these need to be understood within their own context of their passages, the idea remains true. There is a struggle in life. It can be defined by *labor, a challenge,* or *to fight against*, all of which are a part of the struggle we are in.

If there is anyone who is at war with the opposing force, it is Paul. He knows it and discusses it in his letters to the Ephesians and Colossians brethren (Eph. 1:21; 3:10; 6:12; Col. 1:16; 2:15). At this point, to turn Paul away from the Lord would be a great accomplishment for Satan.

The Struggle Is Real!

However, Paul's struggle is equally his fight, which is why toward the end of his life he wrote, *"I have fought the good fight, I have finished the course, I have kept the faith"* (2 Tim. 4:7).

Something that we should gain from this is that we have leaders in the Lord's church, some with the title of a shepherd or deacon, some preachers, and some with no title at all, but they are nevertheless great leaders within the kingdom. Every good leader has people or souls that they fight for each day—encouraging, teaching, correcting, and training for the Lord. Their lives are filled with prayer and concern for the brethren around them and abroad as well. What we must think about is that while they spend much time in thought of your spiritual well-being, who is thinking about theirs? Is their struggle not just as real as your own?

Our struggles come from every direction, and truthfully, none of us can overcome them by ourselves. Spiritually strong or not, we need each other to fight the fight of faith. For Paul, the struggle was real in the fact that he, too, was facing the reality of sinful tendencies in life. It didn't make him a bad person, but it did make him a real person, one who needed Jesus is the same way that you and I do.

Third, we can only find true strength in Jesus. We are simply not strong enough on our own. In reality, we cannot even fight for ourselves as there was no hope for us in the world without His act of obedience to the will of the Father. While Paul may be struggling with sin in his life, he is more thankful that he knows Jesus has taken care of that sin. It is simply no more.

Paul writes to the Ephesian brethren at the close, *"Finally, be strong in the Lord and in the strength of His might"* (Eph. 6:10). How can he say that? Because he, too, has found his strength in Him. Therefore, he states, *"I joyfully concur with the law of God in the inner man"* (7:22; cf. Ps. 119:97). Denny and others have noted that the *"inner man"* is the real Paul, and the real Paul is joyfully ready in every way to follow the will of the Lord and all else that he may be asked to do. While he sees himself as a prisoner in one way, he also understands himself as a warrior in another sense. Here, however, the struggle is real, and that is what he is focusing on.

But Paul knows that just as sin has taken its opportunity through the law, he must take his opportunity through Jesus. As we have stated before, there is a real battle for the soul, and Satan is seeking every opportunity to exploit Paul's weakness and turn him away from righteousness (cf. 1 Pet. 5:8).

In reference to sin, we must remember that first, sin will destroy the innocent (7:8-12); second, sin will take over (7:13-20); and finally, sin will frustrate (7:21-24).[9] Is Paul feeling these things? Absolutely. Is he innocent of the sin? No. But the blood of Christ makes him innocent before God. Is sin trying to overtake him? Yes. Is he strong enough by himself to overcome? No, but with Jesus, he can! Is Paul frustrated with himself and his actions? Yes. Can he push through that frustration? Possibly, but with Jesus he can remain confident in who he is and what he has. Salvation.

---

9. Winkler, Dan. "Just-If-Ied Never Sinned and Determined to Stay That Way, Romans 6:1-7:25." *Life Changing Studies with an Open Bible, Just-If-Ied Never Sinned, A Study of Romans*. Madison: Winkler Publications, Inc., 2005, 40.

Our strength in every way is found in the Lord. From Paul's perspective, he knows more than anything that he must rely on Him in all times of his life. To recall his words to the Colossian brethren, he wrote, *"Therefore if you have been raised up with Christ, keep seeking the things above, where Christ is, seated at the right hand of God. Set your mind on the things above, not on the things that are on earth"* (Col. 3:1-2), and then he says in Colossians 3:15, *"Let the peace of Christ rule in your hearts, to which indeed you were called in one body; and be thankful."*

To reiterate our point here, remember. The struggle of sin is real! No man is exempt from this very fact. So, as Paul did, and as we all should do, fight the good fight against the spiritual forces in the armor of God (Eph. 6), with the brethren (Phil. 4:3) and for each other (Col. 2:1). While Satan tries to attack us from every angle of our lives, if we can stay together unified with our Lord, the struggle may be real, but it will not hinder us from reaching our eternal goal.

ACTIVITY

Gather into equal groups. Be sure that each person has the worksheet, something to write with, and his/her Bible. There will need to be one spokesperson for each table.

This activity is designed for group discussion and team building as you answer the questions together as a team and discuss. You are looking for:

1. Best Practices
2. Ways to Edify
3. Opportunities to Encourage
4. Strategies to Overcome
5. Ways to Positively Affect the Body

Through each question given, seek an answer that will fulfill each of these obligations that we have to either a person, group, or congregation who is struggling with sin. Be sure to note some things that **will not work** and all the things that **will work**.

The #1 priority we should have in mind is the soul of the individual who is struggling. The struggle of sin is real, and no matter how strong you are, that will never change.

Once the designated time is up for the group discussions, which will be set by the teacher/instructor, he or she will call on any of the tables for their feedback to present the discussion they had. Do this for each question.

Once the activity is done, it would be worth having a prayer for all who have taken part in this activity and for those who are struggling greatly within your congregation.

Use the tools that you gain from this activity and put them into practice. The more we can fight against the schemes of Satan, do it together and fight for one another, the better off we will be!

The Struggle Is Real!

WORKSHEET

1. What sins do you struggle with? Remember, as Paul was open about his struggle, we should be too.

2. Why is it that you struggle with those particular sins? Remember, Paul couldn't understand, but it is worthy of examination.

3. Do you believe you are the only one struggling with sin? Sometimes, we can feel as if we are alone on an island; know that you are not alone. Talk about it if you are struggling with something like someone else!

4. What can we do to overcome the sin struggle in our lives? Think of practical ways as a group and as individuals that you can add to the conversation.

5. What can you do to help someone else in their struggle with these sins in their life? Be sure to apply the list given in the activity instructions.

6. What are the possible outcomes if we do not work to help ourselves and each other win the battle over our sinful struggles? (Be sure to list them.)

7. Why is it essential for us to work through our struggles together? Why do we need to keep our focus on Jesus in the process?

Building

Excel Still More Bible Workshop

Building

NO CONDEMNATION!

ROMANS 8

BILLY CLABAUGH

"Therefore there is now no condemnation for those who are in Christ Jesus."

- Romans 8:1 -

INTRODUCTION

There may be no more reassuring words ever read or heard than those the apostle Paul pens in Romans 8:1! *"Therefore there is now no condemnation for those who are in Christ Jesus."* We need to go back to Romans 7 to help us understand why this declaration of no condemnation is so amazing. In Romans 7 the apostle Paul describes the impossible task of trying to keep the Law perfectly. It's a pointless effort that results only in frustration and continued separation from God. It's a constant battle of doing what he doesn't want to do and not doing what he does want to do. But thankfully Paul ends chapter 7 by acknowledging His only hope and the only one who can set him free from the 'body of this death,' when he says, *"Thanks be to God through Jesus Christ our Lord!"* (Rom. 7:25a). He then continues this thought into chapter 8 by beginning with the word *therefore*. So because Jesus Christ paid the ultimate price on the cross for our sins, **there is now no condemnation for those who are in Christ Jesus**! Jesus suffered the consequence for our sins, so that we wouldn't have to! Jesus suffered death to give us life! There can be no greater gift and there can be no greater news than that! It's the kind of news that changes how we view our lives and makes clear our purpose for being on this earth! Once we get into Christ, we become a part of an eternal kingdom made up of those who by God's grace, now stand justified before Him, eager to use this life to honor the Savior.

FOCUS

When a disciple of Jesus acts on his belief in Jesus Christ as the Son of God and is clothed with Him in that watery grave of baptism, he is surrendering his life. He no longer lives by the desires of the flesh or walk according to the flesh; he now walks according to the Spirit (Rom. 8:4). It's no longer a life controlled by sin, but by the Spirit of God, because he's been set free from his sin to live according to God's will. God allows us to choose who or what controls our lives, and Paul gives two options in Romans 8:5-8:

> *For those who are according to the flesh set their minds on the things of the flesh, but those who are according to the Spirit, the things of the Spirit. For the mind set on the flesh is death, but the mind set on the Spirit is life and peace, because the mind set on the flesh is hostile toward God; for it does not subject itself to the law of God, for it is not even able to do so, and those who are in the flesh cannot please God.*

Whether or not people live by the flesh or live by the Spirit is determined by what they set their mind on—what their thoughts are dwelling on. If the mind is set on the flesh, then that mind is death, it is hostile toward God, and it does not subject itself to the law of God, nor can it please God. On the other hand, the mind set on the Spirit is life and peace. Unlike the mind set on the flesh, it will subject itself to God and seek to please Him.

The *Truth for Today Commentary* on Romans 1–8 describes the difference in the mind set on the flesh and the mind set on the Spirit in this way: "To 'set their minds' on the things of the flesh means that those who do so, are absorbed with this life, earthbound. They concentrate only on what they can see, taste, or feel."[1] "'The things of the Spirit' are the spiritual concerns of God, matters that pertain to eternity. As a rule, these cannot be seen, but they are more real than that which can be seen. They will last when the things of this world vanish forever."[2]

> Since there is now no condemnation in Christ Jesus, a person should be eager to set his mind on the Spirit, which is life and peace, instead of the flesh which is death.

This life comes down to two basic choices: we either live this life focusing on the flesh, or we live this life focusing on the Spirit. We either trust in the things of this world that can be seen, tasted, and felt, or we trust in what can't be seen, but that we know to be true through faith!

Focus Statement: Since there is now no condemnation in Christ Jesus, a person should be eager to set his mind on the Spirit, which is life and peace, instead of the flesh which is death.

---

1. Roper, David L. "Romans 8-16, A Doctrinal Study," *Truth for Today Commentary: An Exegesis and Application of the Holy Scriptures.* Searcy: Resource Publications, 18.
2. Roper 19.

STUDY KEYS

Note: Take some time as you study through chapter 8 to mark each of these words and phrases individually with different color pens, markers, colored pencils, or highlighters of your choice. If possible, make notes in your margins to reflect the meanings of these words or phrases that may help you understand the overall context to a better degree.

Words or Phrases of Importance

- **No condemnation**...vv. 1, 34
- **Christ/Christ Jesus**...vv. 1, 2, 9, 10, 11, 17, 34, 35, 39
- **Law of the Spirit of life**...v. 2
- **Law of the spirit of sin and death**...v. 2
- **Sons of God**...vv. 14, 16
- **Free**...vv. 2, 21
- **Life**...vv. 2, 6
- **Sin**...vv. 2, 3, 10,
- **Hostile**...v. 7
- **The Spirit**...vv. 2, 4, 5, 9, 11, 13, 14, 16, 23, 26, 27
- **Flesh**...vv. 3, 4, 5, 6, 7, 8, 9, 12, 13
- **Mind**...vv. 5, 6, 7

STUDY

Having no condemnation in Christ means we are found not guilty of our sin! It means not having to pay the penalty that we rightfully owe for our sin. The price has already been paid in full at the cross, and He's removed the eternal consequences of sin for all those in Christ. It's a gift provided only in Jesus because of the amazing grace of God. They are no longer under the law of the spirit of sin and death, but under the law of the Spirit of life. They are led by the Spirit of God and are made sons of God or children of God! Praise God for His grace and mercy and the once for all sacrifice at Calvary which saves us from condemnation!

Adopted Sons

Paul in chapter 8 indicates that these Roman Christians had been slaves to fear because of their sin. Unfortunately, anytime a person is a slave to sin, it will lead to fear and doubt about this present life and the future life to come in eternity. But now, Paul writes that their freedom from sin has brought about a spirit of adoption as sons by which Paul says, *"We cry out, 'Abba! Father!'"* So instead of slaves to fear, God adopted them and made them His sons! He made them His children! (v. 15). Paul follows up by saying: *"If children, heirs also, heirs of God and fellow heirs with Christ, if indeed we suffer with Him so that we may also be glorified with Him"* (v. 17).

A person goes from being a slave to sin to being a child of the Almighty Creator! Through Christ, God has freed us from the bondage of sin and made us His children and heirs. Not only that, but we are also made fellow heirs with Christ. Jesus is our Savior and He certainly deserves to be an heir of God, but by His grace, we too have the privilege of being an heir of God with Christ!

Suffer with Him

One of the conditions to be a fellow heir with Christ is to be a fellow sufferer with Him! Faithful disciples are willing to follow Jesus despite any opposition or suffering. In the Sermon on the Mount, Jesus says rejoice and be glad when you are insulted and persecuted:

> *Blessed are those who have been persecuted for the sake of righteousness, for theirs is the kingdom of heaven. Blessed are you when people insult you and persecute you, and falsely say all kinds of evil against you because of Me. Rejoice and be glad, for your reward in heaven is great; for in the same way they persecuted the prophets who were before you* (Matt. 5:10-12).

There is a great reward in Heaven for all those who have been persecuted for the sake of righteousness, or for the sake of Christ. Jesus also makes the point that they were not alone in the suffering: *"In the same way they persecuted the prophets who were before you."* Jesus has always made it clear that following Him is not easy. His way is the narrow way, and most people will choose NOT to take it. And for those who do choose to follow Jesus, there will always be those they encounter who will oppose them and even hate them. Jesus even warned His disciples of this in John 15:18: *"If the world hates you, you know that it has hated Me before it hated you."*

Peter and the apostles in Acts 5 serve as a fitting example in how to deal with suffering for the sake of Christ. These men had been arrested for teaching Jesus and then they were flogged and ordered not to speak in the name of Jesus. But they didn't let any of that discourage them: *"So they went on their way from the presence of the Council, rejoicing that they had been considered worthy to suffer shame for His name. And every day, in the temple and from house to house, they kept right on teaching and preaching Jesus as the Christ* (Acts 5:41-42). It has been said that "we must be willing to bear the cross in order to wear the crown." [3]

---

3. Roper 41.

No Condemnation

The more we appreciate the great suffering our Lord endured for us, the more joy and peace we should find in our own suffering for Him!

CONCLUSION

Paul in this chapter declares that all who are *"in Christ Jesus"* have no condemnation. They stand before a holy God justified by the ultimate sacrifice Christ has made. They have been freed from the law of sin and death so that that they can live according to the Spirit of God and not the flesh. Those *"in Christ Jesus"* no longer set their mind on the flesh or on their earthly desires, but they set their mind on the Spirit which is life and peace! It's a mind that is set on things above (Col. 3:2). God has chosen all those in Christ to be His adopted children and coheirs with Christ of the eternal inheritance that Peter says *"…is imperishable, undefiled, and will not fade away, reserved in heaven or you"* (1 Pet. 1:4). It's an inheritance that is guaranteed and is worth whatever we need to give up materially or whatever suffering we must face on this earth.

Jesus has done what the Law couldn't do and what man couldn't do for himself. Since He took the punishment for our sins, if we are in Christ, we find salvation from the condemnation that comes because of our sins! We can be assured that we have been made right before God, and we can look forward to when Jesus returns that He will take us back with Him to that eternal home He's prepared!

Excel Still More **Bible Workshop**

ACTIVITY

1. What does the word therefore indicate in verse 1? What is the connection between these verses to the previous verses?

2. What is true of those who belong to Christ?

3. What does it mean to "set their mind on the things of the flesh"? Give some examples.

4. What does it mean to "set one's mind on the things of the Spirit"? Give some examples.

5. What are the consequences of the two different mindsets? In other words, where do they lead?

6. What are the differences in the spirit of slavery and the spirit of adoption?

7. How does the truth of no condemnation in Jesus Christ shape your understanding of your life on this earth and your hope of salvation?

Biblical Text

Romans Chapter 1

1 Paul, a bond-servant of Christ Jesus, called as an apostle, set apart for the gospel of God, **2** which He promised beforehand through His prophets in the holy Scriptures, **3** concerning His Son, who was born of a descendant of David according to the flesh, **4** who was declared the Son of God with power by the resurrection from the dead, according to the Spirit of holiness, Jesus Christ our Lord, **5** through whom we have received grace and apostleship to bring about the obedience of faith among all the Gentiles for His name's sake, **6** among whom you also are the called of Jesus Christ;

7 to all who are beloved of God in Rome, called as saints: Grace to you and peace from God our Father and the Lord Jesus Christ.

8 First, I thank my God through Jesus Christ for you all, because your faith is being proclaimed throughout the whole world. **9** For God, whom I serve in my spirit in the preaching of the gospel of His Son, is my witness as to how unceasingly I make mention of you, **10** always in my prayers making request, if perhaps now at last by the will of God I may succeed in coming to you. **11** For I long to see you so that I may impart some spiritual gift to you, that you may be established; **12** that is, that I may be encouraged together with you while among you, each of us by the other's faith, both yours and mine. **13** I do not want you to be unaware, brethren, that often I have planned to come to you (and have been prevented so far) so that I may obtain some fruit among you also, even as among the rest of the Gentiles. **14** I am under obligation both to Greeks and to barbarians, both to the wise and to the foolish.

15 So, for my part, I am eager to preach the gospel to you also who are in Rome.

16 For I am not ashamed of the gospel, for it is the power of God for salvation to everyone who believes, to the Jew first and also to the Greek. **17** For in it the righteousness of God is revealed from faith to faith; as it is written, "BUT THE RIGHTEOUS man SHALL LIVE BY FAITH."

18 For the wrath of God is revealed from heaven against all ungodliness and unrighteousness of men who suppress the truth in unrighteousness, **19** because that which is known about God is evident within them; for God made it evident to them. **20** For since the creation of the world His invisible attributes, His eternal power and divine nature, have been clearly seen, being understood through what has been made, so that they are without excuse. **21** For even though they knew God, they did not honor Him as God or give thanks, but they became futile in their speculations, and their foolish heart was darkened. **22** Professing to be wise, they became fools, **23** and exchanged the glory of the incorruptible God for an image in the form of corruptible man and of birds and four-footed animals and crawling creatures.

24 Therefore God gave them over in the lusts of their hearts to impurity, so that their bodies would be dishonored among them. **25** For they exchanged the truth of God for a lie, and worshiped and served the creature rather than the Creator, who is blessed forever. Amen.

26 For this reason God gave them over to degrading passions; for their women exchanged the natural function for that which is unnatural, **27** and in the same way also the men abandoned the natural function of the woman and burned in their desire toward one another, men with men committing indecent acts and receiving in their own persons the due penalty of their error.

28 And just as they did not see fit to acknowledge God any longer, God gave them over to a depraved mind, to do those things which are not proper, **29** being filled with all unrighteousness, wickedness, greed, evil; full of envy, murder, strife, deceit, malice; they are gossips, **30** slanderers, haters of God, insolent, arrogant, boastful, inventors of evil, disobedient to parents, **31** without understanding, untrustworthy, unloving, unmerciful; **32** and although they know the ordinance of God, that those who practice such things are worthy of death, they not only do the same, but also give hearty approval to those who practice them.

Romans Chapter 2

1 Therefore you have no excuse, everyone of you who passes judgment, for in that which you judge another, you condemn yourself; for you who judge practice the same things. **2** And we know that the judgment of God rightly falls upon those who practice such things. **3** But do you suppose this, O man, when you pass judgment on those who practice such things and do the same yourself, that you will escape the judgment of God? **4** Or do you think lightly of the riches of His kindness and tolerance and patience, not knowing that the kindness of God leads you to repentance? **5** But because of your stubbornness and unrepentant heart you are storing up wrath for yourself in the day of wrath and revelation of the righteous judgment of God, **6** who WILL RENDER TO EACH PERSON ACCORDING TO HIS DEEDS: **7** to those who by perseverance in doing good seek for glory and honor and immortality, eternal life; **8** but to those who are selfishly ambitious and do not obey the truth, but obey unrighteousness, wrath and indignation. **9** There will be tribulation and distress for every soul of man who does evil, of the Jew first and also of the Greek, **10** but glory and honor and peace to everyone who does good, to the Jew first and also to the Greek. **11** For there is no partiality with God.

12 For all who have sinned without the Law will also perish without the Law, and all who have sinned under the Law will be judged by the Law; **13** for it is not the hearers of the Law who are just before God, but the doers of the Law will be justified. **14** For when Gentiles who do not have the Law do instinctively the things of the Law, these, not having the Law, are a law to themselves, **15** in that they show the work of the Law written in their hearts, their conscience bearing witness and their thoughts alternately accusing or else defending them, **16** on the day when, according to my gospel, God will judge the secrets of men through Christ Jesus.

17 But if you bear the name "Jew" and rely upon the Law and boast in God, **18** and know His will and approve the things that are essential, being instructed out of the Law, **19** and are confident that you yourself are a guide to the blind, a light to those who are in darkness, **20** a corrector of the foolish, a teacher of the immature, having in the Law the embodiment of knowledge and of the truth, **21** you, therefore, who teach another, do you not teach yourself? You who preach that one shall not steal, do you steal? **22** You who say that one should not commit adultery, do you commit adultery? You who abhor idols, do you rob temples? **23** You who boast in the Law, through your breaking the Law, do you dishonor God? **24** For "THE NAME OF GOD IS BLASPHEMED AMONG THE GENTILES BECAUSE OF YOU," just as it is written.

25 For indeed circumcision is of value if you practice the Law; but if you are a transgressor of the Law, your circumcision has become uncircumcision. **26** So if the uncircumcised man keeps the requirements of the Law, will not his uncircumcision be regarded as circumcision? **27** And he who is physically uncircumcised, if he keeps the Law, will he not judge you who though having the letter of the Law and circumcision are a transgressor of the Law? **28** For he is not a Jew who is one outwardly, nor is circumcision that which is outward in the flesh. **29** But he is a Jew who is one inwardly; and circumcision is that which is of the heart, by the Spirit, not by the letter; and his praise is not from men, but from God.

Romans Chapter 3

1 Then what advantage has the Jew? Or what is the benefit of circumcision? **2** Great in every respect. First of all, that they were entrusted with the oracles of God. **3** What then? If some did not believe, their unbelief will not nullify the faithfulness of God, will it? **4** May it never be! Rather, let God be found true, though every man be found a liar, as it is written,

"THAT YOU MAY BE JUSTIFIED IN YOUR WORDS,

AND PREVAIL WHEN YOU ARE JUDGED."

5 But if our unrighteousness demonstrates the righteousness of God, what shall we say? The God who inflicts wrath is not unrighteous, is He? (I am speaking in human terms.) **6** May it never be! For otherwise, how will God judge the world? **7** But if through my lie the truth of God abounded to His glory, why am I also still being judged as a sinner? **8** And why not say (as we are slanderously reported and as some claim that we say), "Let us do evil that good may come"? Their condemnation is just.

9 What then? Are we better than they? Not at all; for we have already charged that both Jews and Greeks are all under sin; **10** as it is written,

"THERE IS NONE RIGHTEOUS, NOT EVEN ONE;

11 THERE IS NONE WHO UNDERSTANDS,

THERE IS NONE WHO SEEKS FOR GOD;

12 ALL HAVE TURNED ASIDE, TOGETHER THEY HAVE BECOME USELESS;

THERE IS NONE WHO DOES GOOD,

THERE IS NOT EVEN ONE."

13 "THEIR THROAT IS AN OPEN GRAVE,

WITH THEIR TONGUES THEY KEEP DECEIVING,"

"THE POISON OF ASPS IS UNDER THEIR LIPS";

14 "WHOSE MOUTH IS FULL OF CURSING AND BITTERNESS";

15 "THEIR FEET ARE SWIFT TO SHED BLOOD,

16 DESTRUCTION AND MISERY ARE IN THEIR PATHS,

17 AND THE PATH OF PEACE THEY HAVE NOT KNOWN."

18 "THERE IS NO FEAR OF GOD BEFORE THEIR EYES."

19 Now we know that whatever the Law says, it speaks to those who are under the Law, so that every mouth may be closed and all the world may become accountable to God; 20 because by the works of the Law no flesh will be justified in His sight; for through the Law comes the knowledge of sin.

21 But now apart from the Law the righteousness of God has been manifested, being witnessed by the Law and the Prophets, 22 even the righteousness of God through faith in Jesus Christ for all those who believe; for there is no distinction; 23 for all have sinned and fall short of the glory of God, 24 being justified as a gift by His grace through the redemption which is in Christ Jesus; 25 whom God displayed publicly as a propitiation in His blood through faith. This was to demonstrate His righteousness, because in the forbearance of God He passed over the sins previously committed; 26 for the demonstration, I say, of His righteousness at the present time, so that He would be just and the justifier of the one who has faith in Jesus.

27 Where then is boasting? It is excluded. By what kind of law? Of works? No, but by a law of faith. 28 For we maintain that a man is justified by faith apart from works of the Law. 29 Or is God the God of Jews only? Is He not the God of Gentiles also? Yes, of Gentiles also, 30 since indeed God who will justify the circumcised by faith and the uncircumcised through faith is one.

31 Do we then nullify the Law through faith? May it never be! On the contrary, we establish the Law.

Romans Chapter 4

1 What then shall we say that Abraham, our forefather according to the flesh, has found? **2** For if Abraham was justified by works, he has something to boast about, but not before God. **3** For what does the Scripture say? "ABRAHAM BELIEVED GOD, AND IT WAS CREDITED TO HIM AS RIGHTEOUSNESS." **4** Now to the one who works, his wage is not credited as a favor, but as what is due. **5** But to the one who does not work, but believes in Him who justifies the ungodly, his faith is credited as righteousness, **6** just as David also speaks of the blessing on the man to whom God credits righteousness apart from works:

7 "BLESSED ARE THOSE WHOSE LAWLESS DEEDS HAVE BEEN FORGIVEN,

AND WHOSE SINS HAVE BEEN COVERED.

8 "BLESSED IS THE MAN WHOSE SIN THE LORD WILL NOT TAKE INTO ACCOUNT."

9 Is this blessing then on the circumcised, or on the uncircumcised also? For we say, "FAITH WAS CREDITED TO ABRAHAM AS RIGHTEOUSNESS." **10** How then was it credited? While he was circumcised, or uncircumcised? Not while circumcised, but while uncircumcised; **11** and he received the sign of circumcision, a seal of the righteousness of the faith which he had while uncircumcised, so that he might be the father of all who believe without being circumcised, that righteousness might be credited to them, **12** and the father of circumcision to those who not only are of the circumcision, but who also follow in the steps of the faith of our father Abraham which he had while uncircumcised.

13 For the promise to Abraham or to his descendants that he would be heir of the world was not through the Law, but through the righteousness of faith. 14 For if those who are of the Law are heirs, faith is made void and the promise is nullified; 15 for the Law brings about wrath, but where there is no law, there also is no violation.

16 For this reason it is by faith, in order that it may be in accordance with grace, so that the promise will be guaranteed to all the descendants, not only to those who are of the Law, but also to those who are of the faith of Abraham, who is the father of us all, 17 (as it is written, "A FATHER OF MANY NATIONS HAVE I MADE YOU") in the presence of Him whom he believed, even God, who gives life to the dead and calls into being that which does not exist. 18 In hope against hope he believed, so that he might become a father of many nations according to that which had been spoken, "SO SHALL YOUR DESCENDANTS BE." 19 Without becoming weak in faith he contemplated his own body, now as good as dead since he was about a hundred years old, and the deadness of Sarah's womb; 20 yet, with respect to the promise of God, he did not waver in unbelief but grew strong in faith, giving glory to God, 21 and being fully assured that what God had promised, He was able also to perform. 22 Therefore IT WAS ALSO CREDITED TO HIM AS RIGHTEOUSNESS. 23 Now not for his sake only was it written that it was credited to him, 24 but for our sake also, to whom it will be credited, as those who believe in Him who raised Jesus our Lord from the dead, 25 He who was delivered over because of our transgressions, and was raised because of our justification.

Romans Chapter 5

1 Therefore, having been justified by faith, we have peace with God through our Lord Jesus Christ, 2 through whom also we have obtained our introduction by faith into this grace in which we stand; and we exult in hope of the glory of God. 3 And

not only this, but we also exult in our tribulations, knowing that tribulation brings about perseverance; **4** and perseverance, proven character; and proven character, hope; **5** and hope does not disappoint, because the love of God has been poured out within our hearts through the Holy Spirit who was given to us.

6 For while we were still helpless, at the right time Christ died for the ungodly. **7** For one will hardly die for a righteous man; though perhaps for the good man someone would dare even to die. **8** But God demonstrates His own love toward us, in that while we were yet sinners, Christ died for us. **9** Much more then, having now been justified by His blood, we shall be saved from the wrath of God through Him. **10** For if while we were enemies we were reconciled to God through the death of His Son, much more, having been reconciled, we shall be saved by His life. **11** And not only this, but we also exult in God through our Lord Jesus Christ, through whom we have now received the reconciliation.

12 Therefore, just as through one man sin entered into the world, and death through sin, and so death spread to all men, because all sinned— **13** for until the Law sin was in the world, but sin is not imputed when there is no law. **14** Nevertheless death reigned from Adam until Moses, even over those who had not sinned in the likeness of the offense of Adam, who is a type of Him who was to come.

15 But the free gift is not like the transgression. For if by the transgression of the one the many died, much more did the grace of God and the gift by the grace of the one Man, Jesus Christ, abound to the many. **16** The gift is not like that which came through the one who sinned; for on the one hand the judgment arose from one transgression resulting in condemnation, but on the other hand the free gift arose from many transgressions resulting in justification. **17** For if by the transgression of the one, death reigned through the one, much more those who receive the abundance of grace and of the gift of righteousness will reign in life through the One, Jesus Christ.

18 So then as through one transgression there resulted condemnation to all men, even so through one act of righteousness there resulted justification of life to all men. **19** For as through the one man's disobedience the many were made sinners, even so through the obedience of the One the many will be made righteous. **20** The Law came in so that the transgression would increase; but where sin increased, grace abounded all the more, **21** so that, as sin reigned in death, even so grace would reign through righteousness to eternal life through Jesus Christ our Lord.

Romans Chapter 6

1 What shall we say then? Are we to continue in sin so that grace may increase? **2** May it never be! How shall we who died to sin still live in it? **3** Or do you not know that all of us who have been baptized into Christ Jesus have been baptized into His death? **4** Therefore we have been buried with Him through baptism into death, so that as Christ was raised from the dead through the glory of the Father, so we too might walk in newness of life. **5** For if we have become united with Him in the likeness of His death, certainly we shall also be in the likeness of His resurrection, **6** knowing this, that our old self was crucified with Him, in order that our body of sin might be done away with, so that we would no longer be slaves to sin; **7** for he who has died is freed from sin.

8 Now if we have died with Christ, we believe that we shall also live with Him, **9** knowing that Christ, having been raised from the dead, is never to die again; death no longer is master over Him. **10** For the death that He died, He died to sin once for all; but the life that He lives, He lives to God. **11** Even so consider yourselves to be dead to sin, but alive to God in Christ Jesus.

12 Therefore do not let sin reign in your mortal body so that you obey its lusts, **13** and do not go on presenting the members of your body to sin as instruments of unrighteousness; but present yourselves to God as those alive from the dead, and your members as instruments of righteousness to God. **14** For sin shall not be master over you, for you are not under law but under grace.

15 What then? Shall we sin because we are not under law but under grace? May it never be! **16** Do you not know that when you present yourselves to someone as slaves for obedience, you are slaves of the one whom you obey, either of sin resulting in death, or of obedience resulting in righteousness? **17** But thanks be to God that though you were slaves of sin, you became obedient from the heart to that form of teaching to which you were committed, **18** and having been freed from sin, you became slaves of righteousness. **19** I am speaking in human terms because of the weakness of your flesh. For just as you presented your members as slaves to impurity and to lawlessness, resulting in further lawlessness, so now present your members as slaves to righteousness, resulting in sanctification.

20 For when you were slaves of sin, you were free in regard to righteousness. **21** Therefore what benefit were you then deriving from the things of which you are now ashamed? For the outcome of those things is death. **22** But now having been freed from sin and enslaved to God, you derive your benefit, resulting in sanctification, and the outcome, eternal life. **23** For the wages of sin is death, but the free gift of God is eternal life in Christ Jesus our Lord.

Romans Chapter 7

1 Or do you not know, brethren (for I am speaking to those who know the law), that the law has jurisdiction over a person as long as he lives? **2** For the married woman is bound by law to her husband while he is living; but if her husband dies, she is released from the law concerning the husband. **3** So then, if while her husband is living she is joined to another man, she shall be called an adulteress; but if her husband dies, she is free from the law, so that she is not an adulteress though she is joined to another man.

4 Therefore, my brethren, you also were made to die to the Law through the body of Christ, so that you might be joined to another, to Him who was raised from the dead, in order that we might bear fruit for God. **5** For while we were in the flesh, the sinful passions, which were aroused by the Law, were at work in the members of our body to bear fruit for death. **6** But now we have been released from the Law, having died to that by which we were bound, so that we serve in newness of the Spirit and not in oldness of the letter.

7 What shall we say then? Is the Law sin? May it never be! On the contrary, I would not have come to know sin except through the Law; for I would not have known about coveting if the Law had not said, "YOU SHALL NOT COVET." **8** But sin, taking opportunity through the commandment, produced in me coveting of every kind; for apart from the Law sin is dead. **9** I was once alive apart from the Law; but when the commandment came, sin became alive and I died; **10** and this commandment, which was to result in life, proved to result in death for me; **11** for sin, taking an opportunity through the commandment, deceived me and through it killed me. **12** So then, the Law is holy, and the commandment is holy and righteous and good.

13 Therefore did that which is good become a cause of death for me? May it never be! Rather it was sin, in order that it might be shown to be sin by effecting my death through that which is good, so that through the commandment sin would become utterly sinful.

14 For we know that the Law is spiritual, but I am of flesh, sold into bondage to sin. **15** For what I am doing, I do not understand; for I am not practicing what I would like to do, but I am doing the very thing I hate. **16** But if I do the very thing I do not want to do, I agree with the Law, confessing that the Law is good. **17** So now, no longer am I the one doing it, but sin which dwells in me. **18** For I know that nothing good dwells in me, that is, in my flesh; for the willing is present in me, but the doing of the good is not. **19** For the good that I want, I do not do, but I practice the very evil that I do not want. **20** But if I am doing the very thing I do not want, I am no longer the one doing it, but sin which dwells in me.

21 I find then the principle that evil is present in me, the one who wants to do good. **22** For I joyfully concur with the law of God in the inner man, **23** but I see a different law in the members of my body, waging war against the law of my mind and making me a prisoner of the law of sin which is in my members. **24** Wretched man that I am! Who will set me free from the body of this death? **25** Thanks be to God through Jesus Christ our Lord! So then, on the one hand I myself with my mind am serving the law of God, but on the other, with my flesh the law of sin.

Romans Chapter 8

1 Therefore there is now no condemnation for those who are in Christ Jesus. **2** For the law of the Spirit of life in Christ Jesus has set you free from the law of sin and of death. **3** For what the Law could not do, weak as it was through the flesh, God did: sending His own Son in the likeness of sinful flesh and as an offering for sin, He condemned sin in the flesh, **4** so that the requirement of the Law might be fulfilled in us, who do not walk according to the flesh but according to the Spirit. **5** For those who are according to the flesh set their minds on the things of the flesh, but those who are according to the Spirit, the things of the Spirit. **6** For the mind set on the flesh is death, but the mind set on the Spirit is life and peace, **7** because the mind set on the flesh is hostile toward God; for it does not subject itself to the law of God, for it is not even able to do so, **8** and those who are in the flesh cannot please God.

9 However, you are not in the flesh but in the Spirit, if indeed the Spirit of God dwells in you. But if anyone does not have the Spirit of Christ, he does not belong to Him. **10** If Christ is in you, though the body is dead because of sin, yet the spirit is alive because of righteousness. **11** But if the Spirit of Him who raised Jesus from the dead dwells in you, He who raised Christ Jesus from the dead will also give life to your mortal bodies through His Spirit who dwells in you.

12 So then, brethren, we are under obligation, not to the flesh, to live according to the flesh— **13** for if you are living according to the flesh, you must die; but if by the Spirit you are putting to death the deeds of the body, you will live. **14** For all who are being led by the Spirit of God, these are sons of God. **15** For you have not received a spirit of slavery leading to fear again, but you have received a spirit of adoption as sons by which we cry out, "Abba! Father!" **16** The Spirit Himself testifies with our spirit that we are children of God, **17** and if children, heirs also, heirs of God and fellow heirs with Christ, if indeed we suffer with Him so that we may also be glorified with Him.

18 For I consider that the sufferings of this present time are not worthy to be compared with the glory that is to be revealed to us. **19** For the anxious longing of the creation waits eagerly for the revealing of the sons of God. **20** For the creation was subjected to futility, not willingly, but because of Him who subjected it, in hope **21** that the creation itself also will be set free from its slavery to corruption into the freedom of the glory of the children of God. **22** For we know that the whole creation groans and suffers the pains of childbirth together until now. **23** And not only this, but also we ourselves, having the first fruits of the Spirit, even we ourselves groan within ourselves, waiting eagerly for our adoption as sons, the redemption of our body. **24** For in hope we have been saved, but hope that is seen is not hope; for who hopes for what he already sees? **25** But if we hope for what we do not see, with perseverance we wait eagerly for it.

26 In the same way the Spirit also helps our weakness; for we do not know how to pray as we should, but the Spirit Himself intercedes for us with groanings too deep for words; **27** and He who searches the hearts knows what the mind of the Spirit is, because He intercedes for the saints according to the will of God.

Romans 1-8

28 And we know that God causes all things to work together for good to those who love God, to those who are called according to His purpose. **29** For those whom He foreknew, He also predestined to become conformed to the image of His Son, so that He would be the firstborn among many brethren; **30** and these whom He predestined, He also called; and these whom He called, He also justified; and these whom He justified, He also glorified.

31 What then shall we say to these things? If God is for us, who is against us? **32** He who did not spare His own Son, but delivered Him over for us all, how will He not also with Him freely give us all things? **33** Who will bring a charge against God's elect? God is the one who justifies; **34** who is the one who condemns? Christ Jesus is He who died, yes, rather who was raised, who is at the right hand of God, who also intercedes for us. **35** Who will separate us from the love of Christ? Will tribulation, or distress, or persecution, or famine, or nakedness, or peril, or sword? **36** Just as it is written,

"FOR YOUR SAKE WE ARE BEING PUT TO DEATH ALL DAY LONG;

WE WERE CONSIDERED AS SHEEP TO BE SLAUGHTERED."

37 But in all these things we overwhelmingly conquer through Him who loved us. **38** For I am convinced that neither death, nor life, nor angels, nor principalities, nor things present, nor things to come, nor powers, **39** nor height, nor depth, nor any other created thing, will be able to separate us from the love of God, which is in Christ Jesus our Lord.

Scripture quotations taken from the (NASB®) New American Standard Bible®, Copyright © 1960, 1971, 1977, 1995 by The Lockman Foundation. Used by permission. All rights reserved. lockman.org

Authors

DENNY PETRILLO

Denny is married to the former Kathy Roberts. They have been married since January 1978. They have three children (Lance, Brett, and Laura), and six grandchildren (Chloe, Ashlyn, Sophie, Easton, Brelyn, and Kyson). He has served as the President of the Bear Valley Bible Institute since 2004 and has been a full-time instructor since 1985. He has preached in Mississippi, Arkansas, Nebraska, and Colorado. He has taught numerous classes for the World Video Bible School and has authored several books and commentaries. He graduated from the Bear Valley School of Preaching (now the Bear Valley Bible Institute), received an AA degree in Bible (York College), BA in Bible and Biblical Languages (Harding University), MA in Old and New Testaments (Harding Graduate School of Religion), and a Ph.D. in Religious Education (University of Nebraska).

JOE WELLS

Joe Wells holds an earned B.S. degree in Science along with a completion certificate from the Nashville School of Preaching and Biblical Studies and a Masters of Ministry degree from Freed Hardeman University. Joe travels the country as a frequent speaker for youth and family events, men's days, as well as Gospel meetings. He is the co-founder of Kaio Publications, publishers of the Family Devotional series as well as the Finer Grounds Bible Study series for women. Joe is also the author of the book Complete: Becoming the Man God Purposes You to Be and Game Plan: Developing a Spiritually Winning Strategy for Adults and Teens in Today's Culture. Along with this, he and Erin are the co-host of The Hey Joe Show, a podcast designed to challenge and strengthen families and teens across America. Joe has served God in a public way since 2000 in the capacity of youth minister and Gospel preacher, helping people make the connection with the Word of God and encouraging them to be transformed for Christ. He is blessed to the husband to the former Erin O'Hara, and they are the proud parents of four beautiful children: Colton, Michala, Camden, and Bennett.

GARRETT BERNETHY

Garrett married his wife, Cristen, in December 2005, and together, they have four wonderful boys: Parker, who is married to his beautiful wife, Claire, and their daughter, Taytum, as well as Cohen, Ryder, and Kamden. Garrett has been actively involved in directing and participating in numerous camps, retreats, conferences, and workshops. In addition, he is the Executive Director of Excel Still More Inc. and contributes annually as a writer and instructor for the Excel Still More Bible Workshop and Excel Publications articles. Currently, Garrett serves as the pulpit minister for the Hydro Church of Christ in Hydro, Oklahoma, where he and his family reside.

BILLY CLABAUGH

Billy, his wife Shayla, and their son Caleb live in Sayre, Oklahoma, where he has been blessed to preach since 2012. He has a bachelor's degree in Math Education from Oklahoma Christian University and a master's degree in Sports Administration from Eastern New Mexico University. He enjoys reading, watching the Oklahoma Sooners, spending time with his family, and serving in the Kingdom of God. Billy also serves on the board of directors for Excel Still More and is a regular speaker and writer for the workshop and other publications.

www.ingramcontent.com/pod-product-compliance
Lightning Source LLC
Chambersburg PA
CBHW081441070526
44586CB00019B/2195